COMBATING POVERTY

Quebec's Pursuit of a Distinctive Welfare State

Studies in Comparative Political Economy and Public Policy

Editors: MICHAEL HOWLETT, DAVID LAYCOCK (Simon Fraser University), and STEPHEN MCBRIDE (McMaster University)

Studies in Comparative Political Economy and Public Policy is designed to showcase innovative approaches to political economy and public policy from a comparative perspective. While originating in Canada, the series will provide attractive offerings to a wide international audience, featuring studies with local, subnational, cross-national, and international empirical bases and theoretical frameworks.

Editorial Advisory Board

Jeffrey Ayres, St Michael's College, Vermont
Neil Bradford, Western University
Janine Brodie, University of Alberta
William Carroll, University of Victoria
William Coleman, University of Waterloo
Rodney Haddow, University of Toronto
Jane Jenson, Université de Montréal
Laura Macdonald, Carleton University
Rianne Mahon, Wilfrid Laurier University
Michael Mintrom, Monash University
Grace Skogstad, University of Toronto
Leah Vosko, York University
Kent Weaver, Georgetown University
Linda White, University of Toronto
Robert Young, Western University

For a list of books published in the series, see page 215.

Combating Poverty

Quebec's Pursuit of a Distinctive Welfare State

Axel van den Berg, Charles Plante,
Hicham Raïq, Christine Proulx,
and Samuel Faustmann

UNIVERSITY OF TORONTO PRESS
Toronto Buffalo London

ISBN 978-1-4875-0156-3

(Studies in Comparative Political Economy and Public Policy)

Library and Archives Canada Cataloguing in Publication

van den Berg, Axel, 1950–, author
Combating poverty : Quebec's pursuit of a distinctive welfare state / Axel
van den Berg, Charles Plante, Hicham Raïq, Christine Proulx,
and Samuel Faustmann.

(Studies in comparative political economy and public policy ; 53) Includes
bibliographical references and index.
ISBN 978-1-4875-0156-3 (hardcover)

1. Poverty–Canada–Provinces. 2. Poverty–Canada–Provinces–Prevention.
3. Canada–Provinces–Social policy. 4. Canada–Provinces–Economic policy. I.
Raïq, Hicham, 1970–, author II. Proulx, Christine, 1985–, author
III. Plante, Charles, 1985–, author IV. Faustmann, Samuel, 1987–, author V.
Title. VI. Series: Studies in comparative political economy and public policy ; 53

HC79.P63V36 2017   362.5'80971   C2017-902220-2

This book has been published with the help of a grant from the Federation
for the Humanities and Social Sciences, through the Awards to Scholarly
Publications Program, using funds provided by the Social Sciences and
Humanities Research Council of Canada.

University of Toronto Press acknowledges the financial assistance to its
publishing program of the Canada Council for the Arts and the Ontario
Arts Council, an agency of the Government of Ontario.

Canada Council   Conseil des Arts
for the Arts   du Canada

ONTARIO ARTS COUNCIL
CONSEIL DES ARTS DE L'ONTARIO
an Ontario government agency
un organisme du gouvernement de l'Ontario

Funded by the   Financé par le
Government   gouvernement
of Canada   du Canada

Canadä

Contents

Figures and Tables

Figures

Tables

Acknowledgments

This book is dedicated to the memory of our good friend, collaborator, teacher, and mentor Paul Bernard. The research for the book started as far back as 2008, when Paul and Axel van den Berg jointly received research grants from the Social Sciences and Humanities Research Council of Canada (SSHRC) and the Ministère de Développement économique, Innovation et Exportation du Québec (MDEIE) to conduct work on interprovincial differences in social and labour market policies in Canada and comparisons with a number of other countries. We gathered a group of talented PhD students to help us with the research and embarked on two years of preliminary data gathering. This proved to be a demanding and often frustrating process. The work of piecing together the histories of different policies and programs from provincial budgetary sources, through endless reversals and reforms, some real, some mostly cosmetic, was particularly arduous. But however daunting the obstacles we faced, thanks in large part to Paul's infectious enthusiasm, we managed to overcome them all one way or another.

Sadly, that wonderful period of excitement and enthusiasm, marked by frequent meetings to solve technical problems as much as to enjoy wide-ranging discussions of political, social, and even culinary matters, came to an end when Paul was diagnosed with a virulent bone cancer to which he succumbed in February 2011. Paul's passing was a huge personal loss to each and every one of us. And it was also a huge setback to our project as Paul was not only our master morale booster but also our principal statistician. After Paul's passing we had to regroup and try to continue the project as much as possible in the manner he had intended. Fortunately, Paul was as superb a teacher as he was a mentor and project leader, so that several of our team members were able to continue working on the quantitative analyses in a way that Paul would have approved.

As was evident from the outpouring of tributes following his death, Paul Bernard occupied a central and unique position in Canadian sociology. He was one of our leading researchers on social inequality in all its facets and on the policies that might mitigate it and its consequences. He was truly a public intellectual in the best sense of the word, deeply committed to helping improve the lives of the least well off, yet equally committed to the highest scientific standards. He was also a consummate builder of bridges between different disciplines and domains, equally comfortable counselling cabinet ministers or undergraduates, leading research groups or sitting in on high-level committee meetings at Statistics Canada. His exceptional qualities as an initiator and builder of bridges were especially in evidence in the key role he played in the creation of the national network of Research Data Centres that today gives researchers across the country direct access to Statistics Canada's immense store of data. And last but far from least, Paul Bernard was an amazing teacher and mentor who inspired a whole new generation of Canadian sociologists.

In writing this book we intend to add another small contribution to the lasting legacy of our dear friend. We can only hope that the end product is up to his demanding standards and a worthy farewell. We still miss him very much.

Our quantitative research was conducted at the Quebec Interuniversity Centre for Social Statistics and the Saskatchewan Research Data Centre, both of which are part of the Canadian Research Data Centre Network (CRDCN) Paul helped create. These centres' services are made possible by the financial or in-kind support of the SSHRC, the Canadian Institutes of Health Research (CIHR), the Canada Foundation for Innovation (CFI), Statistics Canada, the Fonds de Recherche Québecois Société et Culture (FRQSC), and the universities of the provinces of Quebec and Saskatchewan. We are also indebted to the Luxemburg Income Study for the data that allowed us to conduct our international comparisons. As noted, the research was funded by research grants from the SSHRC and the MDEIE, for which we are most grateful.

We are also greatly indebted to Douglas Hildebrand, acquisitions editor at the University of Toronto Press, for his unwavering support and encouragement throughout the long process of turning our project into this book. In response to the extraordinarily thorough evaluation reports of three anonymous reviewers the initial manuscript underwent several major revisions which have immensely improved the final product. We also want to thank Elizabeth Thompson, who did an excellent job of copy-editing the final version of the manuscript. We owe them all a great debt for the many improvements and corrections they have helped us make.

Finally, we want to express our gratitude to our respective families for the incredible patience with which they have endured all the ups and downs of this seemingly never-ending project. We owe them a great deal. But our greatest debt, which we will sadly never be able to repay, is to our dear friend Paul.

Axel van den Berg
Charles Plante
Hicham Raïq
Christine Proulx
Sam Faustmann

Montreal, Saskatoon, and Toronto
November 2016

COMBATING POVERTY

Quebec's Pursuit of a Distinctive Welfare State

Introduction: Quebec's Exceptionalism in Context

Diverging Welfare Regimes?

How sturdy *is* the Canadian federation? This question is never far from the centre of debate in Canadian federal and provincial politics. Whether the issue is language rights, the gun registry, environmental policy, pensions, crime, national security, or health care, strong centrifugal forces pull the major regions and provinces in opposite directions. As federations go, Canada is unquestionably among the most decentralized, with the provinces enjoying greater autonomy and relatively larger fiscal resources than their counterparts in most other federal systems (see Haddow 2015, 31–4). In principle at least, Canada's provincial governments are able to choose their own, possibly divergent, paths in a wide range of policy domains. And if and when they do so, they inevitably provoke alarm in some quarters about the corrosive effect on the federation as a whole.

In this book, we consider the question from the angle of social and employment policy. We assess to what extent Canada's largest provinces have grown apart in their approaches to such policies. We are particularly interested in gauging the extent to which Quebec has diverged from the policy patterns of the other provinces and the federal government, as a result of what some observers call its 'social democratic turn' (*virage sociodémocratique*) during the 1990s.

Concerns about the potential fragmentation of the Canadian federation have become increasingly pressing as the federal government has gradually reduced its role in a number of domains and devolved responsibilities onto the provincial governments (Banting and Myles 2013a; Wood 2013). The gradual federal retrenchment set in motion by the Liberal federal governments of Jean Chrétien and Paul Martin in the 1990s and early 2000s was mostly motivated by a desire to eliminate federal deficits and reduce the federal debt. But, if anything, the following Conservative government of Stephen Harper pursued the policy even more energetically, as it was ideologically committed to reducing the role of the federal government in the Canadian polity. No wonder, then, that opponents to the left have repeatedly accused the Harper government of undermining the very fabric that holds the federation together.

One important area in which the federal government began to cut back to balance its books was that of social and employment policy. Two reforms in particular, both implemented in 1996, amounted to a major devolution of social policy responsibility onto the provinces. The first of these replaced the Canada Assistance Plan (CAP), a federal cost-sharing plan to support provincial social assistance programs implemented in 1966, with a block grant called the Canada Social and Health Transfer (CSHT), covering the federal government's contribution to all provincial social and health programs. The total amount of federal funding for these programs was cut significantly while the federal government gave up much of its regulatory power over the manner in which the provinces chose to spend the funds. In the second reform, the federal government undertook a major overhaul of the Unemployment Insurance program, redubbing it Employment Insurance (EI), tightening eligibility criteria, reducing benefit levels and durations, and devolving a large part of the responsibility for the 'activating' part of the program onto the provinces through individual federal-provincial Labour Market Development Agreements (LMDAs) (see van den Berg et al. 2008). The net effect of these reforms and cutbacks was the significant reduction of the federal government's financial and regulatory involvement in core parts of the social and employment policy domain. The provinces were increasingly made to fend for themselves, leading many observers to fear increasing fragmentation and diversification (Boychuk 2015, 83–6; Haddow 2015, 31–2). Chapter 1 returns to these federal government reforms.

To be sure, the devolution of responsibility for social and employment policy to the provinces is in keeping with the spirit and the letter of the Canadian Constitution. In the British North America Act of 1867, Canada's effective Constitution, the country's founding fathers explicitly relegated jurisdiction over health, welfare, property and civil rights, and 'all matters of a merely local or private nature' to the provinces, while retaining principal taxation powers for the federal government (Banting 1982, 2005, 2008; Haddow 2015, 31; van den Berg and Jensen 2015). In the wake of the US Civil War the Fathers of Confederation sought to craft a union in which the federal government would be the most powerful and important institution, leaving the provinces with what at the time seemed to be the lesser responsibilities of caring for the poor and sick and other 'local' concerns. As a result, 'in formal terms, authority over social policy is divided between the federal and the provincial governments in ways that make Canada one of the most decentralized federations in the world' (Banting 2008, 137–8). And to some extent, this is true in *substantive* terms as well. As Imbeau et al. (2000, 738) note, the variation in provincial welfare expenditures within Canada is greater than it is among OECD countries. Similarly, Boychuk (1998) describes Canada as having a 'patchwork' of provincial social assistance programs, each with its own history, principal features, and goals.

At the same time, there is no question that Canada's federal government has repeatedly succeeded in circumventing constitutional obstacles to impose, or at least coax the provinces into accepting, major nationwide social policies, such as public health care, pensions, and unemployment insurance (see, e.g., Banting 2005, 2008; Maioni 1998; Théret 2002a, 2002b, 2003; van den Berg and Jensen 2015). While the Canadian provinces enjoy the jurisdictional power to pursue social policies of their own making and orientation, then, powerful centripetal forces have historically pushed the country towards some degree of convergence, at least until the early 1990s, when the federal government began its gradual retreat from the field of social and employment policy.

Since then, however, a number of observers have drawn attention to Quebec's growing 'exceptionalism' in the field of social and employment policy. Its 'distinctive policy model' has, it is argued, produced a 'growing dualism between Quebec and the rest of the country ... In the late 1990s, when the rest of Canada was moving in a neoliberal direction, reducing the redistributive role of the state, Quebec moved in the opposite direction' (Banting 2012, 25). Quebec, it is claimed, has made a major turn towards a more generous kind of welfare state, one that is beginning to resemble the much-admired Nordic social democratic 'models.' Meanwhile, the other provinces have followed the general trend towards neoliberal cutbacks characteristic of the Anglo-Saxon liberal market regimes, with ultra-laissez-faire Alberta taking the lead

(Beaujot, Du, and Ravanera 2013; Bernard and Raïq 2011; Bernard and Saint-Arnaud 2004; Fortin 2010; Godbout and St-Cerny 2008; Jenson 2002; Noël 2011, 2013; Roy and Bernier 2006; Vaillancourt 2012).

Most of those emphasizing Quebec's exceptionalism do so with approval, as they tend to subscribe to the same social democratic values informing the new 'Quebec model' (see, e.g., Noël 2012, 427–9). But others view the growing divergence between Quebec's and the other provinces' social policy regimes with alarm (Kershaw 2006; Boychuk 1998). For instance, Wood and Klassen fear that the increasingly differentiated bilateral federal-provincial labour market policy agreements included in the new EI system 'have the potential to balkanize programs across the country, hollow out the centre, and undermine Canada's political union' (Wood and Klassen 2009, 267). Such a 'provincialization of social policy,' Osberg warns, constitutes a major threat to the Canadian 'social union' (Osberg 2000, 214). In effect, Canadian social policy has been transformed from an instrument of nation-building into one of 'province-building' (Jenson 2013, 50).

In Esping-Andersen's famous classification of 'welfare regimes' (Esping-Andersen 1990), Canada is routinely classified as a 'liberal market' regime together with the United States and, increasingly, Great Britain, Ireland, and New Zealand (see, e.g., Banting and Myles 2013b, 4–7). According to Esping-Andersen, regime types can be distinguished by whether they emphasize the state, the market, or the family as the principal provider of social welfare, by their extent of 'decommodification'[1] of labour, and by their egalitarianism. These criteria yielded his three ideal-typical welfare regimes. The liberal regimes, mostly the Anglo-Saxon countries including Canada, are characterized by a relatively strong reliance on the market as the principal determinant of income and welfare. Welfare programs are typically residual in nature and relatively ungenerous, producing the lowest degree of decommodification and the greatest amount of income inequality and relative poverty of the three regime types. The conservative/corporatist/Continental regimes, consisting mainly of the countries on the European continent, are characterized by intermediate decommodification and inequality. They rely relatively more heavily on the family for the provision of welfare, and they favour social protection programs based on mandatory occupational insurance schemes. The social democratic regimes, finally, are mostly Nordic. Theirs are the most decommodifying and egalitarian, relying primarily on the state to provide universal social protection and reduce inequality and poverty.

While immensely influential, Esping-Andersen's three-regime typology and methodology have met with a great deal of criticism. In fact, there is now a veritable cottage industry (Abrahamson 1999) testing, debating, and amending his initial argument. Critics have identified a number of important differences *within* Esping-Andersen's three groups of welfare regimes, leading them to add new types to the initial classification, including a 'Latin' or 'familialist' regime type comprising mostly the countries on the Mediterranean rim (Bonoli 1997; Ferrera 1996); a 'radical' wage earners' regime type for the Antipodes and Great Britain (Castles and Mitchell 1993); and even a Southeast Asian regime type (Warburton and Grassman 2011). Others have questioned Esping-Andersen's location of specific countries in his scheme.[2] Still others have criticized his methodology and the way he codes and interprets his data. When one corrects for these flaws, so these critics argue, it is not at all clear that there really are three distinct clusters of welfare regimes (Bambra 2005, 2006; Scruggs and Allan 2006, 183; see also Arts and Gelissen 2002).

Thus, after an exhaustive review of the debates triggered by Esping-Andersen's original work, Arts and Gelissen (2002) conclude that real welfare states are almost all hybrid cases defying any simple classification on theoretical grounds. Certainly a case can be made that Canada is a hybrid welfare regime, given its more extensive public provision of welfare than the 'liberal' United States.

One basic assumption underlying the Esping-Andersen scheme has *not* come in for sustained criticism until recently:[3] the notion that the countries in question are sufficiently internally homogeneous with respect to social policy that they can be characterized as unitary welfare regimes of one type or another in the first place. This assumption is particularly questionable for a federation like Canada, where much social and employment policy is conducted at the provincial level. If those who point to an increasing divergence in matters of social and employment policy between provinces are correct, the possibility that Canada contains more than one distinct welfare regime must be taken seriously. In a paper addressing the issue, Bernard and Saint-Arnaud analyse a set of quantitative social indicators for the 1990s for Canada's four largest provinces. On the basis of their findings they conclude that, on the whole, the country fits the liberal market label, despite significant variations, ranging from Alberta's regime, which approaches US liberalism, to Quebec's more European and social democratic model (Bernard and Saint-Arnaud 2004). Yet a growing literature documents the differences in social and employment policies between Canada's provinces (see, e.g., Boychuk 1998; Haddow 2015; Béland and Daigneault 2015; Banting and Myles 2013a; Raïq and van den Berg 2012, 2014; van den Berg and Raïq 2014). In fact, as we go on to show, there is considerable evidence of growing divergence.

The question of whether Canada can still be considered a single welfare regime as opposed to a collection of distinct provincial regimes is of more than academic interest. There are reasons to believe the linkage between national identity and culture on the one hand and the welfare regime on the other is much more intimate than hitherto noted in the literature on the development of the modern welfare state.

Until recently, that literature has focused overwhelmingly on the political forces and struggles influencing the implementation of welfare policies and their retrenchment. The principal emphasis has been on the relative strengths of various social actors, movements, and political parties and their ability to shape policy outcomes (Castles 1985; Castles and Mitchell 1993; Esping-Andersen 1985; Korpi 1983; Pierson 2001). It has generally shied away from linking differences between countries in terms of cultural values or national identities too closely to the character of the welfare state, emphasizing economic interests and political mobilization in the service of such interests instead (see, e.g., Olsen 2002, Ch. 5).

At the same time, a large literature documents considerable differences in the types of values and preferences held by the populations and subgroups within countries, and these are surely relevant for social policy formation (Mau and Veghte 2007; Sundberg and Taylor-Gooby 2013; Svallfors 1997, 2003, 2012; Taylor-Gooby 1985, 2011; van Oorschot, Opielka, and Pfau-Effinger 2008). Much of this literature starts from the assumption, explicit or implicit, that such differences matter because they affect the character and extent of national social policies, however mediated by the political process (Brooks and Manza 2007). But the converse may be true as well, that is, values and preferences may be shaped by the policies already in force (Larsen 2007; Olsen 2002, Ch. 5).

Whatever the direction of causation, these researchers posit a relatively straightforward linkage between public preferences and social policies. A small but growing group of researchers, however, has begun to examine the possibility of a much more profound relationship between national identity and welfare state regimes. In this line of thinking, the relationship is one of mutual reinforcement: social policy is deeply and necessarily rooted in a profound sense of national identity and solidarity, while the resulting welfare state institutions and programs serve as instruments to forge a shared set of values in national populations. Thus, in a recent assessment of the long and arduous road towards a 'social Europe,' Barbier emphasizes the extent to which social policies are rooted in a sense of national solidarity that cannot be easily reproduced at the transnational level (Barbier 2013; see also Béland and Lecours 2008).

This line of argument could have far-reaching implications for the character and long-term viability of Canada as a country. For if Canada's provinces are, in fact, growing further apart in terms of their social policy regimes, and if it is indeed the case that such regimes can profoundly alter the sense of national identity and solidarity of the population in question, then Canadians have good reason to worry about the 'balkanization' of their welfare state. For some observers, this is precisely the point; in their view, Quebec's social democratic *virage* is both an expression and a further elaboration of the values that make it a *distinct society*. It is, they argue, part and parcel of Quebec's long-term nation-building aspirations (Béland and Lecours 2004, 2006; cf. Banting 2005, 132).[4] The concluding chapter revisits this interesting question.

There may be powerful economic forces at work that severely limit the extent to which Canada's provinces *are able* to follow distinct paths in their social and employment policies, however. A massive literature now suggests that the wave of globalization sweeping over the capitalist world since the 1970s has closely circumscribed the degree to which jurisdictions are able to pursue social policies that deviate greatly from those of their neighbours and trading partners. The liberalization of international trade and financial markets, so it is argued, are forcing welfare states to converge towards a lowest common denominator lest they be left behind by footloose capital and technology – the 'race to the bottom' (Bowles and Wagman 1997; Brady, Beckfield and Seeleib-Kaiser 2005; Genschel 2004; Huber and Stephens 2001; Mishra 1999; Tanzi 2002).

There is no consensus on the exact mechanisms by which growing openness to international trade and financial markets puts pressure on governments to reduce their spending on welfare programs. Some authors assume the majority of programs have a direct negative effect on the international competitiveness of a country's economy by diverting capital from more 'productive' uses and generating less than optimally flexible labour markets (see, e.g., Kenworthy 1995, 227–30 and the sources cited there). Others emphasize the shift in the balance of *political* power between capital and labour resulting from the greater mobility of capital and governments' increased dependence on international capital markets (Bretschger and Hettich 2002; Korpi and Palme 2003; see also Swank 2005). But all agree that the net effect of trade and financial market liberalization and internationalization is to force governments to reduce taxation levels and shift from taxing mobile factors such as capital to less mobile ones such as labour and domestic consumption. As a result, we should observe a general retrenchment of social programs and policies – the largest component of public expenditures – and a broad convergence of welfare states towards a leaner, more competition- and productivity-oriented model. Such arguments suggest Canada's provinces will be forced to converge towards greater retrenchment in social and employment policies, despite their formal autonomy in these domains (cf. Haddow 2015, 15–17).

As it stands, the evidence for the thesis that globalization leads to massive welfare state retrenchment is mixed.[5] While there may be some cross-national convergence in overall expenditure levels, there is no convincing evidence of a dramatic race to the bottom. Since the recession of the early 1990s, the Nordic countries, which used to be well ahead of other advanced countries in terms of the generosity of their social programs and overall expenditure levels, have implemented a series of reforms amounting to a sizeable retrenchment in both spending and program generosity. At the same time, social spending as a proportion of GDP has continued to rise in Continental regimes and has remained broadly stable in the 'liberal market-oriented' countries. In short, there appears to be a convergence towards the middle rather than the bottom (Achterberg and Yerkes 2009; Hemerijck 2013; Palier 2010; Starke 2006).

Another major trend affecting all advanced welfare states to varying degrees consists of changes in the composition of the 'typical' family and the rising labour force participation of women, including mothers of young children. This massive transformation is occurring even in the most conservative familialistic welfare regimes of Southern Europe. Inevitably, it has a number of important consequences for employment and social protection policies. The once dominant single-breadwinner, two-parent family has been in decline and is gradually being replaced by double-earner families and single-parent (mostly single-mother) families. While the former are perhaps less vulnerable to the loss of employment of one of their income earners, the latter have come to constitute the single largest group at risk of poverty. According to some authors, these developments have led to a 'feminization of poverty,' a phenomenon once thought limited to the developing world (Kim and Choi 2013).

Welfare and employment policies have adapted to these new realities to varying degrees across countries and jurisdictions. The Scandinavian countries were the first to pursue a range of policies to encourage the labour force participation of women with children, partly to broaden the tax base of their expanding welfare states. The Anglo-Saxon liberal market regimes have not pursued any coherent strategy, but both the labour force participation of women with children and the growth of single-parent families have not lagged far behind those of the Nordic countries. The Continental countries, especially those forming the Mediterranean rim, have been slower to recognize the overall trend, but they have not been able to stop it either. Thus, there are substantial differences in the policies meant to influence the labour force behaviour of women with children and to combat poverty among single-parent families. And these differences, in turn, have produced a range of outcomes for different types of families (Bernard and Raïq 2011; Budig, Misra, and Böckmann 2010; Raïq, Plante, and van den Berg 2011; Smeeding 2006; Rovny 2014). In the following chapters, we ask whether and to what extent the largest Canadian provinces have pursued different policy approaches to meet the new challenges posed by these transformations in family composition and labour force participation, and whether and to what extent these approaches have yielded significantly different results.

To sum up, then, evidence of a cross-regime convergence in social and employment policy in the face of globalization is mixed. Whether different regimes have been forced to adopt similar policies in view of the changing composition of the family remains to be seen. But in one respect, the discourse of policymakers and analysts has shifted across the advanced welfare states. Perhaps as part of a growing general concern with productivity and competitiveness, and certainly driven, in part at least, by energetic campaigns conducted by international or transnational entities such as the OECD and the EU, there has been a general drift in employment policy, across countries and regime types, towards 'activation' (see, e.g., Banting 2006; Banting and Myles 2015, 16; Lindvall 2010; Pascual and Magnusson 2007). That is, governments across the ideological spectrum have increasingly turned to measures aimed at encouraging or coaxing the unemployed back into the labour market, treating employment as preferable to 'passive' income support

(Bonoli and Natali 2012; Jenson 2013, 53–4). In effect, there is a push towards a kind of integration of the social and labour market policy domains in which the labour market is viewed as the principal source of solutions for social problems like poverty, unemployment, and growing inequality (Béland and Daigneault 2015, 556), as proposed under a variety of banners, including 'flexicurity,' 'transitional labour markets,' 'making work pay,' and 'social investment' (de Gier and van den Berg 2005; Gazier 2003; Jenson 2013; Morel, Palier, and Palme 2012; Schmid 2006; Schmid and Gazier 2002; van den Berg 2009).

To be sure, not all activation approaches are cut from the same cloth. In some countries, mainly the Anglo-Saxon liberal market-oriented regimes, activation has amounted to what critics call 'workfare.' The main goal is to reduce social program expenditures by cutting the value and duration of passive program benefits like social assistance and unemployment insurance, reducing access to those benefits by tightening eligibility requirements, and making benefits subject to strictly enforced willingness-to-work conditions. Critics claim it perpetuates the Poor Law principle of 'less eligibility,' according to which no social benefits should be high enough to discourage beneficiaries from seeking gainful employment (see Daigneault 2014, 4; Somers and Block 2005; Peck 2001). While it may reduce public expenditures on passive programs, such critics maintain, it does not help to reduce overall poverty, but merely pushes the poor out of social programs and into the ranks of the 'working poor' (see, e.g., Barbier 2009; Bengtsson 2014; Berthet and Bourgeois 2014; Bonoli 2012; de la Porte and Jacobsson 2012; Dostal 2008; Lødemel and Trickey 2001; Morel 2002). While reference to the Elizabethan Poor Laws surely overstates the case, some governments have been much more energetic in pursuing the workfare route to activation than others, as we shall see in more detail in Chapter 1.

At the other end of the spectrum, we have the social investment perspective, according to which social policy need not be a deadweight cost to society. In fact, if properly designed, activating policies can be a productive force. Advocates of social investment argue the only way to combat poverty and long-term unemployment is to provide those who need it with the skills and training necessary to succeed in the current labour market. Thus, instead of cutting social protection benefits, a social investment approach focuses on providing citizens at risk of unemployment and/or poverty with training facilities to upgrade their skills, services to assist in job searches, subsidized day care to allow mothers with young children to join the labour force, and support for families with children to combat long-term poverty risks. In the long run, it is argued, such policies will achieve both greater equity *and* a more fiscally sustainable welfare state (Hemerijck 2013, 165–9; Jenson 2013, 54–6; Jenson and Saint-Martin 2006; Morel, Palier, and Palme 2012; Nolan 2013).

While the punitive workfare variant of activation has been mostly adopted in liberal, market-oriented welfare regimes, the social investment approach has been followed primarily in the Nordic social democratic welfare states (Dingeldey 2007; Hemerijck 2013; Huo, Nelson, and Stephens 2008; Morel, Palier, and Palme 2012). As noted above, Canada is generally regarded as a liberal, market-oriented welfare state. Yet here, too, the social investment perspective 'has been powerfully evident in policy debates regarding social policy' (Boychuk 2015, 87). It served as a justification for the federal government's National Child Benefit (NCB) in 1998 (ibid., 87–8) and, even more prominently, as the basis for the major overhaul of the federal Unemployment Insurance program in 1996, as indicated by the name change to Employment Insurance. But as our brief discussion of this reform has already hinted, there is room for debate as to how much of this allegedly epic transformation was rhetorical (van den Berg et al. 2008). And, in fact, for all the public talk about social investment, most observers agree Canada's approach has remained closer to the workfare end of the spectrum (Banting and Myles 2013a; Béland and Daigneault 2015).

Then again, in view of what we have said about the decentralized nature of the Canadian welfare state, such an assessment may not do justice to the variations *within* the federation with respect to the type of activation orientation. In this book, we are interested in finding out whether and to what extent there are significant differences between the country's major provinces in this respect. Have they all adopted the workfare approach, or are there elements of the social investment approach? If so, which provinces have gone farthest in that direction? We are particularly interested in gauging the degree to which Quebec's exceptionalism can be described as a social investment–oriented approach.

As mentioned, many observers point to a considerable and growing distance between Quebec and the rest of Canada with respect to social and employment policy. Quebec's distinctive approach to family policy, especially its celebrated system of subsidized day care and its relatively generous parental leave program, has garnered a fair amount of attention (Beaujot, Du, and Ravanera 2013; Jenson 2002; Godbout and

St-Cerny 2008; Stalker and Ornstein 2013; Haddow 2015). In addition, the growing divergence between Quebec and the other provinces with respect to (un)employment policy and, as we shall see in the remainder of this book, anti-poverty policy, is the subject of a growing literature (Banting and Medow 2012; Bernard and Raïq 2011; Boychuk 1998; Fortin 2010; Mondou 2009; Noël 2002; Noël 2011). At the same time, the few more comprehensive analyses of the differences in social and employment policy between Quebec and the other Canadian provinces precede the period of the supposed divergence (Dufour, Noël, and Boismenu 2003; Tellier 2005; Théret 2002a, 2002b, 2003).

Despite earlier calls for more interprovincial comparative policy analyses (Imbeau et al. 2000), differences in social policies between Canada's provinces have only recently received sustained attention. Several of the chapters in a recent collection on the fading of redistributive politics in Canada highlight the differences in provincial redistributive efforts (Banting and Myles 2013a). The contributions to a volume edited by Béland and Daigneault (2015) trace the somewhat divergent recent developments in the provinces' social assistance policies. In a meticulous study comparing the evolution of Quebec's and Ontario's policies in several domains – social assistance, day care and child benefits, economic development policies, and taxation – Haddow (2015) documents the different paths taken by the two provinces, their political and institutional causes, and their distributional outcomes.

In the following chapters, we contribute towards this burgeoning interprovincial comparative literature. Our aim is to present a systematic and comprehensive overview of a wide range of social and employment policies pursued and implemented by Canada's four most populous provinces since the turn of the century. Our principal concern is to assess to what extent these policy orientations have come to diverge in terms of the policies adopted and their outcomes. In the presentation and analysis of our findings we will be guided by the issues and distinctions raised in the Introduction. Thus, we will try to establish to what extent the general policy shift towards activation is reflected in provincial programs and expenditures. But beyond this, we want to find out whether and to what extent such activation has been of the workfare rather than the social investment variety. In particular, we wish to gauge the extent to which Quebec's alleged *virage sociodé-mocratique* has actually moved that province's welfare regime closer to those of the Nordic countries. This will require a detailed assessment of not only the features of Quebec's social and employment policies but also of their outcomes. In view of our earlier discussion of the different approaches to activation and family-friendly policies characterizing the social investment approach, we will focus on the evolution of poverty rates and employment patterns and their distribution across family types, as well as the role played by the different institutional domains (state, family, and market) in combating or exacerbating poverty levels.

At this point we need to say a few words about our choice of provinces. We have selected Canada's four most populous provinces, Ontario, Quebec, British Columbia, and Alberta, mostly for pragmatic reasons. As other researchers have found, collecting the kind of provincial program and expenditure data we need for our analyses is 'surprisingly challenging' (Kneebone and White 2015, 137). The ways provincial governments report on the specifics of their social and employment programs and on their expenditures on those programs make it extremely hard for the researcher to establish what exactly was spent on what program. The problem is compounded when one tries to trace the fate of specific programs and expenditure patterns over time, as governments constantly rename, reorganize, and reclassify their programs from budget to budget in response to the political pressures of the day. As a result, our mapping of the evolution of social and employment policies over a ten-year period for the four provinces in question was the best we were able to do with the resources available. Any attempt to include the other provinces would have required a level of funding and resources far exceeding the maximum amounts generally available for social science research in this country.

There are also positive reasons for choosing these four provinces as our comparison cases. These are, by far, the most populous provinces in Canada, representing together some 85% of the Canadian population. Moreover, between them, they span the entire range of political orientations and traditions in the country, from free-market and until recently solidly Conservative Alberta, to relatively interventionist and possibly social democratic Quebec, with Ontario and British Columbia more or less in between these two extremes. Saskatchewan and Manitoba have had left-leaning NDP governments, but so have British Columbia and Ontario. For their part, the Maritime provinces have remained well within the range of the conventional political traditions in the country and have been significantly more dependent on the federal government with respect to social and employment policies than the other provinces. A final pragmatic reason for restricting our analyses to the four largest provinces is that the populations in all other provinces are too small to allow us to conduct the comparative statistical analyses required in our later chapters.

In addition to comparing Quebec's policies and policy outcomes to those of the other three largest Canadian provinces, we compare them to those of a selection of advanced countries representing the range of policy regimes. Starting in Chapter 2, we include comparisons with poverty rates in the United States, France, the Netherlands, and Denmark, and in Chapters 5 and 6, Finland. We have selected these countries for both theoretical and pragmatic reasons. First, they represent the range of Esping-Andersen's welfare regime types; thus, they differ considerably in their social and employment policies and their outcomes in terms of poverty rates. At one end of the spectrum, we include the United States, the most liberal, market-oriented of the advanced countries with the least generous social and employment policies. At the other, we have Denmark, one of the archetypical social democratic countries which have brought poverty down to the lowest levels observed anywhere. It is more common to use Sweden as the iconic representative of the social democratic regime type in these kinds of international comparisons – and the 'Swedish model' has been prominent in Quebec's social policy discourse – but unfortunately the internationally comparable data we are using are not available for Sweden for the period under consideration. But in any case, we know the Danish figures are quite close to the Swedish ones; hence, Denmark is an appropriate representative of the social democratic type. For similar reasons, we were forced to replace Denmark with Finland in Chapters 5 and 6: the requisite information on labour force participation patterns is not available for Denmark. But while Finland is a typical social democratic country in terms of those patterns, its poverty rate reduction record is not as exemplary as Denmark's; for this reason, we have kept the latter as our comparison case in the earlier chapters. Finally, France and the Netherlands represent the Continental welfare state type whose levels of poverty are traditionally relatively low but whose patterns of labour force participation compare interestingly to those of Quebec.

This book will, we hope, contribute to the current debates about whether, and the extent to which, Quebec has embarked on a path of its own in the domain of social and employment policy. Beyond that, we hope to shed light on the widely debated issues concerning the supposed limits to welfare state growth resulting from globalization as well as the supposed institutional roots of persistent and sustainable difference between welfare states and regimes. From the Canadian and

Québécois points of view, the stakes are even higher. If those who have emphasized the strong, mutually reinforcing effects of social policy and national identity are correct, the extent to which Quebec has succeeded in pursuing distinct policies in social and employment policy, thereby drifting farther apart from the rest of Canada, is of the utmost importance. Far from having settled into an uneasy acceptance of its asymmetrical position within the Canadian federation, Quebec may be forging its *distinct society* by other means. We hardly expect to settle the matter in this short book, and we do not, in any case, wish to take any position on whether this is a good thing or a bad thing. But we believe addressing this larger set of issues requires assessing the extent to which Quebec has actually distinguished itself from the rest of Canada in matters of social and employment policy.

Chapter Overview

In Chapter 1 we compare the social and employment policy trajectories of Alberta, British Columbia, Ontario, and Quebec. We begin with an overview of the political history of the policies adopted in each province, starting in the late 1980s. We then catalogue a wide range of policies in force from 2002 onward. Finally, we present data on the expenditures on these programs for each province from the fiscal year 2002 onward, organized by categories of programs that reflect the issues discussed in this introduction. Our findings in Chapter 1 generally support Quebec's exceptionalism. Starting in the mid-1990s, but particularly after the mid-2000s, the scope and range of Quebec's policies and programs increasingly exceeded those of the other three provinces, particularly Alberta. In terms of expenditures as a proportion of provincial GDP, Quebec also far outspent the other provinces, with Alberta again standing out as the lowest spender. Moreover, the overall policy approach in Quebec is in keeping with the social investment perspective, with a strong emphasis on enabling support to encourage labour force participation, especially by women with young children. By contrast, the other three provinces have adopted the more punitive workfare approach to activation, with an increasingly sharp distinction between the 'deserving' and 'undeserving' poor.

In Chapter 2 we turn to the question of whether and to what extent the different policy approaches in the four provinces have produced different outcomes, particularly with respect to poverty rates. We compare these provincial outcomes with outcomes in a selection of countries representing different welfare regimes in Esping-Andersen's sense. We find that trends in provincial poverty rates correspond rather well to the differences in policy trajectories documented in Chapter 1. Poverty rates exhibit a modest decline in Quebec from the mid-1990s onward, while rising or remaining stable, at significantly higher levels than in Quebec, in the other three provinces and Canada as a whole. But when we compare these poverty rates to their equivalents in other countries, Quebec's poverty rates remain closer to those of the liberal market-oriented regimes, though at the low end of the cluster, than to the considerably lower rates of the European comparison countries.

Such gross poverty rates may obscure variations in the poverty rates of different types of households. This is an important issue in evaluating anti-poverty policies, as the social investment approach of the Nordic countries, which inspired Quebec's *virage*, heavily emphasizes support for families with children. In Chapter 3, we assess the extent to which this approach has borne fruit in the sense of bringing down the poverty rates of families with children. We find considerable support for the claim that Quebec's family-oriented approach has been successful. Poverty rates among two-parent families with dependent children in Quebec have declined substantially since the mid-1990s, while they have drifted upwards in the other major Canadian provinces and essentially remained stable in our comparison countries. The same is true, to some extent, for single-parent families with dependent children. Even more strikingly, as of about 2002, Quebec's poverty rates for two-parent families have begun to compare favourably to those of the European comparison countries, including solidly social democratic Denmark, and have fallen well below those of the liberal, market-oriented three other provinces and the United States. That said, Quebec's policy mix has done little for childless households and single adults. Their poverty rates are as high as anywhere else in liberal, market-oriented North America.

Critics of generous anti-poverty policies have long argued that such policies raise some families above the poverty threshold but only at the cost of creating a culture of welfare dependency that produces a hard core of chronically poor households (see, e.g., Dean and Taylor-Gooby 2014; Somers and Block 2005). In Chapter 4 we address this issue by looking at poverty durations and trajectories of families with children over a six-year period. Our findings appear to prove the critics wrong. In fact, the rates of chronic poverty are significantly lower in Quebec than in the other three provinces, with the partial exception of Alberta.

As well, Quebec households falling into poverty at one time or another during the six-year period are *more* likely to escape poverty in the short term than households in the other three provinces.

Thus, in Chapters 1–4 we establish the extent of Quebec's exceptionalism with respect to social and employment policies; we present evidence suggesting some of the intended outcomes have been realized. But correlation does not necessarily mean causation. Poverty rates are affected by many things other than provincial government policies. In Chapters 5 and 6, we make some preliminary attempts to nail down the causal relationship between Quebec's distinctive policies and the province's favourable record of poverty reduction among families with dependent children. In Chapter 5, we assess to what extent Quebec's performance in combating poverty can be attributed to successful efforts to increase labour force participation, particularly of women with (young) children – a core aim of the social investment approach. Our evidence confirms this to be the case, especially for two-parent families. Single-parent families in Quebec have similarly benefited from policies facilitating entry into the labour market, but they have also benefited from relatively generous transfer payments. At the same time, underemployed Quebec households suffer rates of poverty that are as high as elsewhere in North America and, thus, considerably higher than in the European comparison countries.

Finally, in Chapter 6, we consider demographic and economic factors not necessarily under the direct control of governments but with an influence on poverty rates and government policies' ability to affect them. By 'standardizing' poverty rates with respect to the composition of households and employment patterns in Quebec, we can ask: what would poverty rates have been in the other three provinces and the comparison countries if they had had the same household composition and employment patterns? This is one way of gauging the effects of policy regimes *net of* differences in population and economic conditions. Our findings in Chapter 6 reinforce those of the preceding chapters. When we standardize the poverty rates in the other three provinces and selected comparison countries in this way, we find their poverty rates would have been higher if they had had the same household composition and employment patterns as Quebec. In other words, the actual poverty figures, if anything, *under*state the degree of divergence between Quebec and the other Canadian provinces. In the final analysis, even after controlling for recent increases in labour force participation, Quebec stands out for its greater generosity.

In our concluding chapter, we return to these findings and draw some conclusions from the issues raised in the Introduction. We also briefly speculate about the long-run fiscal sustainability of the Quebec approach and whether it can serve as a model for other provinces. While we cannot possibly answer these large and contentious questions satisfactorily, we do think the findings and analyses in the following chapters will contribute to a more informed political conversation.

Social and Employment Policies at the Provincial Level: A Survey of Four Provinces

Introduction

In this chapter we take a closer look at the major social and employment policies and programs in Quebec as compared to Ontario, Alberta, and British Columbia. This will allow us to gauge the extent of Quebec's *virage sociodémocratique*, and thus to set the stage for the subsequent chapters analysing the differences between these provinces in terms of policy outcomes. In the next section we briefly review the history of social and employment policymaking in Canada and its four largest provinces. We then present the major policies and programs that were in force in each of these provinces during the period from 2002 until 2012. For reasons explained below we present these policies in broad groups according to whether they provide passive financial support or are intended to activate beneficiaries and whether or not they support families with children. We conclude by presenting the expenditure figures on these broad groups of programs for our four provinces for 2002–12.

Our conclusion from these data is unambiguous: while Quebec has historically been more generous in its spending, since the late 1990s it has diverged much more sharply from the patterns observed in the other three provinces. Moreover, the kinds of policies Quebec has adopted since the mid-1990s strongly emphasize positive activation measures, including policies intended to help reconcile work and family care, stimulate the labour force participation of mothers with young children, and provide support for families with children – policies that are the hallmark of Nordic social democratic welfare states and their social investment approach. British Columbia, Ontario, and Alberta, meanwhile, have taken a different path, moving towards neoliberal retrenchment, with expenditures on social and employment policies remaining relatively flat. In other words, Quebec has gone 'against the current' (Jenson 2002) by taking its *virage sociodémocratique*.

Social and Employment Policy in Canada's Four Largest Provinces: A Brief History

Federal Background: From Taking the Lead to Pulling Back

As noted in the Introduction, in international comparisons Canada is usually classified as a liberal, market-oriented welfare state. Such regimes are characterized by a reliance on the market as the principal institution through which the material needs of individuals and families are to be met (Banting and Myles 2013b, 4–6). The liberal approach to social and employment policy is decidedly 'residualist,' by which state provision of welfare and social protection is a last resort for those truly incapable of providing for themselves, either through employment or family support. This implies a strict distinction between those 'deserving' state support and the 'undeserving' who are, or should be, able to take care of themselves.

In the Anglo-Saxon world, the distinction between deserving and undeserving poor goes back as far as the Elizabethan Poor Laws of 1601 (see Hick 2004, Ch. 2). The principal concern of these Poor Laws, as well as successor laws and programs in Great Britain, was to ensure that *only* those truly unable to work and who had fallen into destitution through no fault of their own – that is, the truly infirm, orphans, widows, and the elderly – would receive publicly provided charity. Those deemed employable were strictly subjected to the principle of 'less eligibility': whatever charity they received should always be less (and the attached conditions less attractive) than the lowest-paying employment available in the local labour market.

With the introduction of the English Poor Law Reform Bill of 1834, able-bodied adults were required to enter the draconian 'workhouses' of Dickensian notoriety to qualify for charity.[1] As Somers and Block (2005, 267) vividly put it, the idea was to make 'welfare so odious that it was less attractive (eligible) than even the most demeaning life without it.' According to some critics, recent workfare reforms inspired by neoliberal thinking are a throwback to the Anglo-Saxon Poor Law tradition (see, e.g., Morel 2002; Daigneault 2014; Somers and Block 2005; Peck 2001).

But given the plethora of social programs serving a wide range of vulnerable populations in even the most liberal welfare state regimes, it would be a gross exaggeration to suggest a return to Dickensian times. Nevertheless, as we shall see, some recent welfare reforms have ended up reinforcing the old distinction between the deserving and the undeserving poor in some jurisdictions.

At any rate, after the Second World War, the Canadian federal government began to introduce a number of policies and programs with a more 'Beveridgean' flavour, based on the principle of citizen entitlement rather than residualism and dire need, including unemployment insurance, public health care, and public pensions.[2] Then, in 1966, it introduced the Canada Assistance Plan (CAP) providing federal-provincial cost-sharing of a range of federally approved provincial social assistance programs in a bid to improve and standardize the level of benefits across provinces (see Boychuk 2015, 70–4). At the same time, however, the provinces were left to define and apply their own eligibility criteria for programs co-financed through CAP, and these criteria remained decidedly residualist, at least outside Quebec.

Quebec's early approach to social policy had slightly different cultural roots, although the net effect in terms of program generosity, or the lack thereof, and outcomes in terms of poverty levels were not very different from the rest of the country.[3] Social policy in Quebec until the 1960s was principally a matter of private charity, dominated by the Catholic Church, with very modest financial support from the provincial government. Here as elsewhere individuals and families deemed able to work received little or no support, although the distinction between deserving and undeserving poor never acquired the punitive elements found in other provinces (Noël 2015, 193). As early as 1937, the government introduced a program providing a modest allowance for needy mothers that established a minimum entitlement for families with children (ibid., 194). The policy was likely inspired by the conservative family-oriented ideology of the church, but it was also a harbinger of things to come; it certainly deviated from the residualist orientation holding sway in other provinces.

The period from the 1960s to the mid-1980s saw the gradual expansion of Canada's social welfare programs, however modest by international standards, particularly at the federal level. But by the late 1980s, this trend began to stall as a result of the severe recession begun earlier that decade and the growing influence of neoliberal thinking in policy circles and national and provincial political discourse. By the early

1990s, Canada's accumulated public debt as a proportion of GDP was one of the highest among the major industrialized countries, causing a great deal of alarm at both the federal and provincial levels. In accordance with the rising tide of neoliberal thinking, Canadian policymakers cut back public expenditures, particularly on passive social protection programs thought to be counterproductive, such as unemployment insurance and social assistance (Banting and Myles 2013b, 12–13).

At the federal level, successive Liberal governments led by Jean Chrétien and Minister of Finance Paul Martin launched a sustained campaign from 1993 onward to reduce the federal deficit and turn it into an annual surplus by cutting back commitments to the provinces and reforming major programs. Two such reforms substantially reduced the federal government's contribution to social protection programs. First, in 1996 the Unemployment Insurance program underwent a major overhaul and was redubbed Employment Insurance. While the reform was widely advertised as a move away from passive support towards the adoption of activating measures, an important motive was cutting expenditures by lowering benefit levels, restricting eligibility, and reducing maximum benefit periods (see, e.g., van den Berg et al. 2008). Second, in the same year, the federal government replaced the CAP, through which it had borne 50% of the cost of provincial social assistance programs, with a block grant called the Canada Social and Health Transfer (CSHT). The CSHT abolished all federal regulation of provincial social assistance programs, except for the prohibition of residency requirements, and significantly reduced the federal contribution to provincially administered welfare programs.[4] Since the provinces were now forced to finance all social programs *as well as* health care from the same reduced block grant, and as health care and education expenditures continued to rise, this put great financial pressure on the provinces' other social programs, particularly social assistance (see, e.g., Boychuk 2015, 70–4; Jenson 2013, 52–3; Myles and Banting 2013b, 22–3).

As will be shown more clearly in the following sections, the provinces, with the significant exception of Quebec, followed the federal lead in cutting back on social spending, albeit with varying degrees of enthusiasm. In Alberta and Ontario, Conservative governments under Premiers Ralph Klein and Mike Harris, respectively, pursued a policy of aggressive cutbacks and reforms of provincial social programs that went well beyond anything the federal Liberals would have endorsed. Their primary motivation was not so much the need to balance the budget as an ideological commitment to reducing the role of government altogether and to eliminating, or at least drastically reducing, what they saw as widespread dependency on unconditional government 'handouts.' The NDP and Liberal governments in power in British Columbia after the defeat of the Social Credit Party in 1991 were not as ideologically committed to an explicitly neoliberal policy agenda. Nevertheless, fiscal and economic pressures caused them to cut back on their social expenditures, with results not all that different from those in Ontario and Alberta.

Ontario: The 'Common Sense Revolution' and Its Legacy[5]

When the Ontario Liberals came to power in 1985 under Premier David Peterson, after several decades of Conservative rule, they raised benefit levels and eased eligibility rules for access to social benefits. The NDP government under Bob Rae, which succeeded the Liberals in 1990, initially intended to continue along this road; for example, they proposed additional reforms to improve benefit levels while emphasizing employability. But these ambitious plans were shelved, as the deep recession of the early 1990s caused social assistance caseloads and costs to soar just as the federal government was putting a cap on CAP. When the Conservatives returned to power under Mike Harris, they set out to reverse these modest reforms with a vengeance as part of their 'Common Sense Revolution.' The Harris government reintroduced the strictest possible distinction between the deserving and undeserving poor by creating two separate programs, Ontario Works (OW) for those able to work and the Ontario Disability Support Program (ODSP) for those not able to work because of severe and prolonged disabilities. Over time, benefits available from OW were slashed, eligibility rules tightened, and benefit receipt made dependent on clear proof of willingness to accept all available employment. ODSP benefits remained relatively untouched.

These cutbacks and reforms resulted in a dramatic decline in social assistance caseloads and expenditures and enjoyed widespread support from the Ontario public despite energetic protests from social assistance rights groups and unions. In fact, they were so popular that the Liberal government coming to power in 2003 under Dalton McGuinty dared only tinker with them at the margins, easing some of their harshest aspects and introducing the far less controversial Ontario Child Benefit (2007) for low-income families with dependent children under the age of 18. Consequently, the essentially residualist architecture of the Harris reforms has remained largely unchanged (for more detail, see Graefe 2015; Haddow 2015, 46–52 and Ch. 4).

Alberta: Supporting the 'Deserving Poor'

While similar, Alberta's story does not involve regime change. The province remained under Conservative rule for decades, until the surprise electoral victory of the NDP under Rachel Notley in May 2015. Until the arrival of Premier Ralph Klein, successive Conservative governments followed the general trend towards modest expansion of welfare benefits within a decidedly residualist framework. But in the wake of the recession of the early 1990s, the new Klein government resolved to eliminate the province's debt and deficits, first and foremost by slashing social program expenditures. In keeping with its residualist tradition, Alberta has had a support program for the deserving poor since 1979; this program, Assured Income for the Severely Handicapped (AISH), has significantly more-generous benefits than the Social Allowance program. In 1990, the latter was renamed Supports for Independence (SFI) to underline its stronger emphasis on pushing potential beneficiaries back into the labour market.

As noted above, almost immediately after taking over in 1993, the Klein government introduced a massive program of budget cuts and constraints, including severe cuts in the benefits and tightening of eligibility criteria of the SFI program but leaving AISH relatively unscathed. Although the reforms were presented as part of a general shift towards more emphasis on employment and employability, the principal aim was to cut government expenditure by drastically reducing welfare rolls (see Reichwein 2003, 27–8). In the following years, the number of SFI recipients fell by 63%, the greatest reduction in the country (Faid 2009, 8; Reichwein 2003, 32; Wood 2015, 238–40).

In the early 2000s, two committees of Conservative MLAs reviewed the province's social policies in response to growing alarm about the deleterious effects of the cutbacks in SFI benefits and caseloads and the erosion of AISH benefits as a result of inflation. The committees' reports inspired another major reform of the SFI program, which in 2004 became Alberta Works Income Support (AW-IS). At the same time, there were some increases in the benefits offered by AISH. AW-IS further strengthened the emphasis on getting beneficiaries back to work, but it had relatively little impact, as caseloads remained quite low due to the buoyant economy of the period. Yet AISH benefits and caseloads continued to rise, so much so that by 2012 Alberta's allowances for citizens with severe disabilities became the highest in the country (Wood 2015, 241). Consequently, by the mid-2000s, Alberta had implemented the strictest separation of deserving and undeserving poor in the country, with very little, if any, support for those deemed capable of taking care of themselves through employment or support from family members on the one hand, and relatively generous support for the severely and permanently disabled on the other (for more detail see Faid 2009; Reichwein 2003; Wood 2015).

British Columbia: Facing Fiscal Constraints

In contrast to Alberta and, to some extent, Ontario, British Columbia was governed by a left-leaning NDP government throughout the 1990s. When it took power in 1991, Mike Harcourt's NDP inherited one of the country's least generous provincial social welfare regimes as a result of the aggressive cuts in welfare programs undertaken during the 1980s by the Social Credit government of Premier Bill Bennett (Graham et al. 2009, 12–13). During its first years in office, the Harcourt government attempted to reform the existing Guaranteed Available Income for Need (GAIN) program with a view of removing its most coercive aspects, improving benefit levels and accessibility, and offering positive incentives of various kinds for beneficiaries to participate in the labour market. But the initial optimism about the government's ability to strengthen the province's social safety net quickly waned under the combined pressures of declining federal funding, the deep recession of the early 1990s, rapidly rising welfare caseloads, and growing provincial public debt. Faced with rising anti-welfare sentiment, the government implemented a major reform in 1996, replacing the GAIN program with BC Benefits to prove that even an NDP government was willing to 'get tough' with welfare clients and impose a stricter family/work enforcement approach (Graham et al. 2009, 13–14; Pulkingham 2015, 214–15). Benefits were cut and workfare more strictly enforced in an effort to reduce the numbers of beneficiaries by making 'work a better deal than welfare' (British Columbia Ministry of Social Services, cited by Pulkingham 2015, 215). As a corollary to this new, harsher treatment of those deemed capable of working, stricter distinctions between those expected to work and those with disabilities were introduced. In other words, whatever their initial policy preferences might have been, NDP governments under Mike Harcourt and his successors were unable to withstand the prevailing economic and political pressures moving them towards social policy retrenchment.

While British Columbia's NDP governments may have implemented a harsher workfare regime with some reluctance, under the Liberals of Premier Gordon Campbell, who took over in 2001, the province moved towards an 'enthusiastic adoption of the neoliberal model' (McBride and McNutt 2007, 177), replacing BC Benefits with a new welfare administration called British Columbia Employment and Assistance (BCEA) in 2002. Under BCEA, benefit levels were cut and restrictions on access to benefits under the category of 'persons with persistent and multiple barriers to employment' were tightened significantly (see Graham et al. 2009, 15–16). As a result, despite some later reversals and relaxation of access criteria and the introduction of some additional housing support for vulnerable populations (ibid., 17–18), British Columbia's social safety net came to closely resemble Alberta's. As one recent observer notes, 'social assistance in BC today is no longer a system that largely supports those deemed to be temporarily unemployed and "expected to work"; it is one that supports those deemed to have a recognized disability, medical condition or other health-related barrier to employment' (Pulkingham 2015, 225).

Quebec: Going against the Current

It is tempting to conclude from this brief survey of social policy history in Ontario, Alberta, and British Columbia that the strong claims in the literature about the irresistible pressures of globalization and 'hard' economic realities on the welfare state are confirmed by the Canadian case. It would appear that by the 1990s, Canada's provincial governments, *whatever* their political stripe and initial policy preferences, were compelled by economic and political forces beyond their control to drastically cut back on the social protection policies so painstakingly built up since the 1960s. As predicted by many, the relentless pressures of global competition and budgetary constraints forced even the most reluctant governments to pursue a neoliberal policy agenda of dismantling the social safety net. But then there is Quebec.

As we have noted already, the historical roots of Quebec's social and employment regime cannot be traced to the Poor Law tradition once dominant in English Canada. To fully appreciate the differences, we will have to look in more detail at the history of *la belle province*.[6]

After having broken the decades-long hegemony of the traditionalist Union Nationale in 1960, the new Liberal government led by Jean Lesage set out to radically recast the role of the state in Quebec society, primarily at the expense of the Catholic Church, in what became known as the Quiet Revolution. On the basis of the 1963 Boucher Commission report, which recommended the complete takeover of social assistance by the Quebec government, and aided by the federal funds made available through the CAP introduced in 1966, Quebec passed the Social Aid Act of 1969. Simply stated, this constituted a major step away from the residualist approach prevalent elsewhere in Canada. The act established the entitlement of all Quebeckers, whether employable or not, to a minimum level of income (see, e.g., Noël 2015, 195). While benefit levels under the act were not able to reduce poverty levels below those of the other major provinces, symbolically at least, it represented a major departure, setting Quebec on a course that would distinguish it more and more sharply from the other provinces. The act has undergone several reforms, most of them broadening the concept of legitimate need and increasingly emphasizing the desirability of helping the poor find employment to lift them out of poverty (see Ulysse and Lesemann 2004, Ch. 2).

Another aspect setting Quebec apart is the long-standing influence of a host of advocacy groups in the social policy area, including the province's powerful unions, women's organizations, community groups representing the poor, organizations advocating housing support for low-income families, and so on. Although a few were influential early on during the conservative Catholic corporatism of the Duplessis years, the Quebec government began to fund and consult more of these groups and organizations in the wake of the Quiet Revolution (Haddow 2015, 42–5; Noël 2013, 261, 2015, 204). As their strength and organizing capacity grew, they became increasingly influential, and were frequently enlisted by the provincial government to help formulate and, of course, legitimate new social policies (see, e.g., Vaillancourt 2012, 126ff.). To give one example of their influence, when Liberal Premier Robert Bourassa implemented a major reform of the Social Aid Act in 1989, introducing distinctions akin to those between deserving and undeserving beneficiaries, a storm of protest ensued from a wide range of social rights organizations. The impressive display of those organizations' capacity to mobilize popular support may help explain why Quebec was spared the retrenchment of social assistance programs occurring elsewhere in Canada (Haddow 2015, 112–13; Noël 2015, 195–6).

To be sure, from the late 1980s onward, Quebec governments have attempted to bring down social assistance caseloads and expenditures by a series of surveillance measures to combat welfare fraud and by introducing stricter eligibility criteria amounting to 'significant long-term retrenchment in its social assistance' (Haddow 2015, 239). But while these measures did have an activating component in that they used financial incentives to encourage social assistance recipients to enrol in employment programs, they never adopted the workfare approach of making benefits conditional on such enrolment (Haddow 2015, 102–3). Moreover, whatever reductions in expenditures on social assistance were achieved by these reforms were more than compensated for by Quebec's shift towards increasing support for low-income families with children, as we shall see below (see also Haddow 2015, Ch. 4 and Ch. 8).

Continuous agitation by social rights organizations and the unions ensured that Bourassa's reforms remained controversial, so when the Parti Québécois regained power in 1994, it was eager to establish its social democratic credentials. It did so by appointing a high-level study group to review the province's entire social program architecture (Noël 2015, 196). By this time, the Quebec government was in the same straightened economic circumstances as the other provinces and had the largest provincial budget deficit. Yet unlike his counterparts in the other major Canadian provinces, Premier Lucien Bouchard was not in a position to slash public program budgets unilaterally. Instead, he called two socio-economic summits in Quebec City in March and October 1996, inviting the employers' organizations, the unions, and *les associations de la société civile* to hammer out a 'social pact' to support deficit reduction balanced by measures supporting employment creation. The summits produced a unique 'social contract' in which the government committed itself to simultaneously balance the budget, create employment, and combat poverty and inequality (see, e.g., Noël 2013, 262–4; Ulysse and Lesemann 2004, 129–31).

The 1996 summits were followed by a flurry of new policies, policy reforms, and government commitments for the near future, all of which pushed Quebec in the opposite direction of its sister provinces and the federal government. In 1997, in addition to a number of lesser reforms, such as the automatic recovery of alimonies and a new family allowance program, the Quebec government inaugurated its much-celebrated $5-a-day subsidized day-care system (see Haddow 2015, 134–46; Roy, Fréchet, and Savard 2008, 60). This was followed in 1998 by the creation of the $334 million Fund to Combat Poverty through Reinsertion into Employment (Fonds de lutte contre la pauvreté par la réinsertion au travail; see Ulysse and Lesemann 2004, 131–2). A series of reforms benefiting families with children followed in subsequent years. The Quebec government also committed itself to creating its own parental leave program, more generous than the one offered through the federal EI program. In addition, combining federal and provincial funds and programs after the devolution of active labour market policies under the 1996 federal EI program (see van den Berg et al. 2008), Quebec created Emploi-Québec, an agency mandated to administer all training and labour market insertion programs in the province, supervised in consultation with provincial and regional representatives of business, labour and educational institutions, and local communities. Integrating employment and training programs for all those wishing to use its services, Emploi-Québec is 'an organization without parallel elsewhere in Canada' (Noël 2015, 199). The consolidation of activation programs and the emphasis on local administration have, according to all carefully conducted evaluation studies, been spectacularly successful in aiding clients who might not otherwise have been able to do so find gainful employment (ibid., 199–201). In short, 'in just a few years, a raft of legislation transformed the situation of women in the labour market, redesigned the support and services offered to families, changed the working conditions and earnings of low-wage earners, and revised social programs aimed at the poorest' (Noël 2013, 263).

The most impressive manifestation of the power of Quebec's social rights advocacy movement came on 13 December 2002, when the Quebec National Assembly unanimously adopted Bill 112, 'An Act to Combat Poverty and Social Exclusion.' The stated purpose of the act was to establish a 'national strategy … intended to progressively make Québec, by 2013, one of the industrialized nations having the least number of persons living in poverty, according to recognized methods for making international comparisons' (Quebec National Assembly 2002, Ch. 2, article 4). According to many observers, Bill 112 and its subsequent implementation in the first five-year action plan, *Reconciling Freedom and Social Justice: A Challenge for the Future* (released in April 2004), constituted a watershed in Quebec's development of a distinctive approach to social policy. More than anything else, it put the province in the avant-garde in the social policy field in Canada, and, for that matter, North America (Noël 2002, 2013; Roy, Fréchet, and Savard 2008).

The action plan called for the consolidation and extension of existing programs and the creation of new ones to combat poverty in the province with the commitment of $2.5 billion over a five-year period. It established two main principles to guide Quebec's anti-poverty strategy: first, employment should, wherever possible, be the primary means of lifting citizens out of poverty; second, social protection for those with limited or no capacity to work should be strengthened. In addition, the plan emphasized that a long-term strategy to combat poverty would require special emphasis on supporting families with children at risk of falling into poverty.

Jean Charest's Liberal government, which took over the reins from Bouchard's PQ in 2003, appeared at first to wish to turn the tide in a more conservative direction. The new premier declared his intention to re-engineer the Quebec government into a new, leaner model appropriate to twenty-first-century reality. But in the face of sustained opposition from the coalition of civil society movements that had coalesced around the 1996 social pact, the government eventually backed down and instead continued along the path set out by its predecessor (see Noël 2013, 265).

In the years that followed, the Quebec Assembly passed a series of laws and adopted a number of programs introducing new activation measures to encourage and support labour force participation of persons at risk of poverty, including investment in training; the facilitation of employment for persons with handicaps; support for families with (young) children; the reconciliation of employment and family care by parents, especially mothers, of young children through an enriched parental leave program; measures designed to guide young people into the labour force; and an ambitious program of affordable-housing construction (see, e.g., Godbout and St-Cerny 2008; Lefèvre, Boismenu, and Dufour 2011, 130ff.; Noël 2013, 266–70; Roy, Fréchet, and Savard 2008; Torjman 2010; Ulysse and Lesemann 2004, Ch. 6). In 2010, Quebec renewed its commitment to its overall poverty reducing strategy by designating $7 billion over five years for its new plan, *Le Québec mobilisé contre la pauvreté* (Ministère de l'emploi et de la solidarité sociale du Québec, 2012).

From Politics to Numbers: Spending Divergence over Time

Although admittedly brief, the above review of provincial policy history since the late 1980s suggests Quebec and the other three provinces have taken quite different policymaking paths. One would expect this to be clearly reflected in the provincial governments' expenditures on social and employment policies, and Figures 1.1 and 1.2 strongly confirm this expectation. In keeping with the distinctions we draw in the remainder of the chapter, we divide provincial expenditures into two

Figure 1.1. Social services expenditures as % of provincial GDP, by province

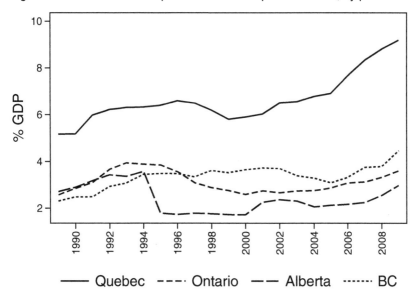

Figure 1.2. Labour, employment, immigration, and special training
expenditures as % of provincial GDP, by province

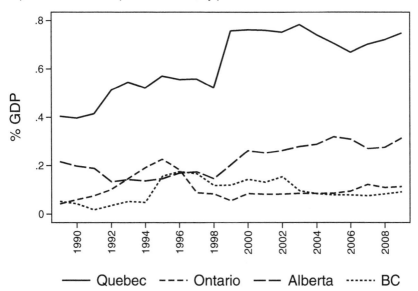

broad categories: social services and housing expenditures, consisting mostly of cash transfers, on one hand, and labour, employment, and retraining expenditures, on the other. (The former are roughly equivalent to our 'income support' category of programs, the latter to our 'activation' one.) We caution, however, against directly comparing the data in these two figures with the more detailed data presented later in this chapter. The present data come from the CANSIM tables provided by Statistics Canada and are limited in two important ways. First, the accounting categories are quite broad and do not permit us to separate out specific social programs of interest, such as, for instance, public expenditures on day care.[7] Second, we can only trace data back to 1989, since that is as far as they go in their present form.

Looking at Figures 1.1 and 1.2, we are immediately struck by the sharp contrast between Quebec and the other provinces. Already in the late 1980s,[8] Quebec is spending considerably more on both social services and employment policies than any of the other provinces. Figure 1.1 indicates that while expenditures on social services fluctuate without any clear upward or downward trend in Ontario, Alberta, and British Columbia from 1989 to 2000, they rise in Quebec, increasing the gap between the other three provinces. Note, also, that the effect of the Harris and Klein cutbacks in Ontario and Alberta are clearly visible, with social service spending declining quite abruptly in Alberta from the mid-1990s until the early 2000s.

Figure 1.2 shows a similar pattern, with Quebec already spending considerably more on activation measures than the other provinces in 1989 and continuing to increase its spending, especially after 1997. Ontario's and British Columbia's spending settles down at about one-eighth of Quebec's level in terms of percentages of provincial GDPs, while Alberta's rises only slightly, to somewhat less than half of Quebec's level. These patterns illustrate the very different orientations of the reforms implemented in the four provinces during this period. As mentioned, in all four provinces, social policy reform was presented as at least partly motivated by a desire to 'activate' those in danger of becoming dependent on the public purse. But whereas the Anglophone provinces pursued this goal by taking a more punitive workfare approach, Quebec opted for something closer to the social investment approach often associated with the Nordic welfare states. We return to these differences below.

Clearly, then, when compared to the other provinces and the federal government, Quebec has taken a distinctive approach to social policymaking for some time. But, while Quebec's unique path has been noted by friend and foe alike, the actual *extent* of its divergence from Canada's other provinces in terms of the character of, and resources devoted to, anti-poverty and employment policies has yet to be fully documented. In the remainder of this chapter, we begin to fill this gap by offering a detailed comparison of the main social and labour market policies and their corresponding expenditure patterns in Canada's four largest provinces during the decade following the adoption of Bill 112 in 2002.

As noted above, a theme of growing importance in Quebec's approach to combating poverty is an emphasis on activation, that is, on measures and programs aimed at helping vulnerable populations (re-)enter and stay in the labour force. A second distinctive feature, at least when compared to the rest of North America, is Quebec's strong focus on supporting families with children at risk of poverty. A third is the attempt to ease the reconciliation of work and family obligations for parents with (young) children through the provision of affordable day care and generous parental leave programs. The latter, of course, are also meant as activation programs for parents of (young) children, especially mothers. These features will become increasingly clear as we proceed.

Program Descriptions

This section describes programs at the provincial level from 2002 to 2012. *Income support programs* are usually comprised of social assistance and its related health benefits, disability support, affordable housing, workplace safety, benefits for seniors, public sector pensions, and tax credits or benefits for families with children. In addition, Quebec has committed public funds to its road safety insurance scheme. *Activation programs* generally include training and apprenticeship, integration and language training for immigrants, disability-related employment assistance, employment programs specifically aimed at youth, employment subsidies and bonuses, and childcare support. As noted, Quebec has complemented the federal parental leave program with provincial funds and added a refundable tax credit for working families. The province also introduced a now well-known program of subsidized low-cost day-care centres.

In what follows we list the existing programs within each broad group for each province for the period 2002–12. While these lists may seem tedious to some, we think it important to present them, both because they provide a sense of the differences in policy orientation across provinces, and because they are the programs and policies we have included in our calculations of provincial expenditures in the next section. Readers interested in our methodology and data sources are referred to the appendix at the end of this chapter. Readers more interested in the resulting expenditure patterns can skip to the section on trends in provincial outlays on these programs.

Income Support Programs

For each province we begin with the general social assistance programs which represent the largest expenditures for income support before moving on to the programs tailored to the needs of specific subpopulations.

ONTARIO

Most of Ontario's income support programs were in effect throughout 2002–12. The social assistance program has two parts: Ontario Works and ODSP. As its name indicates, Ontario Works is a means-tested financial assistance program requiring its beneficiaries to participate in job search activities. In contrast, while also means-tested, the ODSP provides the financial support to pay for basic living expenses and is restricted to individuals with a physical or mental disability that is expected to last at least a year and impedes their ability to participate fully in society. Within the ODSP, the affordable housing program subsidizes the construction of housing units for rent or sale and allocates housing allowances.

The Developmental Services program provides support for individuals who have developmental disabilities from birth or before age 18. These supports enable such individuals to participate in the community; they include residential support, respite services[9] for informal caregivers, and a network of professionals to coordinate care and activities to help them participate in the community once they finish high school. The vast majority of these funds are not intended to help beneficiaries find jobs.

One of the income support programs is specific to seniors. The Guaranteed Annual Income Supplement (GAINS) acts as a supplementary benefit to the federal Old Age Security and Guaranteed Income Supplement for low-income seniors. Another income support program is work related; the Workplace Safety and Insurance Board administers replacement wages for workers injured on the job or who contract an occupational disease. It replaces 85% of income (up to a maximum of $77,600 in 2010).

As noted above, we include public sector pensions in the income support program category: Ontario's Public Service Pension Plan (PSPP), The Ontario Public Service Employees Union pension plan (OPTrust), the Ontario Municipal Employees Retirement System (OMERS), the Healthcare of Ontario Pension Plan (HOOPP), and the Ontario Teachers' Pension Plan (OTPP).

Two relevant programs were implemented during the period 2002–12. First, since 2007–8, the Ontario Child Benefit has provided cash benefits to low-income families with children. Second, since 2008–9, the Ontario Senior Homeowner's Property Tax Grant has offered a tax credit of up to $500 to help home-owning, low-income seniors pay their property taxes.

A final program of note. In 2008, no doubt inspired by the Quebec example and following province-wide public consultations, the government of Ontario released a comprehensive poverty reduction strategy, *Breaking the Cycle: Ontario's Poverty Reduction Strategy* As the name suggests, the strategy emphasizes the need to break the intergenerational cycle of poverty. This was followed by legislative commitment in 2009 when the Poverty Reduction Act passed unanimously in the Legislative Assembly. The act commits the government to targets and timelines (e.g. a 25% reduction of the number of children living in poverty in Ontario by 2013), to continued public consultation, and to regular review of its strategy. The act specifies that 'the Government of Ontario is required to establish a specific poverty reduction target at least every five years.'

BRITISH COLUMBIA

In British Columbia, social assistance is comprised of three parts: temporary, continuous or disability, and supplementary assistance. Temporary assistance is intended for families or individuals who are temporarily unable to work due to a short-term medical condition or another barrier to employment. Continuous assistance is for those who have a longer-term disability or illness and need help with daily living activities. Individuals receiving continuous assistance are not expected to return to employment or to try to find work. Finally, supplementary assistance consists of additional health and other supports for families of individuals who receive temporary or disability social assistance benefits.

Community Living Services (called Community Living BC since fiscal year 2003–4) is the counterpart of Ontario Developmental Services. It is restricted to adults with a developmental disability prior to age 18 and who have difficulties living independently. When needed, it provides residential support, community support and inclusion activities, respite services for the main caregiver, as well as psychological or instrumental support to individuals and their families. Again, employment support is included but represents a very small fraction of spending in this program.

The housing program includes emergency shelter for the homeless, as well as affordable housing for rent or purchase. Its mandate is to ensure a range of housing options exist, so it either adapts existing housing or builds new homes or buildings to fill a gap in affordable housing.

WorkSafeBC is responsible for compensating the loss of income following a work-related injury or disease. It replaces 90% of income for the first ten weeks of benefits regardless of individual circumstances, but these are taken into account in the calculation of benefits beyond 10 weeks.

Other income support programs include public sector pensions: the College Pension Plan, Municipal Pension Plan, Public Service Pension Plan, Teacher's Pension Plan, and WorkSafeBC Pension Plan.

Finally, British Columbia offers a series of tax-related benefits. The BC Family Bonus program provides tax-free monthly benefits to families with children who earn a low or modest income. Another part of the program is a tax credit for families to support the cost of raising children. Starting in 2006–7, the government implemented a progressive non-refundable tax credit for individuals with modest incomes called the BC Tax Reduction Credit. Since 2008–9, British Columbia has offered a Low Income Climate Action Tax Credit, with non-taxable quarterly payments intended to help offset the carbon taxes paid by low-income individuals and families.

ALBERTA

Alberta's social assistance program also consists of three parts: support for people who are working or are expected to work, support for people not expected to work, and support for learners. It includes financial and health care support. We include the support for learners under our category of activation programs because it is similar to an apprenticeship program, and the Alberta government reports separate expenditures for it.

The Persons with Developmental Disabilities program offers services to support eligible Albertans in their homes, their work, as well as in the wider community. As with the Ontario and British Columbia equivalents, the portion of the program that focuses on employment support is very small. Adults with a permanent disability and with household income under a certain threshold are eligible for financial and health benefits under the Assured Income for the Severely Handicapped program.

There are various programs for seniors, another specific subpopulation. The Alberta Seniors Benefit is a financial support program adding benefits for low-income seniors on top of the federal pension programs. The Income Support Widows Program provides financial benefits to low-income widows between the ages of 55 and 64, inclusively (Government of Alberta 2009). The Seniors Dental Assistance Program, which started in the fiscal year 2003–4, and the Seniors Optical Assistance Program, introduced in 2005–6, offer financial support for basic dental and optical services for low- and moderate-income seniors. Starting in 2009–10, the Special Needs Assistance Grants offers a one-time payment for extraordinary expenses to help elderly Albertans with the cost of minor home repairs, appliances, or medical costs; the maximum benefit is $5,000. The same year, School Property Tax Assistance began to provide a yearly rebate to senior homeowners to offset increases in the education property tax.

The affordable housing programs offered by the Alberta government throughout 2002–12 provide subsidized rent or create new affordable housing options for low-income families, seniors or persons with special needs, and support emergency or transitional housing for homeless people.[10]

Coverage of some health services not covered through the Alberta Health Care Insurance scheme was extended to low-income individuals and their children with the Alberta Adult Health Benefit and Alberta Child Health Benefit programs. Additional funding for the special needs of parents of children with disabilities is provided through the Family Support for Children with Disabilities program.

In the area of replacement income, the Alberta Workers' Compensation Board replaces a similar proportion of earnings as its counterpart organizations in other provinces. In 2011, it replaced 90% of earnings up to a maximum of approximately $82,000 per year.

Public sector pensions for Alberta include the Local Authorities Pension Plan, Management Employees Pension Plan, Supplementary

Retirement Plan for Public Service Managers, Public Service Pension Plan, Special Forces Pension Plan, Provincial Judges and Masters in Chambers Registered and Unregistered Pension Plans, and the Teachers' Pension Plan. Most of these plans existed throughout the whole period of interest, except the plan for judges and masters in chambers, which started in 2005.

Finally, in 2012, the government of Alberta committed to creating a comprehensive poverty reduction strategy for the province with the aim of eliminating child poverty by 2017 and reducing overall poverty by 2022. To this end, it orchestrated a series of province-wide consultations throughout 2013–14. Its resulting *Poverty Reduction Strategy Discussion Guide* (Government of Alberta 2013) details seven broad concerns that should be addressed by a poverty reduction strategy tailored to Alberta's needs. One is the role of assets in determining poverty, making Alberta the first province to make this connection (Rothwell and Haveman 2013; cf. Torjman 2008). Despite the promising start, two years on, a comprehensive poverty reduction strategy is still forthcoming.

QUEBEC

The social assistance program in Quebec is known as the Aide aux personnes et aux familles (Assistance-emploi before 2005). As in other provinces, the program is divided into subprograms: social assistance is for individuals considered able to work but facing temporary constraints preventing them from holding a job, such as having young children or a medical condition; social solidarity is for those with more severe constraints.

There are also some specific income support programs for older workers or for workers who become unemployed following a massive layoff in their company or industry, along with several smaller programs for youth to help them gain skills useful on the labour market (Alternative Jeunesse, Devenir, Interagir[11] and Réussir). We would normally classify the latter as activating policies, but because the budget is not divided by subgroups, we include them in our income support measures, as this will not affect the results very much.

The programs assisting disabled persons financially or in accessing services are Aide financière aux personnes handicapées and Soutien à l'intégration des personnes handicappées, respectively. The latter is presented as a personalized approach; an intervention plan is developed with the beneficiary or his or her guardian to ensure his or her needs are met.

As mentioned previously in this chapter, the Société d'assurance automobile du Québec provides income replacement for individuals injured on the road. As of 2011, when workers are injured or incur a workplace-related illness, 90% of their income is replaced, up to a maximum of $64,000, as part of the provincial workplace safety program administered by the Commission de la santé et de la sécurité du Québec (CSST). The CSST also administers a preventive program for early maternity leave for pregnant women whose workplace may represent a risk for their pregnancy.

Quebec is similar to British Columbia, but differs from Ontario, and to an even greater extent from Alberta, in its support of seniors. It does not have specific programs for its elderly population other than what is already included in other, larger programs. However, it does fund public sector pensions through the Commission administrative des régimes de retraite et d'assurances, which includes plans for civil servants, other government employees, teachers, police officers, municipal councillors, mayors, and judges.

In terms of social housing, Quebec offers subsidies to not-for-profit organizations or cooperatives to build or renovate housing for low- or low-to-middle-income households, and it provides subsidized rent in social housing or in housing owned by a cooperative or a not-for-profit organization. This program is called Aide au logement social et communautaire.

The income support programs targeting families with children evolved between 2002 and 2012. Prestations familiales existed until 2004–5, when it was replaced by Soutien aux enfants, a refundable tax credit for families with a child aged less than 18 residing with them. There is also a supplement for a child with disabilities. Up to 2004–5, means-tested family allowances were given to mothers, in addition to an allowance at the birth of a child. This was a much larger program before 1997, but was slowly phased out.

Activation and Work and Family Reconciliation Programs

In this section we list, again for each province, the provincial policies and programs in force during the 2002–12 period that were intended to help individuals enter or stay in the labour force. These programs consist of two broad subgroups: activation programs that help beneficiaries find employment and/or training that will enable them to find employment, and family support policies that facilitate the labour force participation of parents of families with (young) children.

ONTARIO

A few changes in Ontario programs over 2002–12 are intended to encourage individuals to enter or re-enter the labour market. In 2002–3, four main programs dealt with helping people find employment or acquire the skills leading to employment: Employment Preparation, the employment assistance portion of Ontario Works, the province's social assistance scheme, the employment assistance portion of the Ontario Disability Support Program, and Apprenticeship and Training Services. Then, in the fiscal year 2006–7, Employment Assistance and Apprenticeship and Training Services were replaced by two programs serving the same purpose: Labour Market and Training and Workplace Preparation. In 2011–12, these programs were renamed Employment and Training. The program Loans for Tools was implemented in 2006–7; as its name suggests, it offers loans to apprentices who need to buy tools to exercise their trade. From 2006–7 to 2010–11, the Labour Market Development Agreement with the federal government brought in additional funding for employment programs and services.

Specific programs to help immigrants settle in Canada, learn one of the official languages, and eventually join the labour force were in effect throughout the decade. Settlement and Integration Grants funded services delivered through local newcomer settlement agencies. In 2006–7, two additional programs were inaugurated to help immigrants learn English or French and find employment: Language Training and Workplace Training. Finally, Second Language Programs appeared in the provincial budget as of 2006–7; they are available to all adult Ontarians, whether foreign- or Canadian-born.

Ontario's family support programs include childcare and parental leave programs to help parents reconcile work and family obligations. The Ontario budget is not very precise about the purpose of the funds allocated to its Child Care and Early Learning program, but part of the program is related to child development in day cares or in centres where children attend activities with their parents, while another part is allocated to issuing licenses to day-care centres and lending support so that operators meet provincial standards in childcare. In addition, the province offers the Ontario Child Care Supplement for Working Families,[12] a tax-free monthly payment to low- to middle-income parents to offset the cost of childcare and of raising children. Families are eligible regardless of whether a child is in day care. Finally, parental leave benefits are funded under the federal EI program.

BRITISH COLUMBIA

As in Ontario, the activation programs offered by British Columbia assist individuals in finding employment, but unlike Ontario, there is no separate program for persons with disabilities. They simply receive services under a larger program. For example, Employment Programs pay for the salaries of persons with disabilities who receive on-the-job training under the public service employment program.

Several activation programs centre on skills development, training and apprenticeships. Until 2003–4, the Skills Development and Employment Standards program worked to develop and direct strategic plans for skills development. The management of the industry training system was conducted under the Industry Training and Apprenticeship program, but this program ended in 2004–5. In January 2007, the Training Tax Credit was created to provide tax credits to employers and apprentices participating in eligible apprenticeship programs in the province.

Settlement and integration support services are provided by the Aboriginal, Multiculturalism and Immigration program. As the program's title suggests, services are offered to both immigrants and aboriginal persons. Exchanges with the federal government on matters related to immigration, as well as international qualifications programs, are funded under this activation program. It existed throughout the decade under study but was renamed twice, becoming Multiculturalism and Immigration in 2005–6, and Labour Market and Immigration in 2008–9.

British Columbia's family support programs, in the form of childcare and parental leave, are similar to those in Ontario. For childcare, funding is allocated to licensed group and family childcare providers through the Child Care Operating Funding program to assist them with their operating costs. In addition, a Child Care Subsidy is allocated monthly to parents with low- and middle-incomes to offset the cost of childcare.

ALBERTA

As mentioned earlier, we define a portion of Alberta's social assistance program as an activation program, as it is restricted to those requiring skill upgrading or training – in other words, those persons participating in measures leading to an eventual entry in or return to the labour market. Five other programs are concerned with apprenticeship, training, skills development, job search services, and financial assistance while in training: Apprenticeship Delivery Support, Career and Development

Services, Basic Skills and Academic Upgrading, Summer Temporary and Other Employment Programs (for students), and Training for Work.

Alberta has a program to help persons with disabilities access the labour market. More specifically, its Disability Related Employment Support offers job search services, workplace support, such as modifications at the workplace or the provision of assistive technology to enable the person to work, and educational supports, such as interpreters or tutors.

Another program targeting a specific subgroup is Youth Connections. It helps youth who are still in school and youth between the ages of 16 and 24 who are unemployed or underemployed to explore career options by connecting them with potential employers.

Workforce Partnerships is charged with analysis and strategic planning in the labour market, including identifying the need for particular skills to avoid labour shortages. Starting in 2006–7, the Labour Attraction and Supply program has complemented this mandate with three objectives: to increase the skills of Albertans to meet the demands of the labour market; to attract skilled workers from other provinces; and to increase the number of immigrants, especially skilled immigrants, to address labour shortages in specific industries. In a similar program, Aboriginal Development Partnerships has been responsible for strategic planning and economic development in Aboriginal communities since 2006–7 (Aboriginal Relations 2009).

Most programs specific to the integration of immigrants were created or further developed in 2005–6. For example, the International Qualifications Assessment program (which became Qualifications Assessment/ Foreign Qualification Recognition in 2005–6) works to increase access to educational institutions, employment, or professional-association membership by assessing how credentials acquired outside Canada compare to Canadian ones. Other programs focus on settlement services and language training. Immigrant Support Services, created in 2003–4, became Settlement and Integration Services and Enhanced Language Training from 2005–6 onwards. Learning technical language related to the job is within the purview of this program, but learning English is part of the English as an Additional Language program, which also started in 2005–6. For the same number of years, the Bridging Program has assisted recent immigrants in upgrading their skills, the Alberta Immigrant Nominee Program has helped immigrant workers sponsored by an Albertan employer become permanent residents, and a Living Allowance for Immigrants has been provided to economic immigrants who need to upgrade their skills.

Finally, in its family support programs, the Alberta government, like other provincial governments, provides childcare subsidies to parents, but only if they use the following types of day-care services: licensed day-care centres, licensed group family childcare, approved family day homes, licensed out-of-school care centres, licensed preschools and approved early childhood development programs.[13] As in the other provinces, except for Quebec, the federal government provides parental leave benefits as part of the federal EI program.

QUEBEC

The main activation program in Quebec is comprised of the services delivered by Emploi-Québec, including training, subsidies, allowances, skills development, and job searches. Since 2005–6, it has been called Mesures d'aide à l'emploi in the provincial budget. It includes the bilateral labour market development agreements (LMDA) with the federal government. The program Action emploi existed until 2004–5, inclusively; it helped adults who had been beneficiaries of social assistance for a period of at least 36 months to find sustainable employment. Since 2008–9, the Provision pour pourvoir tout crédit pour la mise en oeuvre du Pacte pour l'emploi has added $116 million from the federal government as part of the LMDAs to provide activation measures for individuals not eligible to receive employment insurance or social assistance benefits.

In Quebec's activation programs, we include two smaller programs aimed at training or helping individuals enter or re-enter the workforce by allocating supplementary budgets to training, job search, and the conversion of income support measures into active measures: Provision pour augmenter tout crédit pour la réalisation de projets favourisant l'insertion; la formation et l'aide à l'emploi; and Provision pour augmenter tout crédit pour la création de projets favourisant la conversion de prestations d'aide financière en mesure d'aide à l'emploi.

Other programs are specific to subgroups of the population, such as immigrants, youth, indigenous persons, and persons with disabilities. First, the program Intégration, régionalisation et relations interculturelles aims to help immigrants with social and economic integration, including their acquisition of the French language. Starting in 2004–5, Francisation, the French language course offered to immigrants, essentially became a separate program. From 2007 to 2008, additional funding was devoted to all relevant French language activities under Provision pour augmenter tout crédit pour la réalisation d'activités soutenant l'intégration et la francisation des immigrants. Second, between 2003–4 and 2005–6, Solidarité Jeunesse offered a personalized approach to encourage youth aged 18 to 20 and eligible for employment insurance to finish high school and to find employment in order to facilitate their social and economic integration. Between 2004 and 2011, a small program aimed at promoting summer employment for students called Provision pour augmenter tout crédit pour la réalisation de projets de création d'emplois pour étudiants was part of the budget. Third, the livelihood of Cree indigenous people is supported with funding from the Office de la sécurité du revenu des chasseurs et piégeurs cris. Fourth, specific subsidies to businesses hiring persons with disabilities existed between 2002 and 2005 under the name Subventions aux centres de travail adapté.

A relatively small program to help older workers was added in 2007–8, but it does not appear in subsequent budgets. Since 2006–7, a specific deduction for workers, equivalent to 6% of their employment income up to $1,000, was added to the provincial taxation scheme to encourage people to work and to offset some of the costs related to employment, such as transportation and meals.

Finally, our activation measures for Quebec include a portion of the road safety insurance (SAAQ) devoted to social, educational, and economic integration following a road accident.

Turning to family support programs, a main difference between Quebec and the other provinces is Quebec's subsidization of both public and private day-care centres through Soutien financier aux centres de la petite enfance et aux autres services de garde and Subvention pour le financement des infrastructures des centres de la petite enfance (2008–12). These subsidies have created an affordable day-care system, with exceptionally low daily fees ($7 per child in 2011–12, $5 before 2004).

In addition to subsidies to day-cares, the Quebec government provides a tax credit to offset the cost of childcare, the Crédit d'impôt pour frais de garde d'enfants. In 2005, a new refundable tax credit called Prime au Travail was created to encourage individuals with children to work and to provide additional incentive to social assistance beneficiaries to enter the labour market.

Among Quebec's family support for the purposes of activation, we include the parental leave benefits for a birth or adopted child provided to mothers and fathers by the Régime québécois d'assurance parentale since January 2006. Before 2006, parental leave benefits were provided through the federal EI program.

Figure 1.3. Family support and other expenditures, 2011–12

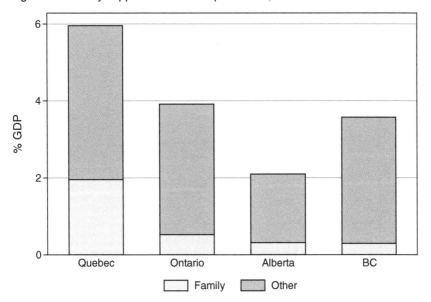

Trends in Public Expenditures

As discussed in the Introduction and the introduction to this chapter, in the past fifteen years Quebec has adopted its own orientation to social policy, putting increasing weight on family support and work-and-family reconciliation policies (F&FR policies hereafter) to achieve its social objectives. As we review the differences in income support and activation policy expenditures between the four major provinces, this will be a recurring theme. To set the stage, we start with a simple comparison: the proportions of GDP devoted to F&FR expenditures versus the proportions spent on all other policies mentioned here.

Data for the fiscal year 2011–12 in Figure 1.3 reveal a very different pattern for Quebec than for Ontario, British Columbia, and Alberta. Quebec spends more as a proportion of its provincial GDP than its counterparts for all programs taken together, especially for its F&FR programs. The province spends approximately 6% of its GDP on income support and activation expenditures together, with a third aimed specifically at families with children. Ontario comes second, in both overall expenditures (3.9% of provincial GDP)[14] and share of expenditures

Figure 1.4. Income support expenditures, fiscal years 2002–3 to 2011–12

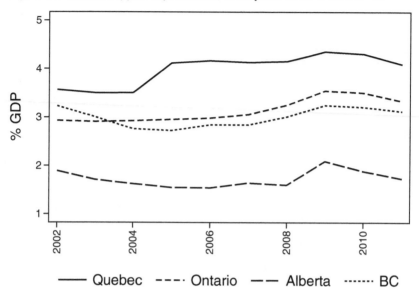

targeting families (13.3% of all expenditures, or slightly less than 0.5% of GDP). British Columbia has a spending pattern similar to Ontario, albeit with lower spending in programs supporting families, while Alberta stands out with its much lower overall spending.

In all four provinces, F&FR policies consist mostly of tax credits, child benefits, and support for childcare, but Quebec is much more generous than the other three, especially when it comes to its public childcare program, parental leave benefits, and refundable tax credit, Soutien aux enfants. As looking at one year of data may not be representative of the long-term differences between the provinces, we now focus on the evolution of each type of expenditure over time, from 2002 to 2012.

Income Support Expenditures

We start with what is generally considered the main instrument to combat poverty: income support programs. Figure 1.4 shows the expenditures on these programs as a percentage of GDP for the fiscal years 2002–3 to 2011–12.

The figure includes all passive income support expenditures, whether they are aimed at families or not. The difference between the provinces is obvious: Quebec spends considerably more than the others, and Alberta spends the least. In both Quebec and Ontario, there is an increase in spending between 2002–3 and 2009–10. However, Quebec takes a different trajectory between these points, showing a sudden increase in 2005–6, due to the Soutien aux Enfants that came into effect in 2005. Over the same period (2002–3 to 2009–10), British Columbia and Alberta experienced a decrease followed by an increase in spending, but the increase is just enough to bring the expenditures back to their 2002–3 level. We then witness a decrease in expenditures for all four provinces in the last two years of the period under study. The increase across provinces between 2008–9 and 2009–10 may in part be attributable to the economic crisis, which resulted in a larger number of Canadians having to rely on income support programs. However, this trend is not sustained in more recent years.

The extent to which Quebec's sudden increase in expenditures in 2005–6 is attributable to programs aimed at supporting families is apparent in Figure 1.5. The figure shows the evolution of income support expenditures specific to families. Notably, we see an increase of nearly 0.6% of GDP, a figure corresponding to findings shown in Figure 1.4. While Alberta remains stable in its family income support expenditures over the decade 2002–12, we see a steady decline for British Columbia, and an increase in the second half of the decade for Ontario. In Ontario, this change can be completely attributed to the creation of a new program, the Ontario Child Benefit. Spending for this program corresponded to 0.03% of GDP in 2007–8 and reached 0.14% in 2011–12. British Columbia and Alberta maintained the same programs throughout the period, but in British Columbia spending declined in dollar terms and as a share of GDP, from $153 million in 2002–03 to only slightly more than $8 million in 2011–12. In Alberta, the reverse occurred, with expenditures increasing in dollar terms but remaining stable as a share of GDP.

Activation and Work and Family Reconciliation Expenditures

Quebec's exceptionalism is confirmed when we consider programs meant to encourage those who are unemployed, or out of the workforce for some other reason, to return to work.[15] Take a look at the trend

Figure 1.5. Family income support expenditures, fiscal years 2002–3 to 2011–12

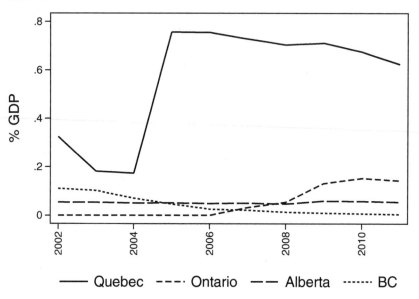

Figure 1.6. Activation expenditures, fiscal years 2002–3 to 2011–12

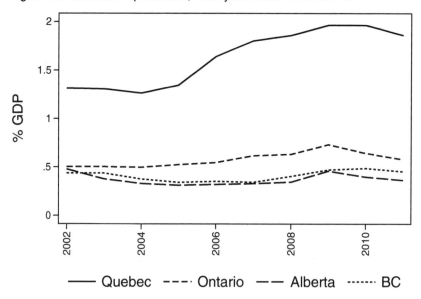

data for activation programs shown in Figure 1.6. For Ontario, Alberta, and British Columbia, trends in spending are largely stable and modest compared to Quebec. A small increase in activation expenditures is noticeable in Ontario in 2009–10, an increase attributable to the doubling of its expenditures in dollar terms on Labour Market and Training. The province spent around $400 million on this program in 2008–9 but increased its expenditures to $822 million the following year. This trend was not sustained in 2010–11, when expenditures decreased to $590 million, corresponding to a drop of 0.045% of GDP. In fact, all provinces, including Quebec, show a small decline in their activation expenditures in the last two years of data presented.

The recent decline notwithstanding, Quebec remains the leader in activation expenditures. It spends relatively more on employment support programs in its Mesures d'aide à l'Emploi. It also has a tax deduction for workers that other provinces do not have, and this has represented almost 0.2% of GDP since its implementation in 2006–7. This accounts for part of the increase shown in Figure 1.6.

But more of the increase is attributable to programs targeting families, helping them balance work and family. Figure 1.7 clarifies the contribution of those programs to the overall expenses incurred by activation programs by presenting spending on work and family reconciliation programs from 2002–3 to 2011–12 for the four provinces. We see that Quebec's expenditures were already much higher at the beginning of the period, largely because of its public day-care program. In fact, the program created in 1997 accounted for 0.5% of GDP in 2002–03 and 0.6% in 2011–12 (or $2.1 billion). Other provinces also subsidized childcare over this entire period, but as mentioned earlier, none developed a public system of day-care centres with such low daily fees for parents. In addition to its subsidized public day-care places, Quebec has consistently provided subsidies directly to parents who send their children to private day cares. This portion of expenditures has been more modest, representing only 0.07% of GDP in 2002–3. However, it increased over the period, starting in 2008–9. By 2011–12, it represented almost 0.1% of Quebec's GDP, slightly more than what British Columbia and Alberta spent on childcare subsidies at the time, but slightly less than Ontario.

The sharp increase in spending we see in Figure 1.7 for Quebec cannot be attributed to childcare. Rather, it is largely due to the provincial expansion of the federal parental leave program. The Régime québécois d'assurance parentale created in January 2006 has accounted for 0.4%

Figure 1.7. Work and family reconciliation expenditures, fiscal years 2002–3 to 2011–12

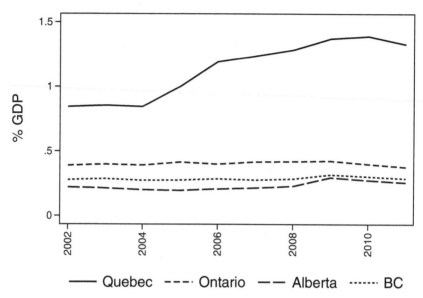

to nearly 0.6% of GDP, depending on the year. Before then, the federal parental leave program accounted for less than 0.3% of Quebec's GDP. It has always been larger as a share of GDP than the federal programs in other provinces, with Ontario following closely behind Quebec, and British Columbia and Alberta third and fourth, respectively, with less than 0.2% of GDP in Alberta. The tax credit Prime au travail also contributed to the increase in Quebec in 2005–6, corresponding to approximately 0.1% of GDP.

The activation expenditures for the other three provinces remained stable over the period observed, especially when we look at programs aimed at families in Figure 1.7. As the figure indicates, Ontario spent slightly more as a share of GDP (although much more in dollar terms) than Alberta and British Columbia on childcare subsidies.

Conclusion

Quebec's growing reputation as North America's only 'social democratic' regime seems, on the basis of the figures presented in this chapter, not entirely unjustified. As we more or less expected, in all comparisons it emerges as the largest program spender. Moreover, the combination of policies pursued by successive Quebec governments has, it seems to us, a decidedly more social democratic flavour than those of the other three provinces we consider here. By contrast, pointing to the gradual retrenchment in Quebec's social assistance programs in favour of targeted family benefits, Haddow casts doubt on Quebec's supposed social democratic turn (see Haddow 2015, 239). And, as we shall see in Chapter 3, not all low-income households have benefited equally from Quebec's approach. But it is still worth noting that, unlike the provinces to which we have compared Quebec, *la belle province* has chosen a combination of family-friendly and positive activation – as opposed to workfare – measures that bears more than a little resemblance to the social democratic, or social investment, approach.

Also as expected, Alberta comes out as the least generous province, confirming its reputation as the most laissez-faire, liberal-market-like Canadian province (Faid 2009; Gibson 2007). British Columbia and Ontario fall somewhere in between, although when compared internationally (Bernard and Saint-Arnaud 2004; Bernard and Raïq 2011), they remain much closer to liberal regimes than to any others.

To be sure, as noted in our brief provincial policy descriptions, both Ontario and Alberta have recently taken (or promised to take) poverty reduction initiatives, possibly inspired by Quebec's example.[16] But these initiatives have yet to be clearly reflected in increases in expenditures comparable to those in Quebec. Moreover, they have been undertaken in a general climate of fiscal prudence and program cutbacks that may well leave the two provinces spending less rather than more on combating poverty and social exclusion in the near future (see, e.g., Banting and Myles 2013a).

Second, Quebec's outlier status is primarily due to its extensive array of policies supporting families with children. Much of our analysis in the following chapters is devoted to assessing how and to what extent these policies have resulted in changes in the material conditions and employment behaviour of families with children in Quebec as opposed to the other provinces. In addition, we assess to what extent Quebec has succeeded in embodying the social democratic type of welfare state – arguably, the inspiration for its exceptionalism (Dandurand and Kempeneers 2002, 52–3).

That said, social outcomes are a complex result of many factors, of which government policy is only one. It is one thing to establish systematic differences in policy priorities between jurisdictions, as manifested in government spending patterns. It is quite another to link these to final outcomes for the populations in question. Therefore, in addition to comparing outcomes in Quebec with those in the other major Canadian provinces and other countries, we assess to what extent these outcomes are attributable to the policy differences documented in this chapter.

APPENDIX: METHODS AND DATA SOURCES

Program Selection

Our principal data consist of program descriptions and expenditure figures for the four provinces under study. We collected information on all policies and programs intended to support the income of vulnerable populations, as well as those intended to support individuals' (re) integration into the labour market. While we have been as inclusive as possible, we have omitted a small number of programs that were a) too small to have a perceptible effect on the overall spending patterns of the province in question; b) not defined clearly enough to qualify as either an income support or an activation policy; or c) both exceedingly small *and* very similar to programs in the other three provinces. Finally, since the object is to examine interprovincial differences in spending priorities, any programs financed by federal funds are excluded to the fullest extent possible, as they simply add like amounts to each province's expenditures.

Fundamentally, *income support programs* aim to prevent vulnerable populations from falling into poverty, however defined. Included in this category are income assistance for the able-bodied and the disabled, programs which provide affordable housing, workplace-injury compensation programs, and benefits and services for the integration into community life of individuals with developmental disabilities. Provincial public-sector pension programs are also included in the poverty reduction category, as they express the different provinces' commitment to supporting the incomes of vulnerable populations.

Programs are defined as aimed at *labour market activation* if they are intended to facilitate integration into paid employment. Included in this category are a) training programs which increase the skill level of participants and programs offering support to facilitate the job-search process; b) programs providing subsidies or bonuses for accepting or holding a job; and c) programs facilitating the integration of immigrant and migrant labour into local labour markets. These programs achieve these goals by providing training directly or by subsidizing the costs of training for employers and students.

Finally, we distinguish policies and programs that seek to provide *support for families with children*, whether by subsidizing the costs of raising children (passive support) or by helping to reconcile the spheres of work and family.

Admittedly, our classification of programs and policies is fairly crude. In practice, there is bound to be considerable overlap between the different types of programs in terms of the criteria used to distinguish between them. Thus, for instance, income support programs commonly contain elements of activation in that their eligibility conditions can be used to coax potential beneficiaries into the labour force. As we have seen, some provinces have made vigorous use of this possibility in recent years by pursuing a workfare approach. Similarly, family support programs comprise both activation and income support elements. But while it is worth keeping this in mind, our rough classification reflects the broad policy orientations and alternatives – active versus passive, families with children versus all households – currently under debate by policymakers and researchers alike in the field of social and employment policy. And as our review of provincial policies makes clear, they also help identify the most significant differences between Quebec and the other Canadian provinces in terms of both programs and outcomes.

Our main data sources are the budgets of the respective provincial governments. In some cases, figures were not available in budget documents at the desired level of detail and had to be drawn from reports published by individual ministries. Some agencies operating under the supervision of their provincial government retain a certain degree of autonomy and manage their own finances. This is the case, for instance, for workers' compensation boards. Expenditure data for the CSST, the Alberta Workers' Compensation Board, the Workplace Safety and Insurance Board of Ontario (WSIB), and WorkSafeBC were collected from the annual reports of those agencies.[17]

Quebec has a compulsory insurance scheme protecting all individuals against loss of income due to a road accident implicating a motorized vehicle. The SAAQ is responsible for administering this insurance scheme, which operates at arm's length from the provincial government. The expenditure data for this agency are available in its annual reports. No insurance scheme of this nature exists in the other three provinces.

Another peculiarity of the province of Quebec is that since 2006 it has extended the federal parental leave program funded through EI to cover a larger population and to provide more generous and flexible income replacement rates and durations. The expenditures for the income replacement benefits of mothers and fathers are found in the official statistics of the Régime québécois d'assurance parentale (RQAP). Elsewhere in Canada, maternity and parental benefits are still funded through the federal EI program. The expenditures in those provinces, although federally funded, are included; we compare their size with RQAP's expenditures to avoid overstating the difference between Quebec and the other provinces. This form of expenditure is found in the annual EI Monitoring and Assessment Reports produced by the Canadian Employment Insurance Commission.

Similarly, some of the provincial expenditures on employment activation policies are financed partly by federal funds secured through federal-provincial LMDAs as part of the federal EI program. Some smaller provincial programs, such as Alberta's housing program, also benefit from some federal support. As these federal contributions are virtually impossible to separate reliably from purely provincial expenditures, and as they either do not differentiate greatly between provinces or differences are of minor significance, we do not try to exclude them from the overall provincial expenditure figures.

Tax credits, like some of the compensation and insurance schemes above, do not always appear in budget documents. We include major tax credit programs in our analysis, both refundable and nonrefundable, if they have the aim of poverty alleviation, work-family reconciliation, or the facilitation of training. The question of how provincial taxation systems as a whole affect poverty and other outcomes is a complex one, well outside the scope of this chapter. Although comparing major tax credit programs would provide insight into provincial spending priorities, any final judgment on the total effect of taxation must await a more complete analysis. We were able to gather data on tax credits for British Columbia, Ontario, and Quebec only.

In Alberta, the Alberta Family Employment Tax Credit is relevant to our research as it encourages parents with children under 18 to work and is a progressive measure that disproportionately benefits low-income families. It was not included, however, as we only found data for 2010.[18]

The final expenditures included here are benefits paid by public-sector pension funds to their retirees, specifically those funded and administered solely by provincial governments. The Canada Pension Plan and Quebec Pension Plan are not included. As with tax credits, the analysis of public-sector pensions must be interpreted with caution. The amount of benefits paid by any given pension plan not only reflects the generosity of contribution by the provincial government but also the rate at which employees pay into the plan, the rate of return obtained by the fund's investments, and the relative proportion of individuals currently paying into the plan versus the number drawing benefits. Despite the complexity of analysis along these variables, however, the differences between provinces are large enough to suggest that a significant component of variation is provincial generosity. All figures used here refer to operating expenses, with the exception of public-sector pensions, workers' compensation boards, the RQAP, and the SAAQ, whose expenditures are measured in terms of benefits paid as a percentage of GDP. Program descriptions are either derived from the same sources as expenditures or from additional sources listed below in this appendix.

We present expenditures as a percentage of provincial GDP, traditionally used as a comparative measure of spending priorities. It could be argued that expenditure per capita would be a better measure, since it shows how much spending reaches the population. However, we analysed trends in per capita social expenditure (not shown) and found no major differences between them and the expenditures as a share of GDP used here.

Data Sources

Ontario

Healthcare of Ontario Pension Plan benefit payment estimates retrieved from http://www.hoopp.com/about/pastreports/index.asp

Ontario Disability Support Program Employment Support Directives
    retrieved from http://www.mcss.gov.on.ca/en/mcss/programs/social/
    directives/
Ontario Municipal Employees Retirement System benefit payment estimates
    retrieved from http://www.omers.com/About_OMERS/Annual_report.htm
Ontario Pension Board/Ontario Public Service Pension Plan benefit payment
    estimates retrieved from annual reports at http://www.opb.on.ca/portal/
Ontario Public Sector Employees Union benefit payment estimates retrieved
    from http://www.optrust.com/AnnualReports/p_annualReports.asp#top
Ontario Teachers' Pension Plan benefit payment estimates retrieved from
    http://www.otpp.com
Public Accounts of Ontario retrieved from http://www.ontla.on.ca/library/
    repository/ser/15767/2009-2010/_
Service Ontario information service, contacted 17 June 2011, at 1-800-267-8097
Workplace Safety and Insurance Board of Ontario's Annual Reports retrieved
    from www.wsib.on.ca
Additional information on programs retrieved from ministries' websites:_
    www.citizenship.gov.on.ca; www.children.gov.on.ca; www.mcss.gov.on.ca;
    www.fin.gov.on.ca; www.mah.gov.on.ca; www.tcu.gov.on.ca

British Columbia

BC Budget and Fiscal Plan retrieved from http://www.bcbudget.gov.bc.ca/
    default.htm
BC Budget estimates retrieved from http://www.bcbudget.gov.bc.ca/
    default.htm
BC College Pension Plan benefit payment estimates retrieved from
    http://www.pensionsbc.ca/portal/page/portal/
BC Municipal Pension Plan benefit payment estimates retrieved from
    http://www.pensionsbc.ca/portal/page/portal/
BC Public Service Pension Plan benefit payment estimates retrieved from
    http://www.pensionsbc.ca/portal/page/portal/
BC Teachers Pension Plan benefit payment estimates retrieved from
    http://www.pensionsbc.ca/portal/page/portal/
British Columbia's Early Years Annual Reports retrieved from http://www.
    mcf.gov.bc.ca/early_childhood/publications.htm
Community Living British Columbia Supported Employment Program
    Review 2007 retrieved from http://www.communitylivingbc.ca/
    individuals-families/employment-initiative/
WorkSafeBC's Annual Reports retrieved from www.worksafebc.com

Additional information on programs retrieved from www.gov.bc.ca; www.bchousing.org

Alberta

Alberta Teachers' Retirement Fund Board's Annual Reports retrieved from www.atrf.com

Email communication with Tim Weinkauf from the Persons with Developmental Disabilities' office on 5 May 2011

Government Estimates retrieved from www.finance.alberta.ca

Local Authorities Pension Plan's Annual Reports retrieved from www.lapp.ca

Management Employees Pension Plan's Annual Reports retrieved from www.mepp.ca

Provincial Judges and Masters in Chambers Pension Plans' Annual Reports retrieved from www.apsc.ca

Public Service Pension Plan's Annual Reports retrieved from www.pspp.ca

Special Forces Pension Plan's Annual Reports retrieved from www.sfpp.ca

Supplementary Retirement Plan for Public Service Managers' Annual Reports retrieved from www.mepp.ca

Workers' Compensation Board's Annual Reports retrieved from www.wcb.ab.ca

Additional information on programs retrieved from www.eae.alberta.ca; www.health.alberta.ca; www.humanservices.alberta.ca; www.municipalaffairs.gov.ab.ca; and communications with public servant Tim Weinkauf

Quebec

Dépenses fiscales retrieved from www.finances.gouv.qc.ca

Expenditure Budget Volume 2: Estimates of the Departments and Agencies retrieved from www.tresor.gouv.qc.ca

Phone conversation with Serge Hamel 1 February 2011 and email communication with Lise Lallemand 8 April 2011 of the Ministère de l'emploi et de la solidarité sociale

Rapports annuels de gestion de la Commission administrative des régimes de retraite et d'assurances retrieved from www.carra.gouv.qc.ca

Rapports annuels de gestion de la Commission de la santé et de la sécurité du travail du Québec retrieved from www.csst.qc.ca

Rapports annuels de gestion de la Société d'assurance automobile du Québec retrieved from www.saaq.gouv.qc.ca

Statistiques officielles sur les prestataires du Régime québécois d'assurance parentale retrieved from www.cgap.gouv.qc.ca

Additional information on programs retrieved from: www.ophq.gouv.qc.ca; www.rrq.gouv.qc.ca; www.habitation.gouv.qc.ca; www.micc.gouv.qc.ca; www.osrcpc.ca; www.mess.gouv.qc.ca; www.emploiquebec.net; www. mfa.gouv.qc.ca; www.rqap.gouv.qc.ca; and communications with public servants Serge Hamel and Lise Lallemand

Chapter Two

Poverty: Measures and Trends

Introduction

Chapter 1 convincingly shows how the province of Quebec has steered a different course from the rest of the country in its social and employment policies since the mid-1990s. While the federal government and the other provinces have kept expenditures down, Quebec has greatly expanded both the scope of its policies and the financial resources devoted to them. Having detailed the growing divergence between Quebec and the other provinces, we now proceed to the obvious next question: to what extent has Quebec's different approach achieved the goals the province has set for itself, in particular, that of bringing down the number of persons living in poverty to levels comparable to the lowest in the industrialized world?

This chapter begins to answer the question of whether Quebec has achieved its goals by comparing its overall poverty rates over several decades with those of the other provinces, as well as a selection of advanced industrialized countries, including some with the lowest poverty rates in the world. Our results show poverty rates have indeed declined in Quebec since the mid-1990s, while they have stagnated or gone up in the three other provinces and in Canada as a whole. This pattern corresponds with the policy trajectories documented in Chapter 1. At the same time, when we compare poverty rates in Quebec to those in a selection of other countries, we find Quebec's rates, while somewhat lower than in comparable liberal market-oriented countries, still remain considerably higher than in the European countries whose performance Quebec set out to match. Thus, with respect to gross poverty rates, Quebec's *virage* appears to have had only modest success.

In subsequent chapters, we take a detailed look at poverty rates for different types of households to see whether this is the case across the board.

Poverty is by its nature one of those 'essentially contested' concepts, 'the proper use of which inevitably involves endless disputes about their proper uses on the part of their users' (Gallie 1955, 169). The literature about poverty is replete with debates about what poverty 'really is,' how it should be conceptualized and, not least, how it should be measured. For reasons that will shortly become clear, different conceptions and measures often carry quite different evaluative and policy implications. Consequently, before presenting our results, we briefly review the 'true' nature of poverty and its measurement. This will allow us to explain what measures we will be employing in our analyses in the rest of this book and why.

What Is Poverty?

Absolute vs. Relative Poverty

Many concepts in common use among policy experts and social scientists receive little attention outside their small circles of discussion and debate. Poverty is not one of them. A 2011 YouTube video entitled 'Poverty Solved' shows Chris Alexander, Conservative MP for Ajax-Pickering, drawing jeers and charges of 'liar' from an audience of community members for claiming poverty had been eliminated in Canada.[1] But by the standard of the World Bank's $2-a-day poverty cut-off he was invoking, Alexander was right. Yet so was his outraged audience, which obviously had quite a different poverty level in mind.

The World Bank's USD$2 poverty cut-off exemplifies what is commonly called an 'absolute' measure of poverty. Two dollars a day is considered the bare minimum needed to afford enough food and shelter to survive. By this absolute measure, anyone whose daily income is less, anywhere in the world, irrespective of local differences in standards of living, is by definition poor.[2] It should be clear, however, that this is a measure of absolute poverty not by virtue of its extremely low level but because it applies the same income threshold across societies with widely varying levels of average income. If we were to set the poverty threshold at, say, the equivalent of USD$20,000 a day, and apply it across countries, irrespective of their differences in GDP per capita, this would be a much higher but equally *absolute* poverty threshold and, of course, by this much higher standard, most of the world's population would qualify as 'poor' (see, e.g., Scruggs and Allan 2006; Kenworthy 1999).

Obviously, indiscriminately applying a measure of absolute poverty as low as $2 per day to poor and rich countries alike makes little sense. As indicated by the angry response to MP Alexander, most Canadians do not think an income of $2 per day is enough to secure the barest necessities for survival in this country. In fact, even the deliberately minimalist 'absolute poverty' lines developed by the Fraser Institute, a conservative, strongly free-market-oriented think tank, put the bare annual minimum on which a family of four can survive in Canada at around $20,000, or around USD$50 a day, depending on the local cost of living (see Sarlo 2001; see also Kneebone and White 2015, 123–5).

But whatever absolute poverty threshold we decide to accept, one major peculiarity is that when the economy grows, barring any counteracting redistribution of income from the poor to the rich, the number of people considered poor *automatically* declines. Thus, simply as a result of Canada's level of economic development, there are no more poor people by Mr. Alexander's absolute measure. Similarly, even by the Fraser Institute's much higher measure of absolute poverty, the number of people qualifying as poor automatically declines as the economy grows, other things being equal. This is why many observers prefer a 'relative' measure of poverty, one that takes into account the (rising) consumption standards in each country or province, particularly in cross-national comparisons (Christopher 2001; Brady 2003, 2009; Misra and Moller 2005; Smeeding 2005a, 2006).[3]

The main rationale for preferring relative measures of poverty is as follows. In a rich country like Canada it takes a lot more than mere subsistence to be able to 'get by,' to participate fully in society, to be 'socially included.' Those who lack the minimum of material resources to do so may be considered poor *relative to* the society of which they are a part. The idea goes back to Adam Smith who, in *The Wealth of Nations*, famously observed that, 'by necessaries, I understand not only the commodities which are indispensably necessary for the support of life, but whatever the custom of the country renders it indecent for creditable people, even the lowest order, to be without ... Custom ... has rendered leather shoes a necessary of life in England. The poorest creditable person of either sex would be ashamed to appear in public without them' (Smith 1776, 351–2; see Sen 1983). Clearly, the roots of relative reasoning around poverty run deep. Even in 1776, Adam Smith anticipated that the same level of income may not provide a person with everything he or she needs to achieve the same standard of living in different contexts.

In fact, the dichotomy often drawn between relative and absolute measures may be a false one. Adam Smith's argument has been recast in terms of 'capabilities' by Nobel Prize–winning economist Amartya Sen (1999). According to Sen, advocates of absolute measures of poverty conceive of poverty as purely a matter of (insufficient) income, which is far too narrow. Well-being does not simply depend on absolute income; poverty is not a matter of 'not having enough' per se, but of 'not being able to *do* enough.' Sen calls the things people are able to do their 'capabilities.' According to him, poverty that is absolute with respect to capabilities is very likely to be relative with respect to things like income. Following Sen's reasoning, our relative measures may capture an absolute standard of poverty more accurately than absolute measures (cf. Brady 2003).

A related concept embraced by researchers and policymakers in the European Union (Atkinson and Da Voudi 2000; Fortin and Gauthier 2011, 126; Muffels, Tsakloglou, and Mayes 2002) is the notion of 'social exclusion,' which is based on the idea, expressed in a much-quoted passage by one of the earliest advocates of the concept, that people are poor when 'their resources are so seriously below those commanded by the average individual or family that they are, in effect, excluded from ordinary living patterns, customs and activities' (Townsend 1979, 31; see also Ringen 1988). Social exclusion is a multidimensional concept going far beyond 'mere' income poverty to include exclusion from the labour market, educational deprivation, poor health, lack of adequate housing and living space, and lack of social support. This is a very broad concept of deprivation indeed and, not surprisingly, there is little consensus in the literature on how to measure it empirically (Hyman et al. 2011). This renders the concept difficult to use satisfactorily in cross-national comparisons. Moreover, in Canada research into the nature and causes of social exclusion in this broad sense remains in its infancy (Fortin and Gauthier 2011), even though the need to combat it is an explicit part of Quebec's celebrated anti-poverty strategy, as noted in Chapter 1.

For these reasons, we do not attempt to measure and compare levels of social exclusion in this book. However, we emphasize that poverty is a matter of deprivation *relative to* what is considered customary or 'ordinary' in the society in which one lives, that is, a *relative* notion of poverty. While there is no doubt that social exclusion, however it is measured, only partly overlaps with income deprivation (Nolan and Whelan 2010,

316–19), we focus on the latter simply because relative income deprivation constitutes a necessary and substantial determinant of the broader state of social exclusion (see also Brady 2003).[4] While there will always be plenty of debate over which of the two types of poverty measures is preferable (Sen 1983), most social scientists studying poverty, particularly in advanced industrialized countries, prefer to use some relative measure of poverty for the purpose of comparisons over time and between places. This means a researcher must choose some measure of income relative to a country's average or median income as the relevant poverty threshold. We opt for this more conventional approach rather than attempting to measure poverty in absolute terms.

Different Measures: LICO vs. MBM vs. LIM

Even when we restrict ourselves to relative poverty measures, there are several different ways we can calculate the relevant poverty threshold. Each relies on a slightly different concept of poverty and appeals to different intuitions regarding want and need. Some researchers aim to identify an explicit standard of consumption, while others focus on whether people are able to keep up with others in society. Some concepts are easily understood and interpreted by researchers and laymen alike, while others are more challenging.

In addition to being based on different concepts of poverty, the various poverty measures on offer to Canadian researchers are also more or less sensitive to whether they capture the same standards of subsistence and social exclusion over time and across the country. Some measures impose the same income standard in dissimilar contexts, with little concern for whether the same amount of income buys the same amount of subsistence and social inclusion in every place. Others are more sensitive to differences in prices and consumption habits. Finally, some measures can easily be related to poverty measures outside Canada, while others cannot.

Statistics Canada releases three sets of low-income thresholds for researchers interested in poverty in Canada (Statistics Canada 2013): the Low Income Cut-Off (LICO), the Market Basket Measure (MBM), and the Low Income Measure (LIM).[5]

The LICO defines the low-income threshold as an income that is 20% above the amount the average Canadian family spends on food, shelter, and clothing in a given year. This requires information on Canadian families' consumption patterns. Statistics Canada uses information from the 1992 Family Expenditures Survey as its basis for calculating the LICO for subsequent years by multiplying the 1992 average amount spent on food, shelter, and clothing by the consumer price index for each year. In addition, the LICO controls for family size and community size to account for differences in the local cost of living (see Statistics Canada 2013, 6–7). Thus, the LICO assumes a Canadian needs to have an income of 20% more than what is necessary to procure the basic necessities of life in order not to be considered poor.

The LICO has several limitations. First, comparing LICOs across provinces and countries requires detailed information about consumption patterns which are not readily available, at least not for other countries. Second, consumption patterns change over time and so does, presumably, the amount of income required for a family to feel socially included. Having to base one's measure on the consumption pattern of Canadian households of more than twenty years ago is obviously less than ideal. Third, while controlling for community size and the rural-urban divide may capture some differences in local costs of living, they do so very imprecisely. The LICO is especially insensitive to differences between regions and provinces in the cost of living which are, as we will see below, considerable. To put it differently, while both Montreal and Toronto are classified as communities with a population of over five hundred thousand inhabitants, the cost of living, particularly when we factor in the cost of housing, is often quite different in the two metropoles (Allen et al. 2009).

The MBM, designed in collaboration with Human Resources and Skills Development Canada (HRSDC), tries to deal with this latter shortcoming. It defines people as poor if they are unable to afford a basket of goods needed to maintain basic levels of subsistence and social inclusion, the cost of which is estimated for each of the forty-nine economic regions throughout the country. In determining the contents of the basket, HRSDC aims 'to identify a standard of living lying between the poles of subsistence and social inclusion. It goes beyond that subsistence standard of living, allowing for the acquisition of resources necessary for taking part in the life of the community' (Michaud, Cotton, and Bishop 2004, 8). The basket contains things like food, clothing, footwear, transportation, and shelter. Families are considered poor if their disposable income cannot buy them this basic basket of goods in their respective economic region.

The MBM is often presented as the most easily understood measure of poverty available to Canadian researchers (cf. CEPE 2009; Zhang 2010). By drawing on a tangible basket of goods needed to meet a minimum standard of subsistence and social inclusion in Canada, the

MBM makes the most intuitive sense to both researchers and laymen. But what should or should not be included in the basket is inherently debatable. Researchers have criticized the MBM for not containing enough (Kolkman 2011) or for insufficiently considering the role of inequality in determining poverty (Hunter and Miazdyck 2006). As noted, consumption patterns change and, as a result, the things people need to be socially included also tend to change, sometimes dramatically. A good example is access to the Internet. The technology is so pervasive that those without it may legitimately be seen as excluded from full social participation. In short, the items included in the basket require frequent revision (see Statistics Canada 2013, 9–13).[6] A final criticism of the MBM is that it, like the LICO, is based on information about Canadian consumption patterns which is not available for other countries.

The most frequently used poverty threshold is the LIM, which defines people as poor if they live in a household whose reported income is less than half of the median Canadian household income in a given year. The LIM is part of a family of measures advocated by many leading comparative researchers (cf. Brady 2003; Förster and D'Ercole 2012). According to the nationally based LIM, an individual is poor if he or she lives in a family reporting an income less than 50% of the median Canadian family (Statistics Canada 2013, 9). Poverty is not defined by a fixed amount of access to income or by consumption but, rather, by the extent to which an individual is able to keep up with most people in the society. The measure assumes 50% of median income is about the threshold at which people begin to fall behind in a way that prevents them from participating as others do. But again, the level of this threshold is debatable. For instance, the EU uses a similar standard for its 'at-risk-of-poverty' measure, but takes 60% of the median national household income as the critical cut-off (Maquet and Stanton 2012). The great advantage of the LIM is that, unlike the MBM and the LICO, it can be estimated in the exact same fashion for every society for which we have reliable income distribution data. It can also be easily adapted to take into account differences in local consumption patterns and costs of living (see below).

In short, the three low-income thresholds used in Canadian poverty research are based on different conceptions of what constitutes poverty and they answer different questions. As Murphy, Zhang, and Dionne (2012) put it in their careful comparison of all three measures:

> The LICO implies that a person is deprived if he or she lives in a family that has to spend significantly more of its income on the necessities of life

Figure 2.1. Poverty rates in Canada using different measures

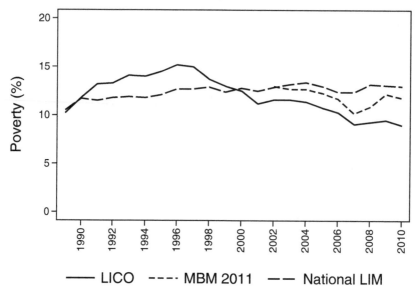

than the average family, and therefore has little discretionary income with which to participate fully in society. The LIM considers one to be deprived if his or her household income is less than half of the income of the median household. With much less income than the mainstream makes, a person would have difficulty participating fully in the society. The MBM considers as deprived individuals whose families lack the disposable income to purchase the goods and services of the 'market basket' that represents a modest yet decent standard of living. (91)

It is not surprising, then, that the three low-income thresholds also yield different results when used to calculate the rate of poverty – that is, the proportion of the population whose income falls below that threshold. This can be seen in Figure 2.1 where we compare the three measures discussed here for Canada for 1990 to 2010.

As the figure shows, the poverty rates based on the MBM and the LICO decline more or less considerably starting sometime in the late 1990s to early 2000s. By contrast, the poverty rates based on the LIM remain steady over time.[7] This makes sense. The period we are covering was one of fairly steady economic growth. The MBM and LICO are, as explained above, measures based on a fixed basket of goods, annually adjusted for the rate of inflation, that is, the combined elements of relative and absolute poverty. As the economy grows, and as long as low-income households benefit at least somewhat from this growth, there will be fewer and fewer households whose income falls below the basket-of-goods threshold. The LIM, however, is a purely relative measure of poverty. No matter how rapidly the economy grows, if the income distribution remains unchanged, so does the poverty rate.

While each of these measures provides valuable, though slightly different, information,[8] we choose the LIM as our principal basis for estimating poverty rates. We do so for the reasons outlined above, but first and foremost because neither the MBM nor the LICO is available for countries other than Canada. LIM-like measures of the poverty threshold are the most frequently used in the international comparative literature, and if we want to make a contribution to the debate about where Quebec and the other Canadian provinces stand with respect to poverty and social exclusion as compared to other countries, we need to follow this firmly established convention.

Relative to What Population? National vs. Provincial LIMs

The next issue we need to address is considerably more contentious. Throughout the 1990s Quebec developed a reputation for having some of the highest provincial poverty rates in Canada. This reputation was mostly based on estimates generated by Statistics Canada's LICO. Quebec's reputation in the 1990s did not sit well with the province's researchers and policymakers, who criticized the LICO for not properly taking into account differences in costs of living between the provinces (Noël 2011; Roy, Fréchet, and Savard 2008). Instead, they have advocated for the use of either the MBM or the *provincially based* variant of Statistics Canada's LIM (CEPE 2009; Noël 2013, 272–3).

If we measure poverty on the basis of the provincially calculated thresholds, we get a far more favourable picture of poverty in Quebec than if we use nationally based measures. This is not surprising. There are considerable differences in the level of economic prosperity between Canadian provinces. As a consequence, the median household income of all Canadians taken together will be lower than the provincial medians of the richest provinces and higher than those of the poorest ones. In other words, taking the Canadian median income as the benchmark for calculating the low income measure will understate the poverty rate in the former and overstate it in the latter.

Conversely, given the differences in provincial GDPs, median provincial incomes are likely to differ considerably. If, say, the median person's income in Alberta is $37,350, as it was in 2011, and $28,690 in Quebec, by the provincially based LIM criterion of 50% of the median, a single Albertan would be considered poor if his or her income was less than $18,675, compared to $14,345 for a Quebecker (Statistics Canada 2014). Similarly, a family of two parents and two children would be considered poor if its income was less than $37,350 and $28,690, respectively. If we had taken the Canada-wide median income as the basis for calculating the 50% threshold, we would have found more people with incomes below the poverty threshold in Quebec and fewer in Alberta.

This is not, in itself, a good enough reason to prefer the provincially based to the nationally based measure, of course. But there are other reasons. First, the provincial medians are more likely to reflect differences in the cost of living, especially housing. Second, our main concern is to assess the effectiveness of Quebec's ambitious strategy to combat poverty and social exclusion by comparing it to the other large Canadian provinces. Since Confederation, the Canadian Constitution has placed social policy under the jurisdiction of the provinces (Banting 1982; Guest 1980). While there is a long history of federal 'intrusions' (Unemployment Insurance, health care, pensions), the policies that most affect social exclusion (social assistance, family support, housing) are, by and large, decided at the provincial level. This is why Quebec has been able to steer such a distinctive course. So if our aim is to assess the effectiveness of *provincial* poverty-combating policies it makes sense to measure poverty using provincially based poverty thresholds.

Third, we intend to measure Quebec's performance not only by comparison with the other large Canadian provinces but also with other advanced industrialized countries, especially those most successful at combating poverty. After all, the Quebec government's explicit aim was to 'make Québec, by 2013, one of the industrialized nations having the least number of persons living in poverty.' It seems more sensible to use provincially based poverty thresholds that are directly comparable to the thresholds we are able to calculate for those particular countries than a Canadian-based threshold that does not adequately reflect living conditions in the province of Quebec. In fact, CEPE (2009) recommends this course of action for exactly this kind of comparison.

There is a subjective issue as well. Relative measures of poverty are, by definition, meant to capture people's position relative to the community with which they identify. While there can be no doubt – pace the interminable debates – that many Quebeckers feel that they are part of the Canadian 'community,' as do Albertans, Ontarians, and British Columbians, when assessing their ability to partake in the life of the community – to be socially included – they are more likely to compare themselves to their fellow Quebeckers than to their fellow Canadians in Alberta or Ontario. While there is plenty of room for disagreement on this more subjective aspect, we think it provides another plausible argument for adopting provincially based poverty thresholds as our yardstick for comparison.

Measurement Specifics: Units and Thresholds

Poverty thresholds are used to identify who is poor and who is not. From them we derive a measure of the extent of poverty. This is commonly measured by the *poverty rate*, the proportion of a population whose income falls below the selected poverty threshold. Thus, if we select 50% of the median income as our poverty threshold, the percentage of the population with incomes lower than this threshold constitutes the poverty rate. In this book, we primarily use the provincially based LIM set at 50% of the provincial median income as our measure of poverty. As noted, this provincially based LIM is widely used by researchers in Quebec but not elsewhere in Canada. To reiterate, then, we use provincially based LIMs to calculate provincial poverty rates for all four provinces compared in this chapter and the chapters that follow.

The poverty rate measures the extent of poverty but not necessarily its *depth*. It tells us what proportion of the population is considered poor but not how poor they are. Most of those counted as poor by our measure may have incomes very close to the threshold; many may have much lower incomes. The latter case is much more serious, of course. A common measure of the depth of the poverty of those with incomes below the poverty threshold is the *poverty gap ratio*. This ratio is calculated as the percentage gap between the low-income threshold and the average income of those who fall below it. If the incomes of the poor are concentrated at the bottom, the poverty gap will be greater than if they are mainly just below the threshold (see Brady 2003; Statistics Canada 2013, 13). While this is a widely used measure of the depth of poverty, we use a similar but intuitively more easily interpretable measure which we call 'extreme' or 'acute' poverty.

Our acute measure of poverty indicates that people or households suffer from extreme poverty if their income falls below 30% of the median income (cf. Raïq, Bernard, and van den Berg 2011; Raïq 2012). After testing different thresholds below 50%, Bernard and Raïq (2011) make the case that 30% of the median best captures variations in extreme poverty across countries. Higher thresholds produce results similar to those obtained using the 50% median threshold, and lower thresholds are too low to capture any extreme poverty in some countries. Note that 30% of the median is about half of the half of median income standard set by the 50% threshold. Studies find policy efforts that result in poverty reduction can actually still fail to reduce acute poverty (Raïq 2012; Raïq, Bernard, and van den Berg 2011). In what follows, we report results for extreme poverty only if they are telling.

Throughout we take the household as our unit of analysis. This is common in poverty research because it is assumed that resources are shared, however unequally, at the household level (cf. Brady 2003, 2009). What matters most in determining what a person can and cannot afford is not necessarily his or her individual income but the income of the household as a whole. In Statistics Canada's usage, the household 'refers to a person or a group of persons (other than foreign residents) who occupy the same dwelling and do not have a usual place of residence elsewhere in Canada. It may consist of a family group (census family) with or without other persons, of two or more families sharing a dwelling, of a group of unrelated persons, or of one person living alone. Household members who are temporarily absent on [the survey date] (e.g., temporarily residing elsewhere) are considered as part of their usual household' (Statistics Canada 2011).

This is slightly different from the definition of the 'economic family,' that is, 'all persons living in the same dwelling and related by blood, marriage, common-law relationship or adoption' (Statistics Canada 2013, 13n12). Most Canadian studies use the economic family rather than the household as the unit of analysis, with the household more commonly used for international comparisons.

As one of our main aims is to examine how Quebec and the other three large Canadian provinces compare with the United States and a selection of European countries, we use the household rather than the economic family as our unit of analysis. The former is the standard unit of analysis used in the international comparative literature

(Statistics Canada 2013, 13n13). Unfortunately, this means our poverty figures cannot be directly compared to those that are most common in the Canadian literature.

Households come in different sizes, and larger households obviously have greater material needs while, at the same time, benefiting from economies of scale. An annual income of $20,000 may be enough for a single person to get by, but may represent a starvation income for a family of four. Thus, we need to control for the size of the household when assessing its income relative to the poverty threshold. We do so by using a so-called *equivalence scale* which is both simple to apply and consistent with international usage. The scale, developed by the Luxemburg Income Study (LIS), and used by the OECD and Statistics Canada, controls for household size by dividing household income by the square root of the number of members in the household (Statistics Canada 2010a, 11).[9]

Finally, we look almost exclusively at *disposable* household income, that is, income after taxes have been deducted and various transfer benefits received. This, too, is common practice in the literature, since the household's *effective* material resources obviously consist of disposable, not gross or market, income (cf. Brady 2009).

For all the sound justifications that may be invoked for the measures we are adopting, the fact remains that disposable income adjusted to household size is a fairly narrow measure with which to gauge a complex phenomenon like poverty, let alone social exclusion. Yet for the reasons given above, it remains the most useful one for our purposes. There is one serious limitation we are not able to overcome in a satisfactory manner, however: countries and provinces differ quite significantly in the kinds and quantities of public goods and social services they provide their citizens through government programs, and these may be particularly salient for households with low incomes. We are thinking, for instance, of free or heavily subsidized public education, subsidized or low-cost housing, free or subsidized day-care facilities, and, when comparing Canada to the United States, public health care. In cross-national comparisons, such differences ought to be factored in, as they can have a significant impact on the effective standard of living of low-income households. Comparisons that do not take such access to public goods into account will inevitably underestimate the poverty rates in countries and provinces that are stingy in the provision of such goods and overestimate them in more generous countries and provinces.

Unfortunately, there is no acceptable method of adding the provision of such goods to household incomes in a satisfactory manner. Any attempt to do so would be fraught with methodological, analytical, and even political problems. Consequently, we have chosen to leave public goods provision out of consideration, however much we regret having to do so. Happily, one consideration slightly mitigates the seriousness of this limitation. As we have already shown, at least when compared to the other Canadian provinces and the United States, Quebec invests considerably more in a variety of public goods that might disproportionately benefit its low-income citizens, such as subsidized day care, training for social assistance beneficiaries, heavily subsidized public education, and social housing. We can rest assured that if there was a way of factoring in all of these elements, Quebec's performance in reducing poverty would look better, not worse, when compared with these other jurisdictions. The reverse may be true when comparing Quebec with European countries, particularly Nordic ones, which, if anything, commit even larger amounts of public funds to the provision of a wide range of social services. While we cannot quantify the difference here, it is worth keeping it in mind as we continue.

Data

The analysis presented here relies on three sets of household income data in common use among poverty researchers in Canada and throughout the world: the LIS (described above), the Survey of Consumer Finances (SCF), and the Survey of Labour and Income Dynamics (SLID).

The SLID is a household-level survey of Canadians carried out by Statistics Canada annually since 1996. From 1976 to 1995, Statistics Canada gathered information on Canadian income using the SCF. Both surveys provide cross-sectional data on household composition, labour market participation, and incomes across Canada. In addition to tracking families cross-sectionally since 1996, the SLID has also tracked families longitudinally for six-year periods. We use the 2001–7 wave for our longitudinal analysis in Chapter 6.

The LIS is an international data set with cross-sectional information on household composition, labour market participation, and incomes. In recent years, the LIS has become the leading resource for cross-sectional international income comparisons. All of the leading researchers in the field of comparative poverty studies in developed nations use the LIS. It incorporates several household income surveys from all over the world and includes data from a handful of cross sections of the SLID for Canada. These surveys are organized into eight waves centred on 1980, 1985, 1990, 1995, 2000, 2004, 2007, and 2010. We use waves 3 through 7 because data are sparse for the earliest and latest waves. The data are available for specific and sometimes different years across countries; hence, country-specific trends in the graphs that follow start and stop in different years.

Although Canadian subsamples of the LIS are based on SLID and SCF data, they are not identical. It is our understanding that this is due, in part, to anonymization carried out by Statistics Canada, as well as some modifications made by LIS for the sake of international standardization. We generated Canadian estimates using SLID and SCF, and used the LIS to check them against one another. On the whole, results were much the same. Long-term trends were identical, with a handful of single country-year exceptions. Single point estimates based on any survey should always be treated with caution. Throughout this book, we defer to the SLID and SCF for Canadian estimates. We should note that while the SLID and SCF provide thirty-five data points for national and provincial income trends, the LIS only provides twelve.

Quebec and Canadian Poverty Trends

Having dealt with the technical issues, we can turn to trends in the poverty rates in Canada and its four largest provinces. Figure 2.2 presents the poverty rates from 1976 until the most recent data available, calculated on the basis of the *provincial* LIMs, that is, 50% of the provincial median individual's equivalent household disposable income.

As we expected, with this provincially based LIM, the province of Quebec does far better than it does with the nationally based LIM (see, for instance, Murphy, Zhang, and Dionne 2012). More importantly, however, the *trends over time* show a divergence between Quebec and the rest of Canada. Overall, national poverty seems to have worsened in the last couple of decades, particularly during the difficult 1990s. But this national average hides a growing divergence between the major provinces. Whereas the provincial poverty rates are very close to each other in the early 1990s, around 12%–13%, they take different paths after that point. The poverty rates for Ontario and British Columbia rise to around 15%, Alberta's rate drifts up 1 or 2 percentage points, to around 13%, but Quebec's rate drops.

In other words, Quebec's recent poverty levels are consistently below the national averages and also below those of Ontario, Alberta, and

Figure 2.2. Poverty rate in Canada and four provinces using the provincially based LIM

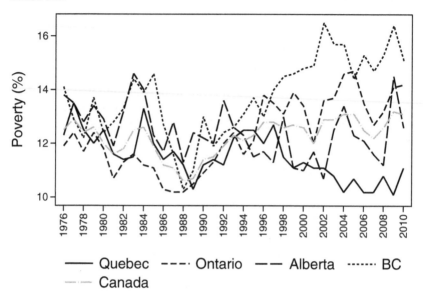

British Columbia. Ontario and Alberta follow the national trend more closely, but British Columbia is an outlier, with consistently higher poverty levels than the other provinces. In fact, British Columbia is the only Canadian province whose poverty rate, which reaches as high as 16%, approaches typical US levels. Ontario's poverty rates are close to the national level, while Alberta's and Quebec's are more or less consistently below the national average. Quebec's rate is actually close to the 10% mark throughout most of the 2000s.

This, then, is our first piece of evidence that Quebec's distinctive approach to poverty reduction may have borne fruit. While poverty rates either stagnated or rose in the other provinces since the mid-1990s, in Quebec, which was broadly facing the same economic climate and federal cutbacks as the other provinces, they declined by several percentage points.

The difference between Quebec and the other provinces stands out more starkly when we look at *acute* poverty rates, that is, the proportion of households with incomes below 30% of the median. This is shown in Figure 2.3.

Figure 2.3. Acute poverty rate in Canada and four provinces using the provincially based LIM

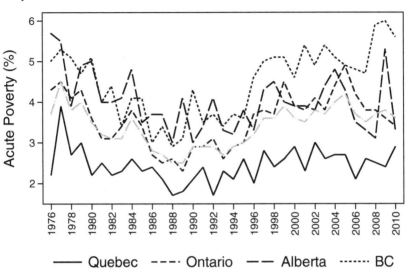

As the figure shows, Quebec's acute poverty rates are consistently considerably lower than those of the other three provinces, going back all the way to 1976. But again, the difference is particularly large from the mid-1990s onward, with Quebec's rate hovering around the 2% mark, Alberta and Ontario's around twice that rate, and British Columbia's occasionally approaching three times the Quebec rate. It should be noted that Quebec's acute poverty rate has been this low for many decades now, so not all the difference can be ascribed to relatively recent policy initiatives. Nonetheless, the fact that Quebec's rates remained this low while rates in the other provinces rose after the mid-1990s may have something to do with Quebec's distinctive policy approach. Finally, Quebec's acute poverty rates compare quite well with those of certain European countries.

Comparing Trends in Other Countries

What about Quebec's ambitious policy target of reaching the ranks of the 'industrialized nations having the least number of persons living in poverty'? While for the sake of readability we limit our comparisons to a few selected countries, it is worth setting these comparisons in a broader context first. Over the past couple of decades or so, we can distinguish three broad groups among the advanced industrialized countries. First, there is the United States all by itself. Persistently greater than 15%, US poverty rates are the highest of any of the advanced countries. In 2010, the most recent year for which we have LIS data, the US poverty rate stood at around 17.5%, the highest it has been over the last two decades. With close to a fifth of the American population living below the poverty line, the United States is a clear outlier when compared to the other countries considered here.

Then there is a group of countries with poverty rates ranging between 10% and 15%. The United Kingdom, Italy, and Spain belong to this group. Over the past twenty years, their poverty rates have been quite similar, although the United Kingdom's has fallen somewhat more recently and Italy's and Spain's have risen.

Finally, a third group of countries, including Germany, France, the Netherlands, Denmark, Sweden, and Norway, have poverty rates below 10%, sometimes approaching 5%. Presumably *these* are the countries against which the Quebec government wishes to gauge the effectiveness of its anti-poverty strategy. Unfortunately, rates for Sweden and France are not available in the LIS beyond 2005. But we know from other sources that poverty rates have risen somewhat in most of these countries in recent years, so the entire group may be converging towards poverty rates just below 10%, with the possible exception of Denmark (see, e.g., Fritzell, Bäckman, and Ritakallio 2012).[10]

In what follows, we compare Quebec and the other three provinces with a small selection of industrialized nations representing different types of welfare regimes, according to Esping-Andersen's classification (Esping-Andersen 1990). The selection includes what is traditionally considered one of the best performing countries in combating poverty (Denmark), the worst performing country (the United States), and two relatively low-poverty continental countries that are frequently compared with Canada and Quebec (France and the Netherlands). We could have added any number of other countries from the LIS data set, but this would have seriously complicated our analyses without affecting the basic results.

The poverty rates from 1990 up to the most recent data available for these countries and the four provinces are shown in Figure 2.4. In all cases, we use 50% of the median household income as our threshold.[11]

Now, where do Canada's largest provinces fit overall? As the figure clearly shows, Ontario, Alberta, and British Columbia fall squarely

Figure 2.4. Poverty rate in provinces and select countries using LIM

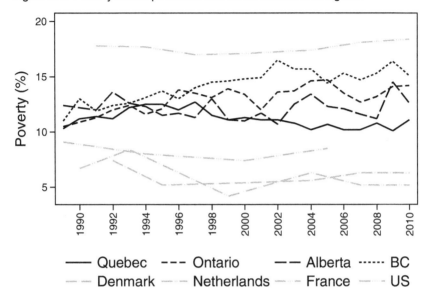

within the group of industrialized states with poverty rates above or well above 10%. Over the time frame, poverty rates are more or less flat in Alberta but slowly rising in Ontario. In British Columbia they rise substantially, from about 12% in the early 1990s, to over 15% in the late 2000s. In fact, British Columbia is the only jurisdiction in the figure whose poverty rates ever approach US ones.

Quebec is the exception. While, as we have already seen, its poverty rates were indistinguishable from those of the other provinces in the early to mid-1990s, as a result of the gradual reduction in Quebec's poverty rate since then and the drift upward in the other provinces, Quebec now stands apart. Although its poverty rate, at just below 10%, now approaches France's, it still remains several percentage points above the Netherlands and Denmark, which hover near 5%. Interestingly, since Swedish poverty rates have risen to close to 10%, Quebec's current rate is very close indeed to that of the country once considered the model to follow by Quebec's policymakers and academics.[12]

The pattern is similar when we look at acute poverty. Figure 2.5 shows acute poverty rates for the four provinces and the same countries as in Figure 2.4. When it comes to reducing the proportion of the

Figure 2.5. Acute poverty rate in provinces and select countries using LIM

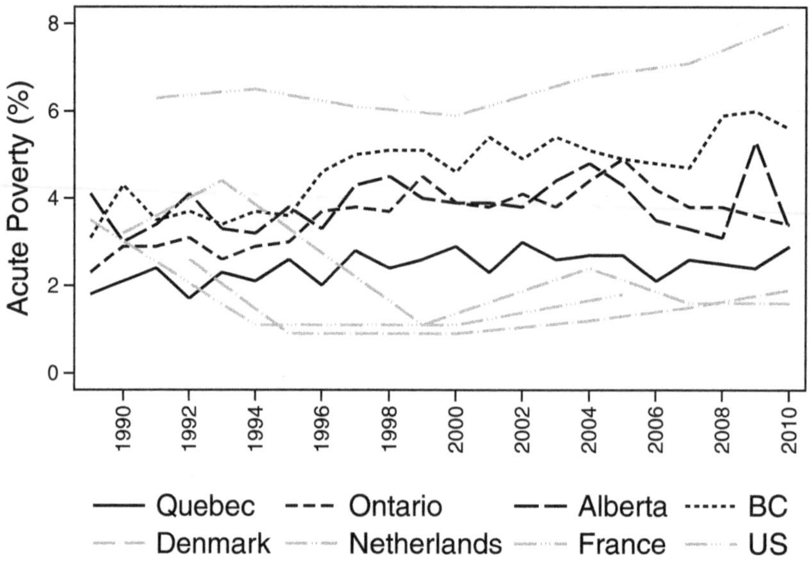

population living on household incomes below 30% of the median, Quebec appears to be doing slightly better than Ontario and Alberta, with acute poverty rates between 2.5% and 2.9% in recent years, but still not quite as well as the best performers, the Netherlands and Denmark, whose rates are usually well below 2%.

By these simple measures, then, Quebec has realized its goal of joining the industrialized countries with the lowest poverty rates – but just barely. Whereas Quebec's poverty rates were around 5%–8% higher than those of the European countries in the mid-1990s they are between 2% and 5% higher in the mid-2000s and mostly well below those of the other provinces and the United States. Quebec is approaching the group with the lowest poverty rates identified above; its rates now compare favourably with the middle-level group of countries, including the United Kingdom, Spain, and Italy.

Conclusion

This chapter is devoted to technical issues of poverty measures and their properties. After considering these, we have opted for a measure that will permit us to compare poverty between provinces and countries while taking into account at least some of the variation in the costs of living across provinces. For the remainder of this book, we use equivalized household disposable incomes of 50% of median household income as the poverty line and 30% as the acute poverty line to calculate the poverty rate. We use the provincial median household income as the benchmark for provincial poverty lines.

When we use these measures to compare Quebec's poverty rates over time with those of the other large Canadian provinces and a handful of comparison countries, we find some preliminary evidence suggesting that Quebec's distinctive approach to combating poverty and social exclusion may be working. While poverty rates elsewhere have remained stable or increased, in Quebec they have been coming down since about the mid-1990s. This corresponds with the evolution of Quebec's distinctive approach described in Chapter 1. But it hardly establishes a causal link between the policies and the outcomes.

Underneath the crude aggregate poverty rates we have been examining in this chapter, there are likely to be large discrepancies between how different groups are affected by the different policies. Many other factors affecting poverty rates among different groups of the population need to be taken into account as well. Nor do the essentially cross-sectional data used here tell us the extent of mobility into and out of poverty in different provinces and countries. Accordingly, in the following chapters, we examine the poverty outcomes for different types of households, the sources of income that permit them to escape poverty, the poverty dynamics over time, and the effect of factors other than government policy for Canada's four largest provinces and a selection of comparison countries.

Chapter Three

Poverty and the Changing Family

Introduction

Today's welfare state is largely the product of the extensive wave of welfare reform sweeping over much of the advanced industrialized world during the three decades following the Second World War – what the French call *les trente glorieuses* (Fourastié 1979). This is true for Canada as well, although the Canadian welfare state was never as extensive or as generous as many of its European counterparts (Banting and Myles 2013b, 4–6). Like the welfare states of other leading Western nations, the Canadian welfare state was based on the male-breadwinner model of the family (Fraser 1994; Millar 1996; Misra, Budig, and Moller 2007; Orloff 1993), guided by the normative concepts of family and labour market participation of the early post-war period (Esping-Andersen 1999; Raïq, Bernard, and van den Berg 2011; Raïq 2012). The ideal family of the day comprised a husband, a wife, and their children. The reigning norm of labour market participation consisted of each family having a single, able-bodied, full-time earner: the husband. The wife was expected to remain in the home, caring for her husband and children. The wage earned by the husband was assumed to be sufficient to secure a comfortable standard of living for his wife and children. The welfare policies of the modern welfare state were designed to ensure against potentially catastrophic income loss as a result of the loss of the family breadwinner. This was the primary purpose of workers' compensation and disability schemes, unemployment insurance, public pensions and, as a last resort, social assistance.

But families and households have been changing since then. The ideal concept of the male breadwinner never applied to all families, but it has applied to fewer and fewer families since the early days of the welfare state. Throughout the advanced industrialized nations, women have entered en masse into the labour market in recent decades, fertility levels have declined, and rates of divorce and separation have increased. These countries have also seen surges in non-standard employment, from rising levels of self-employment and short-term and part-time contract work, to decreasing levels of full-time, secure unionized employment. As the ideal family, and its corresponding labour market participation, no longer apply to the vast majority of households, neither does the secure breadwinner wage. As a consequence, the character of the social risks that welfare state programs are meant to insure against has changed dramatically as well (Banting and Myles 2013b, 25; Daly 2010; Esping-Andersen 2009; Fleckenstein and Lee 2014; Fraser 1994; Goldin 2006; Hemerijck 2013, 62–6; Millar 1996; Misra, Budig, and Moller 2007; Orloff 1993).

In the face of these changes in families and employment conditions, governments in Canada and elsewhere have modified their welfare regimes to varying degrees, attempting to ensure adequate protection against new social risks for an increasing variety of households. Misra, Budig, and Moller (2007) explore how each of Esping-Andersen's ideal-typical welfare regimes has reacted to the changing needs of families. In liberal regimes, individuals are expected to look to the labour market for whatever economic security they are able to obtain. As a result, policy responses to changes in family structure have been minimal and new family types have been left to their own devices. Conservative or 'Bismarckian' regimes have essentially been 'frozen,' continuing to support the family wage ideal, even in the face of countervailing historical currents (Esping-Andersen 1996a; Esping-Andersen 1996b).[1] Finally, social democratic regimes were early to move away from the male-breadwinner ideal by introducing social programs oriented towards supporting individuals, rather than being normatively defined around the traditional family conception, and especially policies aimed at facilitating female labour force participation (Letablier 2003).

As we saw in Chapter 1, Quebec has followed its own distinct policy trajectory, in many ways inspired by the social democratic response to the changing character of social risks, since the mid-1990s. Its subsidized day care, more generous parental leave provisions, family benefits, benefits for low-income workers, and so on, are all aimed at supporting families with children, notably by facilitating and encouraging the labour force participation of mothers and the unemployed.

To be sure, *some* of these policies may well have had their roots in the older Catholic doctrine of the 'family wage,' according to which wages and state-provided benefits ought to be based on family size and responsibilities as laid down in the papal encyclical *Rerum Novarum* (1891). Certainly, Quebec's early introduction of a family allowance, which we noted in passing in Chapter 1, had its origins in that doctrine, and there is no doubt that even the profoundly anti-clerical Quiet Revolution had deep roots in the progressive Catholic movements of the 1940s and 1950s (see Gauvreau 2005). But the lion's share of Quebec's new policies, especially the subsidized day-care program and extended parental leaves, is clearly traceable to a different inspiration, as these policies seek to accommodate and even encourage the trends in family composition and labour force participation that the more familialist, Christian Democratic welfare states have sought to resist (see, e.g., Van Kersbergen 2003).

In theory, such policies should benefit all families with children. But this does not mean they will benefit them all equally. One major trend leading to greater diversity in family types has been the rising divorce rate in most countries and the consequent rise of the proportion of single-parent families, overwhelmingly headed by women. This trend has become a major source of concern for policymakers, as social programs have failed to keep up (Dandurand and Ouellette 1992; Lefaucheur 1993; Raïq 2012). What is more, the trend has disproportionately affected low-income, low-educated families (Esping-Andersen 2014, 18). As a consequence, single-parent, mostly female-headed families have become the single most vulnerable group at risk of poverty in many advanced countries, leading a number of observers to speak of a new, alarming phenomenon: the feminization of poverty (Goldberg 2009; Kim and Choi 2013). The success of policies to combat poverty, then, will depend to a considerable degree on whether they manage to stem this tide by effectively supporting single-parent families with children.

There are additional reasons why welfare programs targeting families with children may be particularly worthwhile. Poverty, especially poverty of long duration, has a way of being passed on to the next generation (Bernard 2007; Bernard and McDaniel 2009). As Esping-Andersen puts it, 'a child from a poor family is more than twice as likely as others to become also a poor parent' (Esping-Andersen 2014, 21; see also Esping-Andersen 2009, Ch. 4). From the life-course perspective, childhood poverty is thus a major factor in producing more poverty in subsequent generations (Duncan et al. 1998). These are strong reasons indeed for policymakers to focus their anti-poverty measures on families with children.

But not all households are comprised of families with children. And for those other types, Quebec's social democratic approach does not appear, at first sight, to offer much succour. Couples without children and single adults do not appear to be of particular concern to Quebec's policymakers. Perhaps these types of households are less vulnerable and, therefore, are less in need of protection and support. But this is hardly self-evident.

In this chapter, we look at how the different emergent family types have fared in terms of poverty rates in Quebec and the three other Canadian provinces, as well as in a selection of comparison countries. Have Quebec's poverty rates for families with children come down to European social democratic levels? What about different family types? How have childless households fared compared to the rest of Canada and the other countries?

Our main findings confirm the importance of Quebec's family-oriented anti-poverty policies in setting it apart from the other Canadian provinces. In fact, the province has succeeded in bringing the poverty rates of families with children under 18 down to levels that compare favourably with even the most social democratic European welfare state. When it comes to households without underage children, especially single adults, however, Quebec's poverty rates are as high as, or even higher than, those in the other high-poverty liberal welfare states. These findings strongly suggest, but do not prove, that Quebec's relatively favourable performance in terms of poverty reduction is in large part due to its specific policy regime.

Changing Families in Canada

Over the course of the twentieth century, a number of social trends affected Canadian families and their composition. Census data from 1921 to 1996 show that the crude marriage rate in Canada peaked at a high of 11 marriages per 1000 population during the Second World War and mostly declined thereafter, except for the early 1970s, but even then it remained at lower levels than in the early 1940s (Milan 2000). The fertility rate rose to reach 3.9 births per woman in 1959 – the decade of the baby boom. The fertility rate has declined since then, to about 1.7 births per woman, a trend generally associated with the expanded use of contraception and the growing participation of women in higher education and the labour force. Women now have fewer children and have those children later in their lives, although the number of women having at least one child has remained stable.

As already noted, higher rates of divorce and separation have led to increases in lone-parent families. In the early twentieth century, most marriages ended with the death of a spouse. Since 1968, the year the Divorce Act was passed, an increasing share of marriages end with divorce (Milan 2000). As a consequence, while the proportion of lone-parent families out of all census families[2] decreased from 12.2% in 1941 to 8.4% in 1961, at which point it started increasing again, finally reaching 16.3% in 2011 (Statistics Canada 2012a). The increasing divorce rate coincided with an increase in the proportion of remarriages in all marriages, as well as an increase in cohabiting unions, for which information was collected for the first time in the 1981 census. In 2001, the proportion of cohabitating unions out of all unions was nearly 30% in Quebec, more than twice that of the other Canadian provinces (Le Bourdais and Lapierre-Adamcyk 2004). There also seem to be provincial differences in the meaning of cohabitation. In Quebec, this type of union constitutes an accepted setting to have children, but it remains very much an entry into marriage elsewhere in Canada. These developments have been a major factor behind the recent surge in family income inequality in Canada (Lu, Morissette, and Schirle 2011) and are likely to have a major impact on poverty rates as well.

Decreasing fertility trends, combined with increases in life expectancy, have also had implications for the age structure of the population. Baby boomers started to reach the age of 65 as of 2010, contributing to the overall aging of the population. The proportion of the Canadian population aged 65 and over has grown from about 8% in the 1970s to over 14% in 2011. The share of couples living in elderly households (households where the youngest member is 65 or older) increased from as low as 4%–6% in the late 1970s to as high as 8%–10% in recent years.[3] Quebec has seen the greatest increases, with the province going from the fewest elderly households among Canada's four largest provinces to the most between 1976 and 2010. These trends are expected to continue. Statistics Canada (2010b) projections suggest that the proportion of seniors[4] within the population will range from 23% to 25% in 2036, a marked increase from 14.4% in 2011.

Families and households in Canada are more diverse than they have ever been. While married couples still account for the largest share of census families, the proportions of common-law couples and lone-parent families have increased over time. Stepfamilies may have increased as well, but they have only been counted in the census since 2011. At that point, simple and complex stepfamilies comprised 7.4% and 5.2%, respectively, of all couples with children, (Statistics Canada 2012b). Simple stepfamilies are families where children are the biological or adoptive children of only one married or cohabiting partner in the couple. Families with at least one child who is the child of both partners and at least one child who is the child of only one of the partners, or families where each partner has at least one child of his/her own, but no child from both partners, are considered to be complex stepfamilies. It should be noted that an increasing proportion of the population does not live within a family. The proportion of the population living in private households, but outside of census families, jumped from 8.6% in 1961 to 17.1% in 2011 (Statistics Canada 2012a). The majority were living alone. The rest were living with relatives or non-relatives.

These massive changes in the composition of families and living arrangements and the growing importance of second earners and women's entry into the labour force have presented policymakers with new challenges. Clearly the old architecture of welfare state programs intended to protect the single-earner family would need to be modified to accommodate these new trends. As early as the 1970s, the Canadian federal government began to make minor adjustments in the social policy repertoire. Thus, the CAP, the federally funded but provincially administered social assistance program, was gradually adjusted to provide support for the working poor and low-income mothers of young children (see Jenson 2013, 51). In the early 1970s, the federal government introduced the Child Care Expense Deduction and the parental leave program as part of the Unemployment Insurance scheme. Much later, during the deficit-cutting 1990s, the federal government implemented a series of reforms to stimulate and facilitate labour force participation and provide greater support for families with children. The mid-1990s saw the replacement of the CAP by the Canada Social and Health Transfer, the introduction of the National Child Benefit, and the revamping of the Unemployment Insurance program to become the Employment Insurance program. While these reforms were, as mentioned, first and foremost part of the federal government's effort to reduce its debt and deficits through the retrenchment of social policy (Banting and Myles 2013a), they also signaled a conversion to a social investment approach (see Jenson 2013, 52–9; Mahon 2013; van den Berg et al. 2008).

In addition, as we saw in Chapter 1, the provinces introduced some relatively minor supplementary programs to support families with children and to encourage greater labour force participation. But when compared to Quebec's social democratic *virage*, these seem relatively modest (Mahon 2013). For instance, as shown in Chapter 1, while the other provinces considered here provide childcare subsidies, and, with the exception of Alberta, subsidies and supports to childcare providers, none come close to matching Quebec's subsidized day cares, enriched parental leave program, and various tax credits for families with children.

With this in mind, we can turn to the evidence on the results of Quebec's distinctive policies in terms of combating poverty for the increasing variety of family types. In the following sections, we compare poverty rates for different types of households in Quebec, the other three Canadian provinces, and a selection of advanced countries to assess to what extent and for what types of households Quebec's policies have met the challenges posed by the new social risks resulting from the trends in family formation and labour force behaviour reviewed above.

Data and Household Types

As explained in Chapter 2, we are limiting our analyses to poverty rates calculated as a percentage of the median disposable household income using the national median for countries and the provincial median for the four largest Canadian provinces. We examine families with children in this chapter, as they are the principal family type of concern to policymakers seeking to reduce poverty and the main focus of Quebec's strategy to combat poverty and social exclusion. But we also look at childless households to gauge the degree to which they have benefited from anti-poverty policies.

We consider six categories of household type: unattached singles, couples, lone-parent families with children, two-parent families with children, elderly households, and a residual 'other' category. Households are defined as families with children if they report at least one member less than 18 years of age (Letablier 2003). Unattached singles or couples without children are households reporting one member, or two members making a couple, between the ages of 18 and 64. Elderly households are those reporting no members under 65 (Smeeding 2006).

All households not meeting any of these criteria are classified as 'other.' This category includes a range of household types, among them those with multiple families, extended relatives, adult children, children living alone, and adult roommates. This classification reflects a demographic definition of household types which, though perhaps not ideal, is in keeping with most of the other research in the field (Christopher 2001, Hakovirta 2001, Misra and Moller 2005, Smeeding 2006). Every household fits into one category, and no household is dropped from the analysis.

As we explained in Chapter 2, we use the household rather than the family as our unit of analysis, in keeping with common practice in international comparative studies of income dynamics, poverty, and the welfare state.[5] While the family – that is, a household in which there is some relation of blood, marriage, or adoption between all members – is a more precise unit of analysis than the household (which in principle could include more than one family), the household is assumed to be the most relevant unit in terms of the sharing of material resources – the main concern in poverty research. But it should be noted here that this approach turns our category of 'other' households into a heterogeneous grouping, including multiple-family households, single young people with roommates, households with adult children, and families caring for live-in elderly parents. Although this category is large and growing, its sheer heterogeneity renders any analysis of poverty rates fairly hazardous. Consequently, while we follow accepted practice in the literature and analyse households rather than families, we leave the detailed analysis of this extremely diverse category for another day.

For the comparisons between Canadian provinces, we use Statistics Canada's Survey of Labour Income Dynamics (SLID) data set described in Chapter 2. As before, we limit comparisons to Canada's four largest provinces: British Columbia, Alberta, Ontario and Quebec. Using SLID, we are able to trace the poverty rates for different family types from 1976 to 2010.

For the international comparisons in this chapter and elsewhere, we use the LIS data, also described in Chapter 2, from 1989 until the latest year available. In order to keep the comparisons manageable, we select the four comparison countries used in Chapter 2: the United States, France, Denmark, and the Netherlands. In addition to the rationale for choosing these four countries given in Chapter 2, France and the Netherlands are of particular interest in that they were relatively late in recognizing the need to redesign anti-poverty policies to reflect the diversification of family types. Once they recognized the trends, they adopted strong policies inspired by the social democratic model of combining passive and active measures to lift families with children out of poverty. Thus, they offer a useful foil to our Canadian provinces. The most recent year for which data are available for both the provinces and the countries, with the exception of France, is 2010. The latest year for which we currently have French data in the LIS data set is 2005.

Before we begin to compare poverty rates among different types of households in these countries and provinces, it is worth noting that their proportions of these different types vary considerably. In recent years,[6] over 9% of Quebeckers formed single-person households, a higher share than in the other provinces, whose proportions are nearer to 6%, 7%, and 8%. The Netherlands, at over 11%, has an even higher proportion than Quebec; in France and the United States, the proportions of individuals living alone are similar to those of the other Canadian provinces. Denmark's is the highest, at almost 12%.

More people reside in households consisting of couples without children. In the provinces, proportions range from a low of 12.5% in Ontario to near 16.5% in Quebec. In our comparison countries, they range from 14% in France to over 18% in Denmark. Across the four provinces, around 3.5%–4.5% of individuals reside in lone-parent households, a proportion similar to that of France. The proportion is lower in the Netherlands (3.3%), but higher in the United States (5.9%) and Denmark (6%).[7] Most people live in a two-parent household with children, that is, 24.2% in British Columbia, 27.5% in Ontario, 28% in Quebec, and 31.3% in Alberta. Denmark's share of individuals residing in this type of household is near Alberta's (32%). The proportion is lower in the United States (29%) and higher in France (33%) and the Netherlands (34%).

The share of people living in elderly households is lower in the provinces and the United States than in the other three comparison countries. It varies from a low of 7% in Alberta to a high of 10% in Quebec, with 9% for the United States. By contrast, 12.5% of the adult population resides in elderly households in the Netherlands, with 14% in France and Denmark.

As mentioned above, 'other' households is a residual category comprising many types of households. Given its extreme heterogeneity, any attempt to analyse poverty rates among these households as a single group is not likely to produce meaningful results. But they constitute a large and growing proportion of all households, and their proportion varies quite considerably between countries and provinces. In the four provinces, between 30% and 40% of all individuals reside in these households, a proportion similar to the United States. The three other countries have significantly lower proportions, with only 18% in Denmark. These differences are not due to classification differences, as we applied the same criteria to households in all our comparison cases. While we have not undertaken an exhaustive analysis of what lies behind the differences, a cursory inspection of our data suggests they are largely due to differences in cohabitation patterns across countries. Thus, for instance, a large part of the difference between the proportion of Danes and the proportion of Quebeckers who live in other households is accounted for by the fact that far more Danish adults (including the elderly) live by themselves and are, thus, classified as single-adult households in our classification.

Families with Children: Canada

The broad poverty trends for families with children in Canada are well documented in the literature. The available research shows that poverty rates of Canadian two-parent families exhibit a more or less trendless fluctuation over the past several decades whereas the single-parent poverty rate has gradually declined, particularly since the late 1990s, although it still remains far higher than the rate for two-parent families (Myles et al. 2009; Osberg and Sharpe 2011; Richards 2010). The latter 'Canadian success story' has been attributed to the 'tough love' welfare-to-work policies enacted in some provinces starting in the 1990s, particularly in Alberta and Ontario (see Richards 2010), and to changes in the composition of lone mothers, as women have become more educated, and lone mothers older (Myles et al. 2009). However, as should already be clear from the findings presented in Chapter 2, we cannot treat such apparent pan-Canadian trends as homogenous and, thus, amenable to pan-Canadian interpretation and policy recommendations. Once we disaggregate the poverty rate trends for families with children to the provincial level, the Canadian picture changes dramatically, as do the most likely explanations and policy implications.

Let us look first, then, at families with children and two parents. Figure 3.1 shows the poverty rates, calculated based on a threshold of 50% of the provincial median household disposable income, for Canada's four major provinces from 1976 until 2010.

Figure 3.1. Poverty rate for two-parent families, Canada and four provinces

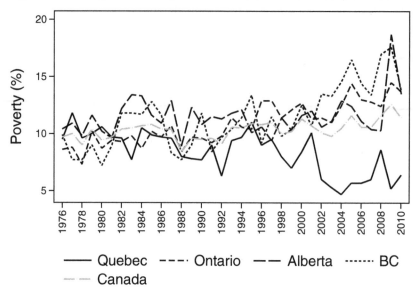

There are a number of notable trends here. First, there appears to be an upward long-term trend in bi-parental family poverty rates in all three English-speaking provinces, though the paths vary somewhat. The steepest climb is in British Columbia, with the poverty rate increasing from just below 8% in 1976 to close to 14% in 2010 (see also Raïq and Plante 2013). The rise has been particularly sharp and steady since the early 1990s, probably as a result of the recession and the subsequent cutbacks by both federal and provincial governments in their commitments to poverty and inequality reduction (Banting and Myles 2013a). Second, at the beginning of the period, Alberta's poverty rate for two-parent families is clearly the highest of the four provinces, fluctuating between 10% and 11%. But while Alberta's rate remains steady until 2006, after which it starts climbing again, British Columbia's and Ontario's continue to climb throughout, so that at the end of the period, Alberta's rate is, at slightly over 12%, about a percentage point above Ontario's but almost 2 percentage points below British Columbia's. In any case, the most important point is the steadily rising poverty rate for two-parent families in all three provinces since 1976.

Figure 3.2. Poverty rate for single-parent families, Canada and four provinces

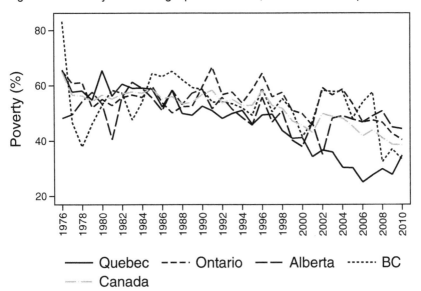

But not in Quebec. In 1976, Quebec's rate was the second highest of the four, less than a percentage point below Alberta's. By the end of the period, Quebec's two-parent family poverty rate is, at just over 6%, about half that of the other three provinces. After a moderate decline from 1976 until 1990 – during which time, it is worth noting, Quebec, unlike Alberta and especially British Columbia, successfully weathered the deep recession of the early 1980s – Quebec's poverty rate briefly increases with the advent of the recession of the early 1990s. But then, starting in 1995, Quebec's rate begins a sharp decline, from close to 9% – less than a percentage point below Alberta's – to close to 4% in 2005, after which it rises again to just over 6%. In short, while Quebec's two-parent family poverty rates are not all that different until the mid-1990s, as of about 1995, the patterns diverge: while the poverty rates in the other three provinces rise, Quebec's declines quite steeply.

By contrast, there is less divergence between the major provinces with respect to poverty rates among single-parent families. As Figure 3.2 shows, poverty rates for lone-parent families are *much* higher than those for two-parent families. This is in keeping with the large literature documenting the high poverty risks faced by this family type virtually everywhere. Until the mid-1990s, poverty affected 40%–50% of all lone-parent families in all four Canadian provinces.

Moreover, the temporal patterns differ significantly from those for bi-parental families shown in Figure 3.1. From the early 1990s onward, the rates begin to decline in all four provinces, albeit more fitfully in British Columbia and Ontario than in Alberta and Quebec. This may reflect the growing effect of piecemeal policy adjustments by the federal and provincial governments to accommodate the changing composition of families noted above. But here as well, Quebec does better, and for a longer period of time, than the other provinces. While Alberta's poverty rates for single-parent families seem to get stuck at just below 40% at the beginning of the new century, and Ontario's falls to about the same level by 2010, British Columbia's rate plunges dramatically in 2004, falling from 40% to 30%. But Quebec's rate, once not really distinguishable from that of the other three provinces, has fallen to 25%, that is, far lower than any of the other provinces. Note, however, that this rate is still about *five times* the rate for two-parent families in *la belle province*. While Quebec's family-focused strategy to combat poverty appears to have benefited all families with children, those with two parents have done far better than lone-parent families.

As noted in Chapter 2, the standard poverty rate tells little about the actual severity of poverty. In Figures 3.3 and 3.4, we attempt to capture the severity of poverty by looking at what we call the *acute poverty* rate, that is, the proportion of the population with a disposable household income of less than 30% of the median for both family types.

With respect to the acute poverty of families with children, Quebec stands out even more starkly from the other three provinces, and for a much longer period of time, than we have seen so far. As Figures 3.3 and 3.4 show, Quebec's acute poverty rates for two-parent and single-parent families have been below those of the other provinces as far back as 1976. To be sure, early in the period, Quebec's acute poverty rate for two-parent families (Figure 3.3) is, at close to 2%, not significantly lower than Ontario's. But this is considerably lower than the rates for British Columbia and Alberta. And it is the closest Quebec comes during this period to the rates for the other provinces. From 1976 onward, each province seems to be on a track of its own. Ontario's acute poverty rate for two-parent families continues to hover around the 2% mark, with a significant rise from the late 1980s until 2004, after which it falls back to the long-term level. Alberta's rate, by contrast, declines steadily from its high point of close to 4% in the late 1970s to about 2.5%

Figure 3.3. Acute poverty rate for two-parent families, Canada and four provinces

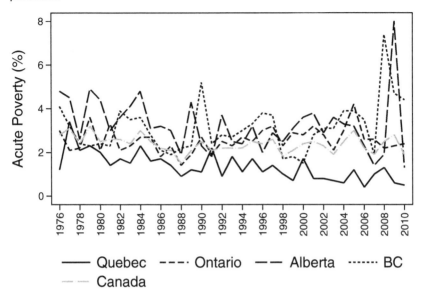

Figure 3.4. Acute poverty rate for single-parent families, Canada and four provinces

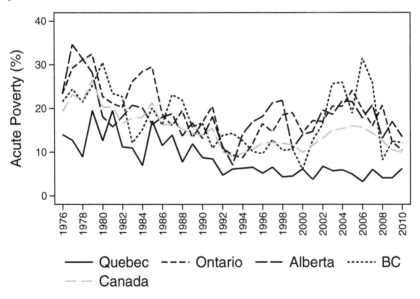

in the mid-1990s, only to climb back up to over 3% by the end of the period, with a sudden peak and drop in the most recent years. British Columbia's overall deteriorating performance is reflected in Figure 3.3 as well. While its rate fluctuates between 2%–3% until the early 2000s, it then soars to close to 5%, the second highest recorded rate for any of the provinces during the entire period.

The acute poverty rates for single-parent families are several times higher than those for two-parent families, even in Quebec. But as Figure 3.4 shows, Quebec's acute poverty rate for lone-parent families is consistently much lower. While the provincial rates converged somewhat from the mid-1970s until the mid-1980s, with Quebec's rate roughly stable at 10% and the other provinces' rates falling from around 20% to 10%–15%, from then on, they begin to diverge again; Quebec's rate drops while the other provinces' rates fluctuate around an upward-sloping trend. As a result, while acute poverty rates for single-parent families decline in all provinces after the mid-1970s, by the end of the period, the gap between Quebec and the other three provinces widens even more. Thus, for both two-parent and single-parent families with children, today's gap in acute poverty levels between Quebec and the other three provinces is the largest it has been over the whole thirty-year period of observation.[8]

When we put all our results together, we find that bi- and lone-parent family poverty rates in Canada have been converging over time, especially during the last ten years, although only modestly. This modest convergence can be attributed to two contrary trends: as two-parent family poverty rates have remained stable or edged upwards outside Quebec, the much higher single-parent family poverty rates have come down. Nonetheless, the gap between the two sets of rates remains substantial. Depending on the poverty rate (standard or acute) and the province, even in the most recent years, lone-parent family rates are between two and four to five times as high as two-parent family ones. Ironically, this gap is proportionately as wide in Quebec as elsewhere. But this is not because Quebec's single-parent families have fared worse than their counterparts in the other provinces. It is the result of its extraordinary success in bringing down the rates for two-parent families combined with its somewhat less impressive results for single-parent families.

Our results cast serious doubt on the validity of examining Canadian poverty trends for the country as whole, not to mention drawing general policy conclusions from them. At least for families with children, aggregate Canadian trends are obviously the product of, and thus mask, unique provincial trends that partly cancel each other out when aggregated into a national trend. In short, the relatively stable poverty rate for Canadian two-parent families until the early 2000s, and its subsequent rise, is actually the product of the countervailing movements of a fairly sharply declining rate in Quebec and a concomitant rise in the rest of the country. Similarly, the great 'Canadian success story' of declining poverty rates for single-parent families may be partly attributable to the declining rates in 'tough love' Alberta, British Columbia, and Ontario, but they are *at least as much* the result of the far greater decline in much more generous Quebec.

These countervailing trends correspond fairly closely to the trends in provincial policy orientation in the course of the past several decades, briefly outlined in Chapter 1. In a recent research report, the Caledon Institute of Social Policy has calculated 'total welfare income,' – that is, the total possible earnings from federal and provincial poverty programs – for four different types of households in all of Canada's provinces from 1986 to 2013 (Tweddle, Battle, and Torjman 2014). Their data show that total welfare income has actually *fallen* in constant dollars over this period in Alberta, particularly sharply for two-parent families, while they remained virtually unchanged in British Columbia and Ontario. Only in Quebec does total welfare income rise over the course of this extended period, albeit by a modest 9%–10% for families with children, (ibid., 79–80, 83–84). Now, given the fact that, despite three major recessions, this was a period of considerable economic growth, this means the total amount of welfare income has declined in relation to the relative poverty threshold which, as we saw in Chapter 2, tends to rise with growth in overall GDP per capita. In other words, with the exception of Quebec, social assistance and related programs have become *less* effective in combating poverty in the past three decades.

Moreover, the difference in welfare generosity between Quebec and the other provinces is even greater if we compare the Caledon Institute's figures to our *provincial* LIMs, as these depend on provincial per capita income, which is significantly higher in the other three provinces than in Quebec. Total possible welfare income for single-parent and two-parent families in Quebec, it turns out, is around 65%–70% of the provincial LIM for those households and over 100% of our provincial acute poverty thresholds. The corresponding ratios are considerably lower for the other three provinces, particularly Alberta.[9] Yet as we shall see in the following chapters, Quebec's relative success in bringing down the poverty rates of families with children compared to the other three provinces is by no means the result of more generous passive social assistance benefits *only*.

This may partly explain why our findings in this chapter differ from those presented by Haddow (2015) in his detailed comparison of the poverty-reducing effects of social assistance, child benefits, and taxes in Quebec and Ontario from 1993 to 2010. Haddow finds that the overall poverty-reducing effects of provincial benefits and taxes were greater in Quebec than in Ontario from about 2000 until 2009 for families with children, but the difference almost disappears in 2010 as a result of the introduction of the 2008 Ontario Child Benefit (see Haddow 2015, 244, 247–8). Moreover, once a series of political and economic variables are controlled for, there is no statistically significant difference in the effects of the two provinces' overall poverty-reducing measures (ibid., 255–7).

Two considerations lead us to think that our findings and Haddow's are less contradictory than they appear to be. First, Haddow estimates the overall poverty-reducing effects in the two provinces for the entire period, whereas we trace the poverty *rates* across the period. As Haddow himself recognizes (ibid., 257), his measure combines the relatively poorer performance of Quebec's policies in the early part of the period with its better performance later on. Second, and more important, Haddow focuses on the effects of transfers and taxes on income levels, whereas we look at poverty rates that are presumably the effect of the combination of such policies with those we call 'activation' policies in Chapter 1, as well as factors not directly influenced by such policies. We will return to this in the following chapters. Given these two considerations, we believe Quebec has still done considerably better than Ontario in bringing down poverty rates for families with children. As we shall see below, this cannot be said for childless households, a finding which parallels Haddow's.

Families with Children: Some Cross-National Comparisons

Our findings suggest, then, that Quebec's distinctive strategy to combat poverty has produced results for families with children that cause it to stand out from the three other provinces. But has it also achieved its ambitious goal of becoming 'one of the industrialized nations having the least number of persons living in poverty' by 2013? In this section we compare Quebec's performance with respect to families with children with that of the United States, Denmark, France, and the Netherlands. Figures 3.5 and 3.6 show the standard poverty rates for

Figure 3.5. Poverty rate for two-parent families in provinces and select countries

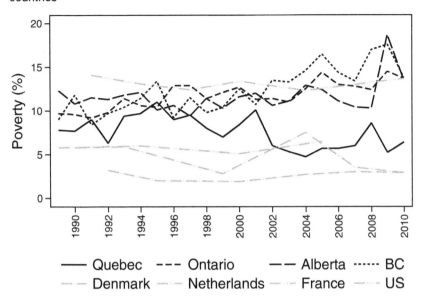

Figure 3.6. Poverty rate for single-parent families in provinces and select countries

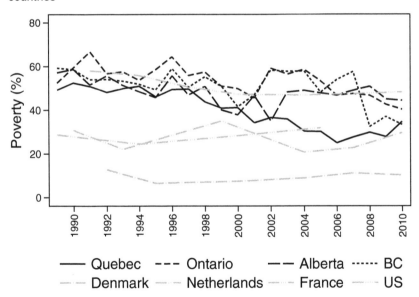

two-parent and single-parent families, respectively, for these four countries and the four Canadian provinces from the early 1990s until the latest figures available.

In Figure 3.5 we see two distinct clusters: the United States and the three Anglophone Canadian provinces, with poverty rates mostly between 10%–15% on the one hand, and the European countries with rates at around 5% or less on the other. Quebec is the only exception. Its poverty rates for two-parent families move from close to the high-poverty group in the early 1990s to around 5% at the end of the period. While still 1 or 2 percentage points above the very low Dutch and Danish rates, Quebec's rates are much closer to the European rates than the North American ones. It is also worth noting that while the latter rates have been stable or rising since the mid- to late 1990s, they have continued to fall in Quebec. In other words, when it comes to two-parent families, Quebec's strategy to combat poverty and social exclusion appears to have achieved its ambitious goal of bringing the poverty rate down to close to the lowest levels anywhere, and well within the anticipated time frame.

The story for single-parent poverty rates is similar but somewhat less dramatic. As shown in Figure 3.6, Quebec's rates fall from North American levels in the early 1990s to those of France and the Netherlands by 2006. But after this they tend to rise again, as do the Dutch rates. Meanwhile, the lone-parent poverty rates for the other North American jurisdictions continue to decline, especially, and somewhat surprisingly, those for British Columbia. As a result, by 2010 Quebec's and British Columbia's rates are, at around 34%, still about 7 to 15 percentage points lower than the other provinces and the United States, but slightly higher than the Netherlands' rates and fully three times Denmark's (around 10%). Put differently, Quebec's success in bringing down the poverty rates for single-parent families is less spectacular than its success for two-parent families. It seems Quebec's single-parent families have not benefited quite as much from the province's anti-poverty programs as its two-parent families. We will suggest reasons for this in Chapter 4.

Yet when it comes to acute poverty – that is, incomes below 30% of the median disposable income – Quebec has done particularly well for both family types, even when compared to the most generous of welfare states. Figures 3.7 and 3.8 trace the acute poverty trajectories from 1989 to 2010 for two- and single-parent families, respectively. In the early 1990s, the rate of acute poverty among two-parent families in Quebec is already lower than all jurisdictions but Denmark. In the following years, this rate declines slowly, nearing lows of 0% in recent

Figure 3.7. Acute poverty rate for two-parent families in provinces and select countries

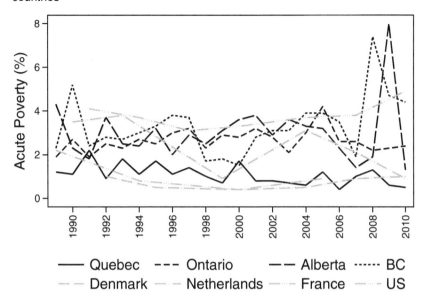

Figure 3.8. Acute poverty rate for single-parent families in provinces and select countries

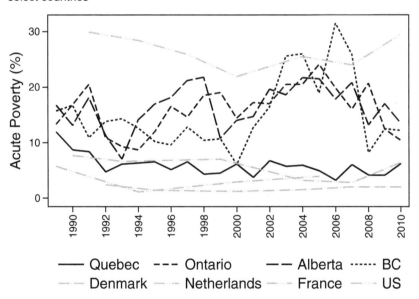

years, even lower than the extremely low rates for the Netherlands and Denmark. The corresponding rates for the United States and British Columbia are over 4%, and Ontario's is over 2%. Only Alberta's rate comes close to Quebec's, albeit after a precipitous rise and decline in the years leading up to 2010.[10] In other words, Quebec appears to have virtually eradicated acute poverty among bi-parent families, with rates dipping even below Denmark's.

Similarly, as the figure shows, Quebec's acute poverty rates for families headed by a single parent are initially relatively lower than those of the rest of Canada and the United States but higher than those of any of the leading European countries. But while these rates either stagnate or rise elsewhere over time, they plummet in Quebec. By the late 2000s, Quebec posts acute single-parent family poverty rates that, at about 5%, compare favourably with those of France and the Netherlands, although they remain a few percentage points above Denmark's low rate (2%). In contrast, between 15% and 20% of lone-parent families in the rest of Canada are shown as living in acute poverty in more recent years, between three and four times the rate in Quebec.

In short, Quebec appears to have realized its ambition of matching or closely approaching the countries that have been most successful in fighting poverty among families with children. To put it in terms of Esping-Andersen's typology of welfare state regimes, in the span of no more than two decades *la belle province* has moved from being virtually indistinguishable from the liberal regimes by which it is surrounded to becoming the near-equal of social democratic Denmark, seen by many in the province's academic and policymaking circles as the model to emulate. The only exception is Quebec's more modest success in bringing down the standard poverty rate for single-parent families, which remains closer to the rates of the Continental countries and some of the North American jurisdictions than to Denmark's. As a consequence, the proportionate gap between single- and two-parent families' poverty rates is, with a ratio of five to one (25% versus 5%, respectively), greater in Quebec than in France and Denmark. But this can be attributed as much to Quebec's success in reducing the poverty rate of two-parent families as to its failure to bring the single-parent rate down further.

Households without Children

As we have mentioned in this chapter and in Chapter 1, researchers and policymakers have been most concerned with documenting and combating poverty among families with children. Quebec's distinctive anti-poverty strategy has heavily targeted such families. Yet as noted in the section about the changing family, other types of families have grown as a proportion of all families at least as rapidly as have single-parent families with children. But the 'other' category refers to a variety of family types: childless couples, single adults living alone, adults living with non-family members, and multigenerational families. Furthermore, childless couples and singles include the elderly, who constitute, from the point of view of poverty reduction, a separate category. Given that anti-poverty policy in most provinces and countries has been heavily tilted towards families with children, how have these other types of families fared?

Some are of relatively little concern, at least in the Canadian and Quebec context. Non-elderly couples without children range from young couples who have not yet had children to couples whose children have grown up and left home, as well as childless couples in between. These households do relatively well in terms of poverty measures in most jurisdictions, ranging from around 3% in Denmark to just below 10% in the United States and Canada. But Quebec's policies have not been any more effective in bringing down the poverty rate than those in the United States and the rest of Canada, with rates ranging from 8% to a little over 10%. This is a first indication that Quebec's family-focused policies have done comparatively little for those without children.

The other group of childless households doing relatively well in Canada and Quebec are the elderly living alone or in a couple. The reduction of the poverty rate among the elderly from around 50% in the 1970s to among the lowest levels in the world today is possibly *the* great success story of the Canadian and Québécois welfare states. This reduction is almost entirely due to the introduction of the Canada and Quebec Pension Plans in the 1960s and the subsequent addition of income-tested complementary programs like Old Age Security and the Guaranteed Income Supplement. Canada's pension system, however much its long-term viability is currently under discussion, is widely viewed as a model for how to eliminate poverty among the elderly, a historically vulnerable population (Schirle 2013).

Single adults living alone fare much more poorly, particularly in Canada and in liberal regimes like the United States. In fact, Canada reports the highest poverty levels among singles in the developed world, with standard poverty rates approaching 40%. Singles who do poorly include young people early in their careers or still in school and

Figure 3.9. Poverty rate for single adults in provinces and select countries

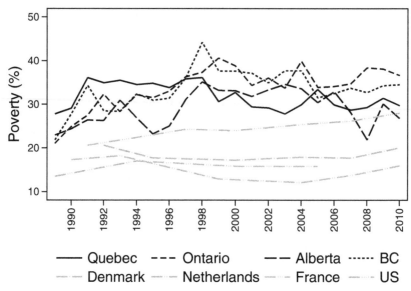

older individuals who find themselves single in later life; older singles, or at least older men, are more likely than their coupled counterparts to suffer from disability, illness, or other life-course altering setbacks (Lund, Nilsson, and Avlund 2010). Figure 3.9 shows poverty rates for unattached individuals aged 18 to 64.

If we compare the curves in Figure 3.9 with those in Figures 3.5 and 3.6, it becomes immediately evident that unattached individuals have considerably higher poverty rates than two-parent families or couples without children. In fact, they come close to the rates for the single-parent families causing the most concern among researchers and policymakers. They come close but are still lower than the single-parent family rates except for ... Quebec. In Quebec, poverty is as prevalent or even *more* so among unattached individuals as among lone-parent families.

Figure 3.9 exhibits the now familiar two clusters, with poverty rates around 30% and at times reaching above 40% in North America, compared to about half that in the European countries. But this time, Quebec is firmly within the North American cluster. In fact, in the most recent years, the poverty rate for unattached individuals in Quebec is, at close to 30%, slightly above Alberta's rate and several percentage points *higher* than the US rate. In other words, unattached individuals appear to have been entirely unaffected by Quebec's vaunted strategy to combat poverty and social exclusion (see also Brochu, Makdissi, and Tahoan 2011; Noël 2011).

In summary, then, the evidence unequivocally confirms the strong pro-family bias of Quebec's *virage sociodémocratique*. Families with children have benefited a great deal from these policies, to the point of putting Quebec, in accordance with the declared goal of Bill 112, among the advanced countries with the lowest levels of poverty. Because they are so narrowly focused on families with children, however, these policies have done little for households without children, and less for single adults. As far as such households are concerned, Quebec remains firmly lodged among the least generous of liberal welfare state regimes.

Conclusion

These findings suggest the broad aggregate trends presented in Chapter 2 are the composite effects of several varying, sometimes divergent or even conflicting, trends among smaller subpopulations. Thus, while in the other provinces, poverty rates of two-parent families have drifted up, they have gone down in Quebec. Single-parent household poverty has declined everywhere, albeit in different patterns, with early declines registered in Alberta, British Columbia, and Ontario, and a much later but more sustained decline in Quebec. The early declines may stem from the new and tougher welfare-to-work policies, but the Canada-wide decline from the mid-1990s can certainly be traced to the decline produced by Quebec's quite different, more generous social democratic policies.

Similarly, the relatively favourable trend in Quebec's poverty rates as compared to the rest of Canada, as documented in Chapter 2, is actually the composite of separate and partially contradictory trends for different types of households in the population. In accordance with Quebec's strong emphasis on lifting families with children out of poverty, such families have done quite well there compared to other Canadian provinces. But this has happened at the expense of a relative neglect of other family or household types. In Quebec, these other households do no better than elsewhere in North America and, in the case of single childless adults, even worse.

But as much as the evidence presented here is congruous with what we know about the policy approaches of Canada's four largest provinces, we cannot automatically attribute differences in outcomes to differences in policies. The causes of poverty are many and the determinants of trends in poverty rates complex; government policies themselves can have a variety of effects, some mutually reinforcing, others conflicting. An important question is whether Quebec's relatively better performance with respect to families with children is the result of its more effective activation policies, particularly its subsidized day care and extended parental leave program, or of its more generous cash benefits to families with dependent children. We address this question in Chapter 5. But final outcomes are also the result of interactions between policies and demographic trends, and it is by no means self-evident that either one or the other is the more important determining factor. In Chapter 6 we assess the extent to which Quebec's relatively successful anti-poverty strategy was helped or hindered by its demographic composition when compared to the other Canadian provinces and the sample countries.

But before we address these questions, we need to consider one additional dimension of poverty: its duration. As many observers argue, welfare states may face a trade-off between the poverty rate and average poverty duration. Policies that make the poor dependent on government cash support may in the long run, it is argued, create a 'culture of dependence' that actually ends up increasing the number of chronically poor households. This kind of argument raises the question of whether Quebec's ability to bring down the poverty rates for families with children has been achieved at the cost of creating a larger class of chronically poor households. For obvious reasons, chronic poverty is, other things being equal, a much more serious problem than 'mere' episodic poverty spells. We turn to this issue in the next chapter.

Chapter Four

Chronic Poverty

Introduction

The results presented in preceding chapters have been exclusively *cross-sectional*. That is, we have compared populations in terms of the incidence of poverty at different points in time. Such consecutive cross-sectional snapshots tell us something about trends in overall proportions of the poor in a population. What they cannot tell us is how long anyone who qualifies as poor at one point in time *remains* poor. That is, cross-sectional comparisons over time do not tell us anything about the duration of poverty. We simply do not know whether the low-income households found at one point in time are the same as those found at the next point. Perhaps they are entirely different households or, more likely, a mixture of the two (Raïq and Plante 2013).

There are a number of reasons why we should be particularly concerned with poverty duration or, conversely, the rate of mobility in and out of poverty. As Picot and Myles note, 'higher rates of low income in one period (or one country) than another is rather more serious if it reflects a rise or difference in long-term, relatively permanent entrapment ('social exclusion')[1] than if it reflects an increase or difference in short term spells of low-income. If we could choose our country of birth, for example, we might be willing to trade off a somewhat higher risk of experiencing 'poverty' or unemployment in country X if we knew that our chances of quickly exiting from that state were higher than in country Y' (Picot and Myles 2005, 21).

Personal preferences aside, for the households in question, chronic poverty is likely to be a radically different experience than an isolated, short spell of low income. In many cases, the latter may be weathered relatively well by making temporary adjustments (Worts, Sacker, and McDonough 2010, 235). By contrast, the many harmful effects of long-term poverty are well documented in the literature (Bane and Ellwood 1986; Fouarge and Layte 2005; Leisering and Walker 1998; Walker 1995). Over time, poverty tends to be cumulative, and initial disadvantages become amplified (Bernard and McDaniel 2009). The situation of poor people is often reproduced not just over the life course but intergenerationally (O'Rand 2009). The longer it lasts, the more poverty breeds instability, trapping families into life patterns that permit less control over their futures (Oxley, Thai-Thanh, and Antolín 2000).

More robust safety nets provide families with the support they need to save them from poverty and its short- and long-term ill-effects, permitting them to focus on making the decisions and commitments that will reduce the risk of future poverty (Laïdi 1999; Saint-Martin 2000). But depending on whether poverty is primarily a transitory state or a persistent and recurrent one, different kinds of safety nets are called for. Transitory poverty may be successfully dealt with by programs providing temporary income support. By contrast, the existence of a sizeable 'underclass' of households suffering long-term social exclusion will require a different policy approach, including a range of social services and activation measures (Finnie and Sweetman 2003, 292; Worts, Sacker, and McDonough 2010, 235).

In this chapter we move from our previous successive cross-sectional analyses to an examination of *poverty dynamics* in Canada's four largest provinces by looking at the poverty trajectories of households between 2002 and 2007. This is the most recent period since Quebec's adoption of its distinctive strategy to combat poverty and social exclusion for which we have the requisite panel data. In preceding chapters we have shown that the strategy *appears* to have borne fruit in terms of reducing overall poverty rates, at least for families with children. Here we are interested in determining whether and to what extent it may have done so by reducing the prevalence of long-term poverty as well.[2]

Our main findings in this chapter suggest that this is indeed the case, at least in part. Our comparisons of poverty durations in the four provinces show that poverty durations are on average actually *shorter* in Quebec than in the other three provinces, with the partial exception of Alberta. Moreover, temporarily poor families in Quebec escape from poverty more quickly, on average, than their counterparts in the other three provinces. In short, poverty in Quebec is less chronic and more transitory.

Poverty Dynamics

The trade-off between the incidence and duration of poverty implied above by Picot and Myles is commonly associated with the 'American Dream.' According to this widely held belief, the relatively high level of poverty and inequality in the United States is rendered acceptable, in part, because Americans know their chances of escaping from poverty and climbing the income ladder are also relatively high. In addition, many have argued that inequality and the threat of poverty are powerful incentives for people to pursue upward income mobility with the utmost energy and resourcefulness. Adherents to this belief add that efforts by the government to reduce inequality and poverty by providing income support for those at the bottom of the income distribution can undermine those incentives. Instead of encouraging independent effort to escape from poverty, such policies produce a culture of dependence on government handouts among the poor and near-poor, reducing upward income mobility and creating a large population of chronically (near-)poor (see, e.g., Murray 1994; see also Dean and Taylor-Gooby 2014).

While such arguments are common in both the literature and political debates, recent cross-national research strongly suggests income inequality is *negatively* related to income mobility. That is, the more unequal the income distribution is, the harder it is for those at the bottom to move up the ladder. Moreover, this research invariably shows the United States to be at the negative extreme of both continua, with the greatest amount of income inequality *as well as* the lowest rate of income mobility of all advanced capitalist countries (Björklund and Jäntti 1997; Blanden 2013, 2014; Corak 2006; Solon 2002; for a review of this literature, see Corak 2013).

Much of the mobility-stifling effect of income inequality appears attributable to the accumulation and intergenerational transmission of privilege at the very top of the income distribution (Corak 2013). However, there is considerable evidence suggesting poverty, especially chronic poverty, is also passed on intergenerationally (see, e.g., Bird 2007; Harper, Marcus, and Moore 2003; Jenkins and Siedler 2007). Unfortunately, we know much less about mobility into and out of poverty in the shorter run, that is, about *intra*generational mobility. Compared to cross-sectional studies of poverty, the number of studies analysing poverty dynamics remains limited, with cross-national comparisons even more so, likely because the necessary data have not been widely available (Oxley, Thai-Thanh, and Antolín 2000, 11; Valletta 2006, 263). To study poverty dynamics, we need panel data, that is, survey data following the same respondents over a substantial period of time.

The available studies of poverty dynamics that focus on a single country have shown that, while most poverty spells are transitory, a significant minority of the population suffers chronic poverty, with some identifiable groups more at risk than others, including single mothers (see, e.g., Bane and Ellwood 1986; Finnie and Sweetman 2003; Stevens 1994). Recent cross-national comparative work on poverty dynamics has documented large differences between countries in the prevalence of long-term poverty, in probabilities of falling into or escaping from poverty, and their correlates. These studies also confirm a connection between inequality and lack of mobility, showing that, contrary to the popular myth, long-term poverty is considerably more prevalent in the United States than in other countries with lower levels of income inequality and poverty (Oxley, Thai-Thanh, and Antolín 2000; Picot and Myles 2005; Valletta 2006; Worts, Sacker, and McDonough 2010).

The results for Canada are mixed. On the one hand, Valletta places Canada close to the United States in terms of poverty persistence and the relatively weak effect of social policies in keeping households out of poverty (Valletta 2006, 268, 274, 282). On the other hand, according to Oxley et al. (2000) and Picot and Myles (2005), the proportions of the poor in Canada who remain poor for a long period of time compare favourably with those in the United States. With around one-quarter of Canada's poor remaining in poverty for five consecutive years, as opposed to close to a third in the United States, and with about 40% of poor Canadians escaping from poverty after one year, as opposed to about 35% in the American context, Canada's performance is closer to that of the United Kingdom. The countries on the European continent perform even better, with most reporting lower long-term poverty rates and higher exit rates after one year of poverty.

We know by now that such results for Canada as a whole probably hide considerable differences between the provinces, especially between Quebec and the rest of Canada. While Quebec may have succeeded in approaching the European welfare states with respect to cross-sectional poverty rates for certain types of households, it remains to be seen to what extent its distinctive policies have been successful in combating long-term poverty. In this chapter we begin to address that question.

Methodology

As noted, to conduct an analysis of typical poverty trajectories, we need panel data. SLID (described in Chapter 2) follows 'waves' of respondents for periods of six years at a time. In this chapter we use the most recent completed wave, from 2002 to 2007, as this is the period when Quebec adopted and implemented its strategy to combat poverty and social exclusion. By following the poverty experience and trajectories of the 2002 cohort of families, we will be able to determine to what extent Quebec's policies have created a distinctive pattern of poverty dynamics when compared to the other Canadian provinces.

We focus on two-parent and single-parent families with children since these are, as shown in Chapters 1 and 3, the types of households specifically targeted by Quebec's policies. As before, we restrict our sample to families who report living as couples or singles, with children under the age of 18 in 2002. But this raises an important methodological issue: the composition of some families will have changed over the six-year survey period. Lone parents may find partners, children may grow up and leave home, and families may move between provinces. Moreover, we know from the literature that such changes in family composition can have important effects on household income (Fleury and Fortin 2006, 82). There is no simple way of examining both changes in income status and changes in family composition simultaneously, so we take *initial* family composition in the year 2002 as the point of reference. The share of families that changes composition – moving from two-parent to one-parent families or the reverse – does not differ significantly from province to province. Consequently, the differences between the provinces in poverty dynamics are primarily due to factors *other than* changes in family composition during the six-year period examined here.

Similarly, we determine provincial estimates based on each family's province of residence in 2002. We further limit our analyses to those respondents for whom we have six complete years of data. Our estimates, then, capture the experiences of the 2002 cohort of families over a six-year period and are generalizable to the entire 2002 cohort of Canadians. We employ the usual Statistics Canada longitudinal survey weights to control for the impact of survey attrition.

Table 4.1 Total number of years in poverty between 2002 and 2007, Canadian provinces

	Two-parent families						
Province	1 year	2 years	3 years	4 years	5 years	6 years	At least 1 year
Quebec	8.0%	2.8%	3.2%	0.4%	0.2%	0.9%	15.5%
Ontario	7.5%	3.3%	4.3%	2.4%	1.7%	2.2%	21.6%
Alberta	8.4%	3.7%	6.7%	3.7%	0.7%	0.9%	24.2%
BC	9.7%	1.9%	4.6%	3.0%	3.8%	4.5%	27.5%
	Single-parent families						
Province	1 year	2 years	3 years	4 years	5 years	6 years	At least 1 year
Quebec	11.2%	15.8%	9.7%	1.9%	2.8%	7.7%	49.1%
Ontario	8.4%	9.1%	5.3%	9.3%	6.5%	18.5%	57.1%
Alberta	11.1%	20.3%	14.1%	1.5%	7.2%	2.5%	56.6%
BC	4.2%	4.7%	17.1%	11.3%	7.1%	15.5%	59.9%

Source: SLID

Poverty: Persistent or Transitory?

Table 4.1 shows the proportions by province of two-parent and one-parent families who were poor, by our criteria, during only one of the six years covered by this wave of SLID data,[3] during two years, three years, and so on, all the way to those who were poor during the entire six-year period. The final column of the table, 'At least one year,' shows the proportions that were *ever* poor over these six years, i.e., the sum of the preceding six row percentages.

At-least-once-poor compared to annual poverty rates: Let us start by considering the final column. Notice how high the numbers are compared to the annual poverty rates for these two family types reported in Chapter 3. While, for instance, we showed in Chapter 3 that the annual poverty rates for two-parent families in Quebec hovered around the 5% mark between 2002 and 2007, from Table 4.1 we can see that fully 15.5% of those living in such families were poor at least one of those years. In other words, the share of families affected at least once by poverty during this six-year period is much larger than the cross-sectional figures suggest. The same is true in the other three provinces.

The fact that far more people experience poverty at some time over a six-year period than there are poor people at any one time means, of course, that there must be a fair amount of mobility across the poverty threshold over time. The proportional discrepancy between the two rates is particularly high for Quebec. There, the ratio between two-parent families ever affected by poverty and those who are poor at any one time is about three to one. The corresponding ratios for the other three provinces are about two to one. These ratios are significantly lower for single-parent families, even though the numbers in the 'At least 1 year' column of Table 4.1 show that staggeringly large percentages were affected by poverty at least once during this six-year period in all four provinces. Yet the ratios of at-least-once-poor to the annual poverty rates reported in Chapter 3 are lower than for two-parent families because the annual poverty rates are so high. Thus, while practically half (49.1%) of Quebec's single-parent families suffered from poverty at least one of the years from 2002 to 2007, the average annual poverty rate for these families was a bit above 25% during this period,[4] yielding an at-least-once-poor to average-poor ratio of about two to one. For the other provinces these ratios are lower still, even though the rates in the 'At least 1 year' column of Table 4.1 are considerably higher because, as we showed in Chapter 3, the average rates of poverty for lone-parent families in these provinces were so high.

The discrepancy between the number of people affected by poverty at least once during the six-year period and those who are poor in any one year is an index, as we have suggested already, of the amount of mobility across the poverty line. The greater this discrepancy – that is, the higher ratios we cite in the preceding paragraphs – the greater the proportion of people who must be moving into and out of poverty. This suggests mobility across the poverty line is more prevalent in Quebec than in the other provinces. But it also suggests that such mobility is significantly lower in all provinces for single-parent than it is for two-parent families.

The other numbers in Table 4.1 shed more light on the actual movement over time in and out of poverty. Somewhat surprisingly, the first column shows the proportion of two-parent families who suffered 'only' one year of poverty during the six-year period in Quebec is in the middle of the pack: Ontario's proportion is half a percentage point lower, and British Columbia has a significantly higher rate, almost 10%.

Long-term poverty: But when we move from the proportions having suffered only one year of poverty to those living in poverty two years, three years, and so on, we observe two distinct patterns. As we might expect, the proportions decline everywhere as we move from the relatively short-term to the long-term poor, but the decline is significantly steeper in Quebec and Alberta. When we get to the proportions of two-parent families suffering *permanent* poverty, that is, who were poor during the entire six-year period,[5] the proportions in Alberta and Quebec are between half and one-fifth of those in Ontario and British Columbia. Comparing the numbers in the six-year column to those in the one-year column, we see that the probability of a two-parent family in Alberta or Quebec suffering permanent poverty is about one-eighth of that same family's probability of suffering a transitional (one-year) bout of poverty, whereas the corresponding likelihood ratios in Ontario and British Columbia are close to one-third and one-half, respectively.

The differences between the provinces are even more marked when we look at the results for single-parent families. The patterns are slightly different, with the overall poverty rates, as expected, considerably higher than for two-parent families. Note, first, that the proportion of single-parent families suffering 'only' one year of poverty varies much more dramatically between the provinces than does the proportion of two-parent families. Interestingly, this time Alberta and Quebec have the highest rates, at 11.1% and 11.2% respectively. Although British Columbia's rate is less than half this number, this is hardly good news for Canada's western-most province. For as we move along the row for British Columbia, the proportions of longer-term poor single-parent families actually go up. That is, British Columbia's single-parent families are *more* likely to suffer long-term than short-term poverty. Similarly, while only 8.4% of Ontario's single-parent families endured a transitional, one-year poverty spell between 2002 and 2007, close to one-fifth (18.5%) of such families lived in poverty during the entire six-year period.

As before, Alberta and Quebec stand out from the rest. The proportions are relatively high for the one-year, two-year, and three-year poor but decline precipitously for longer-term intervals of poverty. In other words, while single-parent family poverty is certainly a serious problem in all four provinces, as the final 'At least 1 year' column makes quite clear, far fewer of these families suffer *very* long periods of poverty in Alberta and Quebec than in Ontario and British Columbia.

The similarity of the Quebec and Alberta patterns may be surprising at first since, as documented in Chapter 1, these two provinces are at opposite ends of the social policy spectrum. But this just goes to show that very different policy regimes are capable of producing similar results. While the relative prevalence of short-term as opposed to long-term poverty among Quebec families is no doubt at least partly the result of Quebec's policies to combat poverty, Alberta's relatively short poverty spells are no doubt explained by the province's buoyant labour markets during this period. There is in fact a growing literature documenting the strong positive spillover effects on job creation and wage levels at the lower end of the income and skill distribution caused by Alberta's sustained oil boom (see, e.g., Marchand 2015; Fortin and Lemieux 2015). This would certainly account for Alberta's relatively good performance both in terms of poverty rates and relatively short poverty durations.

At the same time, Alberta's boom did not necessarily shield its families from poverty. As we would expect from the findings presented in the preceding chapters, the 'At least 1 year' column in Table 4.1 shows the likelihood of single-parent families in Quebec to *ever* be affected by poverty is significantly lower than for Alberta's families. So while Quebec continues to stand out for its overall lower poverty rates and its relatively shorter poverty durations, Alberta resembles the other two Anglophone provinces in the overall chances of a family suffering poverty at least some time during the six-year period. That said, such families are less likely to suffer very long periods of poverty, thanks to Alberta's stronger economy.

Acute poverty: The above patterns are even more pronounced for the proportions of families affected by acute poverty, that is, with incomes below 30% of the median. These are shown in Table 4.2. Acute poverty of more than two years is, happily, quite rare for two-parent families in all four provinces and fairly rare for single-parent families, except for British Columbia, where more than a quarter[6] of single-parent families suffer acute poverty for three years or more.

While Alberta's very long-term (three years or more) rates are generally as low as Quebec's, when we look at shorter terms of acute poverty, the situation changes, with Quebec coming out ahead. The chances of a two-parent family in Quebec suffering from acute poverty at some point during the 2002–7 period are less than half what they are in Alberta, while a single-parent family's risk of experiencing acute poverty for any length of time in Quebec is close to one-third of what it is in Alberta and one-quarter of the BC figure, a staggering 44.8%. Even more strikingly, Alberta single-parent families are about five times more likely to suffer a one-year spell of acute poverty than their counterparts in Quebec,[7] while the ratio for two-parent families is over two to one. Consequently, while overall standard poverty rates are lower in Quebec than in the other provinces, the probability of a

Table 4.2 Total number of years in acute poverty between 2002 and 2007, Canadian provinces

	Two-parent families						
Province	1 year	2 years	3 years	4 years	5 years	6 years	At least 1 year
Quebec	2.1%	0.8%	0.4%	0.0%	0.0%	0.0%	3.3%
Ontario	4.2%	2.1%	1.2%	0.7%	0.0%	0.0%	8.2%
Alberta	4.8%	2.8%	0.0%	0.0%	0.0%	0.0%	7.6%
BC	5.4%	0.4%	0.9%	1.9%	0.0%	0.0%	8.6%
	Single-parent families						
Province	1 year	2 years	3 years	4 years	5 years	6 years	At least 1 year
Quebec	4.6%	5.3%	2.0%	0.0%	0.0%	0.0%	11.9%
Ontario	13.3%	6.1%	0.0%	5.4%	1.7%	0.0%	26.6%
Alberta	25.2%	1.2%	0.0%	3.6%	0.0%	0.0%	29.9%
BC	13.0%	5.0%	8.1%	9.2%	9.5%	0.0%	44.8%

Source: SLID

poor family falling into acute poverty is also significantly lower. These findings confirm the cross-sectional results presented in the preceding chapters. Beyond that, they show that families in Quebec not only run a smaller risk of ending up in poverty than elsewhere in Canada (with the partial exception of Alberta), they also manage to get out of poverty more rapidly.

Who are the chronically poor? As we indicated in the introduction to this chapter, one important reason for being interested in poverty duration and trajectories is to assess whether an identifiable group of families suffers from long-term poverty, and how large a proportion of the poor falls into this category. These chronically poor families are, as a result of the cumulative disadvantages that beset them, most likely to suffer social exclusion, a much broader set of social handicaps than mere income poverty, including exclusion from the labour market, educational deprivation, poor health, lack of adequate housing and living space, and lack of social support. Consequently, they may need quite different forms of support than those experiencing the occasional transitory episode of poverty. The six-year column in Table 4.1 gives a partial answer to this question. It shows the proportions of the respective family types we have labelled 'permanently' poor,[8] by which we mean those who were poor for the entire six-year period.

Note, first, most of the numbers are quite small.[9] Happily, permanent poverty is relatively rare for two-parent families throughout Canada and all but non-existent in Quebec and Alberta. Nevertheless, the 2.2% in Ontario and the 4.5% in British Columbia who experienced poverty in every year from 2002 to 2007 add up to significant numbers. Much more worrying, however, are the results for single-parent families. The share of families in Ontario and British Columbia who did not enjoy a single year out of poverty between 2002 and 2007 is, as noted above, 18.5% and 15.5% respectively. The corresponding figure for Quebec is, at 7.7%, less than half, but it is still *between eight and nine times* the rate for two-parent families in that province. Only Alberta seems to have brought down the permanent poverty rate for single-parent families, but, as we mentioned before, the impressively low 2.5% is no doubt a result of its buoyant and dynamic labour market during this period dominated by its sustained oil boom.

Permanent, chronic and transitory poverty: The proportions of what we have called permanently poor do not necessarily exhaust those who may be considered *chronically* poor. In the case of the latter, although their overall cumulative income over a certain period of time was below the average poverty line for that period, their income may not have been below the poverty line during each and every year.[10] Conversely, some proportion of poverty spells lasting less than the full six years can be defined as transitory in the sense that the families in question managed to stay above the poverty line in the longer term. Table 4.3 captures some of these differences.

In the first three columns, the table displays three rates: the proportion of people living in the respective family types whose incomes were never below the poverty line during 2002–7 ('never'); the proportions whose average incomes were below the poverty line for the period as a whole, irrespective of how many of the six years they are classified as poor ('chronic'); and the proportions who were poor during at least one of the six years but whose income remained above the poverty line for the period as a whole ('transitory'). The fourth column, finally, displays the proportion of those who have suffered any poverty at all during the six-year period (the sum of the chronic and transitory percentages)[11] who are in this 'transitory' category. That is, the figures in this column indicate the proportion of all those who have suffered poverty during at least one year who nevertheless managed to maintain an average income above the poverty line for the period as a whole. The first column, showing the proportions who have never been poor, is

Table 4.3 Poverty duration profiles between 2002 and 2007, Canadian provinces

	Two-parent families			
Province	Never	Chronic	Transitory	Transitory as proportion of ever poor
Quebec	84.5%	2.3%	13.2%	85.2%
Ontario	78.4%	7.0%	14.6%	67.6%
Alberta	75.8%	8.2%	16.0%	66.1%
BC	72.5%	10.1%	17.4%	63.3%
	Single-parent families			
Province	Never	Chronic	Transitory	Transitory as proportion of ever poor
Quebec	50.9%	15.4%	33.8%	68.7%
Ontario	42.9%	32.3%	24.8%	43.4%
Alberta	43.4%	22.4%	34.2%	60.4%
BC	40.1%	37.9%	22.0%	36.7%

Source: SLID

the inverse of the final 'At least 1 year' column in Table 4.1. Thus, for instance, since 15.5% of all two-parent families in Quebec suffered from poverty at least one of the years during the six-year period as shown in Table 4.1, 84.5% of such families never experienced poverty during this period.

Quebec's families are notably better protected against falling into poverty than those elsewhere. The proportions of two-parent families who never suffered poverty in the other provinces are between 6 and 12 percentage points lower than Quebec's 84.5%. For the single-parent families, the difference is even larger, with between close to one-fifth and one-quarter more of these particular Quebeckers never experiencing poverty.

But while fewer families are ever affected by poverty in Quebec, poverty might be disproportionately concentrated among the chronically poor. The second column in Table 4.3, displaying the proportions of the chronically poor, shows this is not the case. To the contrary, a far smaller percentage of both family types in Quebec qualify as chronically poor by our definition than in the other three provinces. The difference is particularly stark for two-parent families: at 2.3%, the proportion of chronically poor in Quebec is about one-fifth of what it is in British

Columbia. But Quebec's single-parent families also stand out: for this group, the chronic poverty rate varies from two-thirds of Alberta's to two-fifths of British Columbia's.

As mentioned, our category of chronic poor is broader than simply including those who were poor during all six years of the period. We call the latter 'permanently' poor. The point of the broader definition is that our category of permanently poor may fail to capture a possibly significant proportion of the long-term poor who are, for the reasons mentioned above, of special concern to researchers and policymakers. What is of particular interest here is how much larger the more inclusive group of chronically poor is in comparison to the always poor, that is, how the figures in the middle column in Table 4.3 compare to the penultimate column of Table 4.1. For two-parent families the effect is quite large. The proportion of long-term poor more than doubles in Quebec and British Columbia when we include all those with an average income below the poverty line over the six-year period, but in Alberta it increases *ninefold*. This is partly a function of the very low proportion of families in Alberta who lived in poverty during all six years, but even more so, of the surprisingly high number of two-parent families in Alberta who, while not poor in every one of the six years, earned an average income below the poverty line during the period as a whole.[12]

For single-parent families the pattern is similar, but as expected, at much higher overall levels. Again, the Alberta rate of chronically poor is about nine times its rate for the six-year poor in Table 4.1. For the other provinces, including Quebec, the number of long-term poor doubles from Table 4.1 to Table 4.3. Again, Quebec's overall rates of chronically poor in Table 4.3 are considerably lower than any of the other provinces, with Alberta's rates the clear next-lowest. Yet Alberta's exceptionally low six-year poverty rate of 2.5% compared to its 22.4% chronic poverty rate means that while very few single-parent families are permanently poor, no less than an additional one-fifth is chronically poor, as opposed to about 8% (15.4%–7.7%) in Quebec.

The third column of Table 4.3 shows the proportion of families experiencing transitory poverty during the 2002–7 period, that is, families hit by poverty at least once during the six years but whose average income for the entire period remained above the poverty line. The figures in this column do not actually present any new information since the transitorily poor are simply the residual after the 'never' and

Table 4.4 Average number of months in poverty and acute poverty between 2002 and 2007 by family type, Canadian provinces

	Two-parent families		Single-parent families	
	Poverty	Acute poverty	Poverty	Acute poverty
Quebec	23.7	17.1	28.9	16.7
Ontario	27.6	19.5	38.5	19.8
Alberta	23.4	15.1	28.0	16.2
BC	32.9	23.6	41.9	29.3

Source: SLID

'chronically' poor have been taken into account. However, if we divide the proportions of the transitorily poor by those who have ever been poor – that is, by the sum of the chronically and transitorily poor – we obtain the percentage of those ever affected by poverty whose poverty was merely transitory. This percentage can be intuitively understood as an index of the proportion of the sometimes poor who are likely to be able to extract themselves from poverty with relatively modest support.

As the final column of Table 4.3 shows, the poverty of more than 85% of two-parent families in Quebec that were ever poor turned out to be transitory, in the sense that their incomes remained above the poverty line for the period as a whole. These proportions are a good one-fifth lower in the other three provinces. The difference is even starker for single-parent families. While the poverty of more than two-thirds of Quebec's single-parent families who fell below the poverty line at some point is transitory by our definition, this is only true for slightly over a third of British Columbia's and two-fifths of Ontario's single-parent families. In other words, in Quebec, and to a lesser extent in Alberta, when poverty does hit a family it is more likely to be transitory than in Ontario or British Columbia.

Average duration of poverty and acute poverty: One way of gauging how difficult it is, on average, for a family that has fallen into poverty to escape it again is to calculate the average duration of poverty spells. Table 4.4 shows the average poverty and acute poverty durations, expressed in months, for the four provinces by family type.

Table 4.4 confirms the findings in the previous tables. Average poverty durations are quite similar in Alberta and Quebec, significantly lower than in Ontario and British Columbia (especially the latter).

While, as we saw in Table 4.1, families in Alberta are much more likely to experience poverty at one time or another than families in Quebec, once poor, Albertans and Quebeckers take about the same amount of time to escape poverty. As we noted before, this suggests that as a result of Alberta's strong economy and tight labour market, its poor are able to find (better paying) work again after a relatively short period of time. But the operative term is 'relatively.' For even in Quebec and Alberta, the average poverty spell for a two-parent family lasted close to two years and almost two and a half years for single-parent families.

Perhaps the real story in Table 4.4 is how astonishingly long the average poverty interval is in British Columbia. Over the time period, its two-parent families suffered average poverty spells of almost 33 months, and single-parent families remained in poverty for a staggering three and a half years on average. Once a family falls below the poverty line, it is apparently very difficult indeed in British Columbia to find a path out of poverty. In fact, since Quebec's average duration figures are actually slightly higher than Alberta's and not uniformly lower than those in Ontario, British Columbia, not Quebec, appears to be the outlier here. Thus, at least in terms of average poverty durations, we find no clear evidence of the exceptionalism we have found elsewhere; if anything, there appears to be evidence of British Columbia's exceptionalism here.

The differences between the provinces in average length of acute poverty are much less pronounced, varying from 15 months in Alberta to two years in British Columbia for two-parent families and from 16 months in Alberta to two and half years in British Columbia for single-parent families. Quebec's figures are on the low end of the range but still somewhat higher than Alberta's. Again, given Alberta's strong labour market, intervals of acute poverty do not last as long as elsewhere. Interestingly, Quebec's figures are closer to Alberta's than to any of the other provinces in spite of Quebec's much less favourable labour market.

Not only do the average acute poverty spells not differ as much between the provinces as the standard poverty spells, but there is significantly less difference between the two family types. While episodes of standard poverty last, on average, considerably longer for single-parent than for two-parent families, acute poverty lasts, on average, about the same number of months for the former as the latter, except in British Columbia. In other words, quite unlike what we have found so far when comparing these two family types, two-parent families in acute poverty find it about as hard as single-parent families to lift themselves out. Our measure of acute poverty may capture some combination of factors that are qualitatively different from those characterizing families suffering from standard poverty. This is rather speculative at this point, but a closer examination of families who suffer severe poverty is certainly warranted.

Different Provinces, Different Trajectories: Does Quebec Do Better?

Recall that Quebec's Bill 112 (Quebec National Assembly 2002) explicitly calls for a strategy to 'combat poverty *and* social exclusion.' In the previous chapters we have shown that *la belle province* has succeeded relatively well in bringing down poverty rates when compared to the three other Canadian provinces, as well as a selection of advanced countries, at least (and, as mentioned in Chapter 3, this is an important qualification) for families with children. How has the province done combating long-term poverty?

Based on the evidence given in this chapter, the answer has to be *rather well*, at least when compared to the other three provinces and, again, for families with children. By virtually every indicator, Quebec has done significantly better than the rest, with the partial exception of Alberta. Not only are fewer Quebeckers living in families with underage children ever exposed to poverty; on average, their poverty spells tend to be significantly shorter as well. The proportion of Quebeckers living in two-parent families suffering from very long-term poverty (four years or more out of six) is a fraction of what we see in the other provinces. The same is true for members of single-parent families, except for Alberta, with figures close to those of Quebec. When we try to distinguish the 'chronically' poor, that is, those poor in all six years covered by our survey data *plus* those whose average income was below the poverty line during the period even if it was not necessarily below that line in every single year, we find a similar pattern. The fraction of individuals living in two-parent families in Quebec who are chronically poor by our definition is much lower – between one-third and one-fifth of the level found in the other three provinces. The difference is only slightly smaller for single-parent families. Conversely, the proportion of all those having suffered from poverty at least once during the period but whose income remained above the poverty line for the period as a whole, the 'transitory' poor, is significantly higher in Quebec than in any of the other provinces.

In short, Quebec's annual poverty rates for families with children are considerably lower than elsewhere in Canada *and* considerably fewer suffer from long-term poverty. Alberta is a partial exception in that some of its long-term poverty rates are as low as Quebec's or close to them. Yet, as we saw in Chapter 1, Alberta has the least developed set of anti-poverty policies and spends considerably less on combating poverty than any of the other provinces. In fact, at first glance, the case of Alberta suggests the trade-off between levels of poverty and income mobility mentioned at the beginning of the chapter. While Alberta's families are much more likely to be affected by poverty than families in Quebec, the episodes of poverty tend to be as short in both provinces and long-term poverty is equally rare. This is clearly not the result of the generosity of Alberta's anti-poverty programs. Rather, as noted above, in all likelihood Alberta's booming economy has enabled poor families to escape poverty by finding (better) employment.

But before we accept Alberta as the Canadian version of the 'American Dream,' a comparison with British Columbia may be instructive. As explained in Chapter 1, British Columbia is very similar to Alberta in its lack of commitment to anti-poverty policies, at least when compared to Quebec and various European countries. Yet as we mention repeatedly and confirm here, British Columbia's record of poverty reduction is the worst of all four provinces. Its long-term poverty figures, for both types of families, are the highest, in some cases by very wide margins indeed. And the average length of poverty spells, including acute poverty, in British Columbia is staggering in comparison with the other provinces.

In other words, in an extremely buoyant economy like Alberta's, the ample availability of relatively well-paying jobs can compensate for the lack of government support for those in danger of falling below the poverty line and, thus, limit long-term poverty. But the lack of Alberta's economic engine and Quebec's generous policies leads to the worst of both worlds in British Columbia, with very high levels of poverty *as well as* a large proportion of chronically poor families. To put it differently, if Quebec is a province where families do not fall into poverty in the first place, and Alberta is a province where those who fall into poverty are quickly able to work their way back out, then British Columbia is a province where families are likely to fall into poverty and remain there.

Worse yet, our results suggest that when families in British Columbia fall into poverty, they fall deeply.

To conclude, then, our results concur with the general conclusions of the literature questioning the 'American Dream' model. The case of Quebec clearly shows that generous anti-poverty programs do not necessarily produce large numbers of chronically poor dependent on government hand-outs, and the case of British Columbia demonstrates that the absence of a strong social safety net does not necessarily produce the right incentives for the poor to struggle their way out of poverty through their own efforts.

Chapter Five

Activation and Poverty

Introduction

As we have mentioned several times, Quebec's distinctive policy approach was inspired by the much-admired example of the Nordic social democratic countries, particularly the 'Swedish model.' At the core of this model was a commitment to maximum employment, or, as the slogan had it, 'work for everyone.' The architects of the Swedish model saw full employment as indispensable to the fiscal foundation of their relatively generous welfare state. As well, full employment would help lift the wages of those at the bottom of the earnings distribution and, thus, help combat poverty. In order to achieve and maintain full employment and maximum labour force participation, Sweden pioneered active labour market policies, as a complement to passive support programs such as unemployment insurance (see, e.g., van den Berg, Furåker, and Johansson 1997).

As the Introduction explains, there has been an international trend away from primary reliance on passive measures and an increasing policy emphasis on activation. But activation comes in different varieties. Some countries have followed a more punitive 'work first' approach by lowering benefit levels and tightening eligibility rules so as to coax those seeking government support into accepting whatever employment is available. This may push people off the welfare rolls but it does not necessarily reduce poverty levels. Quite the contrary, in fact: in countries with a relatively large supply of very low-paying jobs, such policies may simply produce a growing number of 'working poor' (Barbier 2009, 39–40; Cantillon 2011; Hemerijck 2013, 39–40; Morel 2002). Alternatively, those in danger of falling below the poverty line may be offered various forms of support, including measures to facilitate reconciliation of employment and childcare or the means to upgrade employable skills so as to equip them for better-paying jobs. Where such strategies work, an avenue out of poverty opens up through employment rather than dependence on passive support measures.

The latter approach has become associated with the social investment perspective discussed in the Introduction. Advocates reject the widespread assumption that social welfare policy is necessarily a net burden on the economy and the government budget. Rather, social policy, if properly designed, can increase overall prosperity and reduce public expenditure in the long run. Whereas passive social transfer may well be a net burden, many active policies which, by definition, encourage beneficiaries to participate actively and productively in the economy, generate private and public benefits that may well exceed their initial costs. Such policies include 'a child-centred investment strategy, human capital formation, employment activation, labour market flexibility with generous social security and adequate minimum support, gender mainstreaming, family servicing, reconciling work and family life, avoiding early retirement, and encouraging more flexible patterns of retirement, while raising the statutory pension age' (Hemerijck 2013, 36). While such policies provide social protection, they do so by enabling citizens to become (more) productive participants in the economy and society (see, e.g., Esping-Andersen 1999, 2002, 2009; Hemerijck 2013, 35–40; Jenson 2013, 54–6; Morel, Palier, and Palme 2012). They have the considerable added benefit of rendering citizens more financially self-reliant and autonomous, a worthy goal in its own right.[1]

The social investment approach is obviously inspired by the Nordic social democratic regimes and their strong emphasis on active labour market policies, work-and-care reconciliation programs like parental leaves and subsidized day care, life-long learning programs, and support for families with children. As part of its *virage sociodémocratique*, Quebec aspires to follow the Scandinavian countries in pursuing the double-pronged policy of increasing the passive benefits received by families with children while simultaneously encouraging maximum feasible participation in the labour force (Noël 2013, 266–70; Paquin and Lévesque 2014). As mentioned in Chapter 1, Quebec's strategy to combat poverty explicitly calls for an approach combining measures to encourage all those capable of working to seek employment with a strengthening of the social protections for those with limited or no capacity to work. In this chapter, we assess to what extent Quebec's relative success in combating poverty – at least among families with children – has been accomplished by more generous welfare state benefits *and* higher levels of relatively well-paying employment. We assess how well Quebec has done in promoting labour force participation for different family types, and whether it has managed to limit the emergence of a class of 'working poor,' in comparison with Ontario, British Columbia, Alberta, and a selection of European countries. We also ask how households with little or limited attachment to the labour force have fared in view of Quebec's purportedly more generous passive measures, again, as compared with the other provinces and countries.

As in the preceding chapters, the results we present here suggest Quebec's distinctive combination of policies has had dramatically different effects on different types of households. On the one hand, two-parent families with children have benefited from the social investment/activation components of the province's policy package, particularly programs facilitating the labour force participation of women with (young) children, to lift them out of poverty. Employed single-parent families have also benefited from these policies, albeit to a more modest extent, as well as from Quebec's relatively generous transfer payments. On the other hand, underemployed households, with or without children, fare little better in Quebec than those in the other Canadian provinces or the United States and they fare worse than those in European countries.

But before we present our main findings, recall that the most important activation measures in Quebec's policy arsenal include the creation of a system of affordable day-care centres and the implementation of a generous parental leave program. The aim was to facilitate the labour force participation of women with (young) children, thereby lifting many families out of poverty. We will assess this claim later in the chapter. Here we simply observe that Quebec's aim of raising the labour force participation of women with children appears to have succeeded. Until the mid-1990s, the labour force participation rate[2] of working-age women (ages 15 to 64) in Quebec was well below that of the three other provinces and the Canadian average. But while this rate has continued to go up everywhere, it has risen much faster in Quebec. As a result, by 2011 Quebec had more than caught up with the rest of the country, registering a 75% female labour force participation rate for that year (see Fortin, Godbout, and St-Cerny 2012, 6; Fortin, Godbout, and St-Cerny 2013, 7).

But perhaps even more telling is what Quebec's policies have done for women with young children, who are, after all, the primary target group. Figure 5.1 shows the labour force participation rates for women

Figure 5.1. Labour force participation of women with children under six years old, Canadian provinces

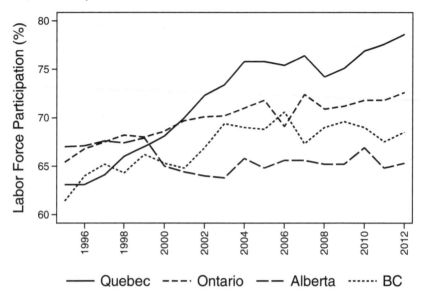

with children below the age of six for the four major provinces from 1995 onward.

As the figure shows, the labour force participation rates of women with young children have risen in all provinces but Alberta. But the increase is *far* more dramatic in Quebec than in any of the other provinces, rising from second-to-last place in 1995 to the highest position in 2012.

A number of recent studies confirm that this dramatic rise is attributable to Quebec's distinct day-care and parental leave policies (Beaujot, Du, and Ravanera 2013, 229–33; Fortin, Godbout, and St-Cerny 2013, 7–13; Lefebvre and Merrigan 2008). The shape of the curve for Quebec in Figure 5.1 is certainly compatible with this interpretation. It starts to rise above those of the other provinces at just around the time of the introduction of Quebec's famed subsidized day-care system in 1997, reaches a plateau and then rises sharply again from just about the time Quebec introduced its parental leave program in 2006. In short, Quebec's activating approach seems to have borne fruit, at least in terms of boosting female labour force participation.

Now, let us return to the central question of this chapter. Chapter 3 finds a dramatic reduction in the poverty rates among Quebec families with children. Has this happened through employment, more generous passive benefits, or *both*?

Methods

The first step in the analysis requires us to distinguish between households in terms of how strong their labour force attachment is – that is, whether and to what extent their members are gainfully employed. The degree of labour force attachment, or simply hours spent in employment in any given period, is, of course, a continuous variable. In principle, we could compare households whose members work, say, a combined 60 hours per week with those who work 61 hours, 62 hours, and so on. But to keep our analyses manageable and intuitively easy to follow, we group our households into a small number of broad classes depending on the extent of combined labour market participation of their members. The classification is admittedly crude, but it allows a relatively straightforward and accessible examination of the resulting patterns.

We measure labour market participation at the household level, as we have done with family income. That is, we simply add up the total number of weeks per year in which any member of the household had a job. This number can range from 0 for households in which no one had a job throughout the year to well over 100 for households with two or more fully employed members. Next, we group households as follows: not working = 0 weeks worked; underemployed = 1–26 weeks worked; single-earner equivalent = 27–52 weeks worked; dual-earner equivalent = 53+ weeks worked. Then we classify households accordingly for each of the household types discussed in Chapter 3, that is, two-parent families with children, single-parent families with children, couples without children, and single adults without children. This classification scheme allows us to examine both the distribution of family types in terms of labour force participation and the poverty rates for each family type/labour market participation combination. This should enable us to assess the extent to which Quebec has reduced poverty levels through activation or increased benefit generosity, or both, when compared to the other provinces and countries. We consider a household to be among the 'working poor' if its members report total labour market participation above 26 weeks of employment in the reference year while earning a total after-tax equivalent family income below the provincial low income measure.[3]

This simple scheme does not permit us to address a number of complexities, such as distinguishing between primary and secondary earners or between full-time and part-time workers, or considering differences in hours worked. Raïq (2012) has shown that the distinction between full-time and part-time workers, defined by hours worked per week, is of some importance in accounting for poverty among single-parent families in France, Canada, and the United States, though less so in the Netherlands, with single-parent part-time workers suffering significantly higher poverty rates than those with full-time jobs. While this is surely an important factor, the data available to us unfortunately do not allow us to distinguish between part-time and full-time workers because the Scandinavian data in the LIS survey do not include complete information on hours worked per week. As it turns out, however, the vast majority of households report either 0, 52, 104, or around 156 weeks worked per year for the household as a whole, with very few falling in between. This gives us some confidence that our classification captures the most important differences between households in terms of the employment patterns

Moreover, our main concern is to assess whether and to what extent activation has alleviated poverty or swelled the ranks of the working poor. That is, we wish to distinguish between those who have worked enough weeks that they should – given reasonably well-paying jobs – be expected to be able to keep their families above the poverty line and those who have not. With these considerations in mind, in the next section we look at how successfully Quebec and the other provinces and countries 'activate' the different family types. Then, in the section after that we examine how badly or how well each of these family types/labour force participation groups does in terms of poverty levels.

Family Types and Employment Patterns

While we know that the labour force participation rate of women with young children in Quebec has risen faster than elsewhere, we do not know how, exactly, this has affected the different types of families. Has it only benefited two-parent families or has it helped single-parent families as well? This is an important question, as the latter are particularly exposed to the risk of falling into poverty. And how do the patterns of labour force participation for the different family types compare to

Figure 5.2. Proportion of single-parent families not working, Canada and select countries

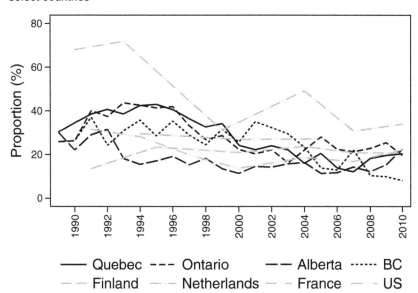

those of the other provinces and countries? These are the questions we address in this section.

Let us take a look at single-parent families first. Figure 5.2 shows the proportion of single-parent families not working at all during the reference year for Quebec, the other three Canadian provinces, and for the United States, Finland, France,[4] and the Netherlands, from 1990 until the latest available year. We are using Finland as the representative of the Nordic social democratic regime because the LIS data set does not contain the information on labour force participation patterns for Denmark required in this chapter. This will not unduly affect our results because Finland is very similar to Denmark in all the respects that matter here, including poverty rates, family composition, and labour force participation, particularly of women with (young) children.

The first thing to note in Figure 5.2 is that the proportion of non-working single-parent families has declined in all cases, spectacularly so in the Netherlands. Interestingly, the Netherlands greatly strengthened the activation component in its employment and social policy repertoires during this period. The only exception is Finland, whose proportion of non-working single-parent families, already quite low, remains broadly stable over the period at just above 20%. A second noteworthy trend is that during most of the period from the early 1990s until 2010, the lowest proportions of non-working single-parent families are found in the most 'liberal' regimes: the United States and Alberta. Finally, Quebec, British Columbia, and Ontario start with similar proportions of non-working lone-parent households; after a brief rise in the early 1990s, all three provinces exhibit a significant decline. By the end of the period, Ontario's and Quebec's proportions are around 20%, pretty much the same as Finland, the United States, and Alberta; British Columbia's proportion are now the lowest, at below 10%.

Thus, while the decline in the proportion of non-working single-parent families in Quebec has been significant since the early 1990s – cut virtually in half from around 40% to around 20% – this is not exceptional: indeed, the trajectory is very similar to Ontario's. Clearly, activation of this type of family can be achieved by different regimes using presumably different means. Moreover, the fact that British Columbia and Ontario also experienced a significant decline of non-working single-parent families suggests some of the decline may be attributable to overall improving economic conditions. At the same time, in Quebec, the decline was accomplished under a welfare state regime that, as we saw in Chapter 1, has been considerably more generous in its support for families with children than those of the other Canadian provinces. At the very least, this shows activation can be successful without imposing punitive restrictions and benefit cuts on those at risk of poverty.

Figure 5.3 shows the other side of the coin, that is, the proportion of single-parent households whose member(s)[5] worked more than 26 weeks during the reference year, the 'single-earner equivalent' category. Recall that Quebec's explicit policy goal was to raise this proportion to protect these types of households against the risk of poverty. Here, as well, it appears that Quebec has been fairly successful. The proportion of single-parent households in which members work 27 weeks or more per year rises from just above 40% in 1991 to above 60% in the 2000s. But the rates rise in the other jurisdictions as well and to similar levels. The fact that the other provinces and the United States have roughly the same proportion of single-earner equivalent single-parent families suggests, again, that it is possible to achieve better employment levels for this section of the population by *either* more restrictive *or* more generous social and employment policies.

Figure 5.3. Proportion of single-earner equivalent single-parent families, Canada and select countries

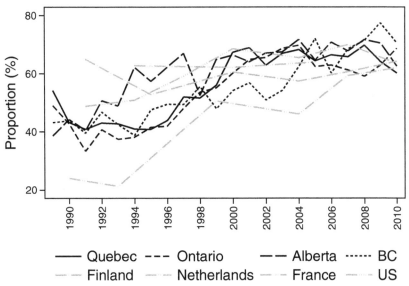

Two-parent families, the principal beneficiaries of Quebec's strategy to combat poverty, appear to have increased their labour supply. This can be seen in Figure 5.4. The proportion of two-parent families with more than one earner equivalent (i.e., with two or more members employed) rises by about 13 percentage points, from around 68% in 1989 to 81% in 2010, higher than any of the other provinces or countries shown in the figure with the exception of the Netherlands, which shows the most spectacular increase in (mostly mothers') labour force participation of two-parent families. While at the beginning of the period, Quebec's proportions of two-parent dual-earner families are already considerably higher than those of the 'Bismarckian' European countries, in this case the Netherlands and France, they are on the low side compared to the other liberal regimes in North America. But by 2010, Quebec has the second highest proportion among these latter regimes, with the proportion remaining roughly stable in the other three Canadian provinces and actually declining in the United States.

Figure 5.4. Proportion of dual-earner equivalent two-parent families, Canada and select countries

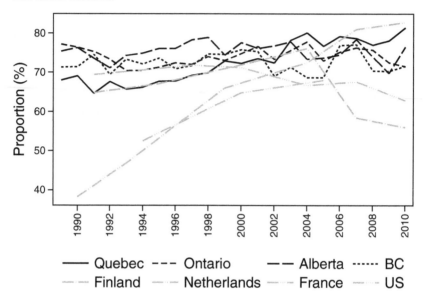

Working and Non-Working Poor

The next question, then, is to what extent this activation has lifted vulnerable households out of poverty, rather than creating a new pool of working poor. This time we consider two-parent families first. Figure 5.5 shows the poverty rates for families with two parents with more than one member employed. This family type has the least risk of falling into poverty anywhere. As can be seen in the figure, poverty rates for this family type do not rise much above 8% in any provinces or countries, and they are considerably lower in several.[6]

Note, however, that the poverty rates for dual-earner equivalent bi-parental families have *risen* in all three comparison provinces, especially in British Columbia and Alberta, while they have declined slightly in Quebec. As economic conditions were not especially more favourable in Quebec than in the other three Canadian provinces during this period, these contrasting trends are most probably the result of the policy differences identified in Chapter 1. What is more, Quebec poverty rates are, at around 2%, much lower than other poverty rates

Figure 5.5. Poverty rate of two-parent families dual-earner equivalent, Canada and select countries

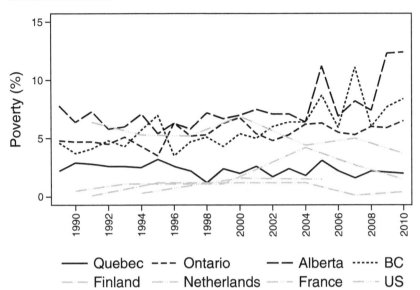

in North America and more or less at par with the European rates. For this class of family at least, Quebec compares quite well with the most generous European welfare states. In addition, while Quebec's poverty rates for two-parent families *with only one earner equivalent* are significantly higher – around 10% (figures not shown) – they are at about the same level as in the European comparison countries and much lower than the other provinces and the United States.

To summarize, in Quebec the proportion of two-parent families with multiple earners has risen slightly more than in Canada's other major provinces, and the poverty rate for this group of families has declined slightly in Quebec while it has risen elsewhere. It appears, then, that a large part of Quebec's success story with respect to two-parent families has to do with the rise in employment levels of the members of such families.

But what about those two-parent households not having at least one member employed for 27 weeks or more? In Quebec, as elsewhere, the proportion of two-parent families that are, by our definition, either underemployed or entirely unemployed is quite small, around 6% of

Figure 5.6. Poverty rate of single-parent families single-earner equivalent, Canada and select countries

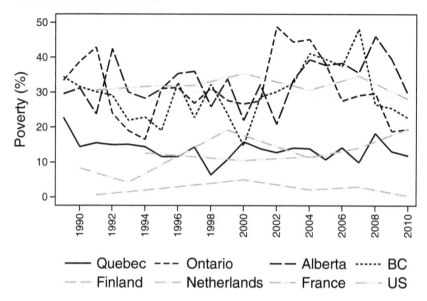

all two-parent families. At somewhere between 10% and 30%, the poverty rates for these families are, not surprisingly, considerably higher than for families with one or more full-earner equivalents. But for these groups as well, Quebec's poverty rates are now comparable to those in the European welfare states and considerably lower than elsewhere in North America, with the exception of Alberta (figures not shown). Quebec's policies of social protection for those who are, for one reason or another, unable to find adequate employment seem to be working, at least for two-parent families with children.

As Chapter 3 explains, Quebec's single-parent families have benefited from its anti-poverty strategy, albeit not as much as two-parent families. Figure 5.6 presents the poverty rates for single-parent families with at least one member employed between 27 and 52 weeks per year (the 'single-earner equivalent'). In Quebec, the poverty rate for this group of households declines only very slightly over the period, from around 15% to between 12% and 13%. This compares well to the Netherlands and France, who have similar working poverty rates for single-parent families, but it is still five to six times the extremely low rates recorded by social democratic Finland. At the same time, the Quebec rate is generally between half and a third of the corresponding rate in the United States, Alberta, British Columbia, and Ontario, the last three of which rise considerably after the late 1990s, before dropping again more recently.

In other words, while until 2005 at least the proportion of working poor among single-parent households increased significantly in the other Canadian provinces, occasionally to levels above 40%, it has held steady in Quebec at around 13%. This strongly suggests Quebec's policies have resisted the trend towards a growing population of working poor single-parent families apparent in Canada's other large provinces. Thus, Quebec may not have brought down its poverty rates for working single-parent families to quite those of 'the industrialized nations having the least number of persons living in poverty,' but it has certainly succeeded in maintaining European-level poverty rates.

But it has actually done better than that. As Chapter 3 shows, the overall poverty rate of lone-parent families, whatever their level of attachment to the labour market, has not just held steady but has actually declined in Quebec while remaining constant in the other provinces and the United States. We can now attribute this success to Quebec's activating policies. As the preceding section shows, the proportion of economically active (single-earner and dual-earner equivalent)[7] single-parent families has increased substantially, at the expense of unemployed and underemployed households. Since the poverty rates for the active families are much lower than for the un- and underemployed families, as we will see shortly, the substantial growth in the proportion of the former at the expense of the latter largely explains the decline in the poverty rates of all single-parent families in Quebec taken together. In other words, a large part of Quebec's relative success is due to the greater activation of its families with one parent.

On the basis of these findings we can say that Quebec's activation policies have *not* been of the punitive kind that has forced those at risk of poverty to accept low-wage employment and join the ranks of the working poor. While the proportion of single- and dual-earner families has increased, the poverty rate for those families has not. At the same time, from the data we have examined so far, we cannot tell whether this favourable result is due to the relatively well-paying jobs obtained by the new entrants into the labour force or by Quebec's relatively generous benefits for families with working members (the Prime au Travail, child benefits, tax credits), or some combination of the two. Recall

Figure 5.7. Market income as a proportion of all disposable income, different household/employment types, Quebec

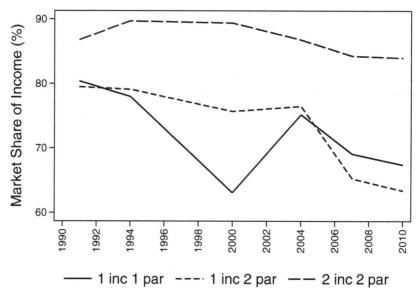

that the original ambition of Quebec's strategy to combat poverty and social exclusion, inspired by the Nordic social democracies, was to lift families with children out of poverty as much as possible by enabling their members to take on sufficiently well-paying jobs to do so, with passive benefits a last resort. This was to be achieved by improving the employable skills of those at risk of falling into poverty, not cutting benefits or tightening eligibility rules for social benefits.

There is no question that Quebec's success in bringing down the poverty rates for households with children has been the result of a combination of successful activation and generous passive benefits. But from a policy perspective it matters a great deal whether the jobs or the social benefits produced these favourable results. One way of addressing this question is to look at the proportion of families' total disposable incomes coming from market earnings[8] rather than social transfers. Figure 5.7 shows the proportions of total disposable household income accounted for by market earnings for three family type/labour market attachment combinations since 1990 in Quebec: single-earner equivalent two-parent families, dual-earner equivalent two-parent families, and single-earner single-parent families.

If Quebec's success in reducing the poverty rates for these types of working families stems from their successful activation into well-paying jobs, this should be reflected in rising market earnings as a proportion of total disposable income. Conversely, if the successful reduction in the poverty rate is mostly the result of Quebec's generous social benefits, we should see this reflected in rising transfer payments as a proportion of disposable income. As Figure 5.7 shows, double-earner two-parent families receive almost all of their income from the market, with slightly above 10% accounted for by other sources of income at the beginning of the period, rising to around 15% in the most recent years. Two-parent families with only one income earner, however, have seen the proportion of market earnings in their disposable income drop from close to 80% in 1990 to less than 65% in the late 2000s. At the same time, poverty rates for this family type go up everywhere, dramatically so in the United States and the other Canadian provinces, to above 20%, but more gently in Quebec and our European comparison countries, to just below 10%. It appears, then, that Quebec's more generous social transfers have come to play a more important role over time in keeping these rates at 'European' levels.

The trend for working single-parent families, those traditionally most at risk of joining the working poor, is similar. As Figure 5.6 shows, the poverty rate for single-earner one-parent families in Quebec has barely declined since 1990, compared to considerable increases elsewhere in North America. Now, when we look at Figure 5.7, we see Quebec has only been able to keep this rate relatively constant by increasing the social transfers to these families. The proportion of household disposable income accounted for by market income drops from close to 80% in 1990 to around 68% in the most recent years. In other words, while as we have seen, the proportion of single-parent households with one income earner increases – and this certainly helps reduce overall poverty rates for single-parent households – keeping poverty rates stable in the long run has required a greater contribution over time by social benefits.[9] For single-earner families, then, activation alone does not keep the poverty rate at European levels.

Now, the fact that the *proportion* of these households' income from government transfer payments has increased does not necessarily mean that those transfer payments have become more generous. In principle at least, the rise could be the result of declining absolute market income

Figure 5.8. Average market and transfer household income, three household types, Quebec

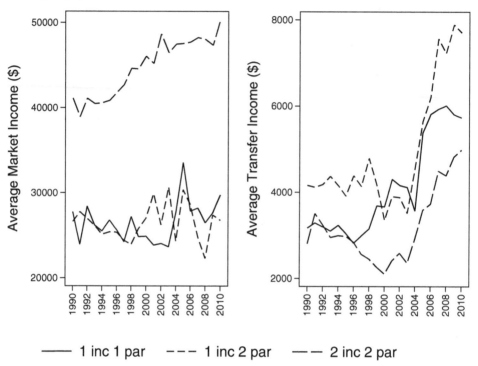

with constant or even (less steeply) declining transfer income. While Quebec's relative success in keeping poverty rates in check for these three types of households suggests the latter possibility is unlikely, it certainly cannot be categorically excluded.

An examination of trends in actual dollar amounts of market and transfer income for these types of households, however, does allow us to exclude that possibility. Figure 5.8 below shows the average equivalized household incomes from the market (mostly employment; left panel) and government transfer payments (right panel) in constant (2011) dollars, from 1990 until 2010 for the same three family types as Figure 5.7.

Let us look at the left panel of Figure 5.8 first. Average market dollar income for households with two income earners has rose moderately but steadily during this period, from $42,000 in 1990 to $50,000 in 2010.

Households with only one income earner did not do so well in terms of market income, however. While there is an ever so slight upward trend, from close to $28,000 in 1990 to almost $30,000 in 2010 for single-earner single-parent families, the average real market income of single-earner dual-parent families actually declined slightly. But for both family types the fluctuations are such over this period that there is effectively no real trend in real average market income.

The trends in average government transfer payments in constant dollars, shown in the right panel of Figure 5.8, are quite different. The average amount of government transfer payments that dual-earner families received actually declined until the year 2000, from $2,800 to $2,100 per annum in constant 2011 dollars. Single-earner single-parent families also experience a modest decline in average transfer payment income, from just over $3,100 to $2,800 per annum, until 1996, while single-earner two-parent families' average transfer payment income fluctuated around $4,000 per annum until 2003. But the most striking feature of the right panel of Figure 5.8 is the steep rise in transfer payments for all three types of households from 2003 onwards – that is, since the adoption of Quebec's strategy to combat poverty. While dual-earner families received around $2,800 per annum in government transfer payments in 1990, this figure rose to $5,000 in 2010. In dollar terms, the increases were even more dramatic for single-earner families, with average transfer payments rising from $3,200 to close to $6,000 for single-earner single-parent families, and from $4,200 to $7,700 for single-earner dual-parent families. Given the single-earner families' much lower overall incomes, the proportional effect of these increases in transfer payments is clearly much greater than it is for dual-earner families. In short, Quebec's relative success in restraining poverty rates for working families with children was clearly due to a combination of constant or rising market income and even more rapidly rising transfer payments, particularly from 2003 onward, and the rise in transfer payments played a relatively larger role in containing poverty rates for single-earner than for dual-earner families.

But what about single-parent households whose members are unable to find 27 or more weeks of employment per year? As Quebec's strategy to combat poverty and social exclusion combines a primary emphasis on activation as a way to escape poverty with a strengthening of the social protection safety net for those partially or entirely unable to work, its success should be measured by the extent to which it has succeeded in bringing down the poverty rates of unemployed or underemployed single-parent families. Figure 5.9 shows the poverty

Figure 5.9. Poverty rate of single-parent families not working, Canada and select countries

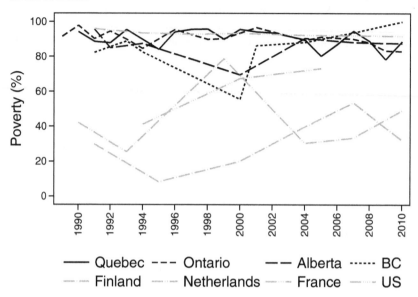

rates for lone-parent families whose members were not working at all during the reference year.

Here, our findings are much less encouraging. While, as we saw above, the proportion of single-parent households with no members working declines to just over 10% in Quebec, these households are not much better off in 2010 than they were in 1990. With a staggering poverty rate of around 90% in most years, the situation of this group of households is truly dismal. The situation for underemployed (i.e., 26 weeks or less per year) lone-parent households are not much better, with a poverty rate of around 70% for the most recent years (not shown). In short, the probability of a single-parent family falling into poverty may have declined over time but only for those with steady employment. Those without it are almost guaranteed to be poor and Quebec's supposedly generous social programs have had little effect.

Moreover, when it comes to single-parent families not working at all, or underemployed for that matter, the Quebec poverty rates are as dismal as they get, indistinguishable from those in the United States and the other Canadian provinces. We are forced to conclude, then, that when it comes to protecting single-parent families who are not able to find employment, or can find only very limited employment, Quebec's social safety net is still very far removed from those of countries with the lowest levels of poverty. In recent years, the rates for the Netherlands and Finland have been almost one third of Quebec's rate, as shown in Figure 5.9.

A Note on Childless Households

As we pointed out in Chapters 1 and 3, and as others have noted as well (Noël 2011), Quebec's strategy to combat poverty and social exclusion has been strongly focused on alleviating poverty for families with children. It has put considerably less emphasis on aiding childless couples and single adults. As Chapter 3 explains, this policy bias manifests itself quite clearly in the poverty outcomes for these types of households. Poverty levels for childless couples tend to be relatively moderate and, as a result, they have not caused a great deal of alarm among policymakers and researchers. But in Quebec, their poverty rates are, at close to 10%, similar to those in the rest of North America and two to three times higher than Denmark.

This general pattern is confirmed when we consider childless couples with different degrees of attachment to the labour market. Dual-earner, single-earner, underemployed or entirely unemployed childless couples in Quebec experience poverty rates that are at North American levels and well above those in the European comparison countries (not shown).

For adults living alone, whether underemployed or fully employed, poverty rates in Quebec are close to or only slightly below the North American rates and far above those in Europe. And the situation of non-working single adults is about as bad as that of non-working single-parent families. As Figure 5.10 shows, the poverty rates for this group of individuals in Quebec have declined since the early 1990s but are still a staggering 70% in 2010. This is very close to the corresponding rates in the rest of North America and far above the European rates.

Thus, more than two-thirds of Quebec's non-working single adults are classifiable as poor. To be sure, the proportion of single adults who did not work at all during the reference year in Quebec has declined somewhat since the early 1990s, from over 30% to around 24%, while the proportion of fully employed singles has risen from 55% to 70%. But even among the latter, the poverty rate has markedly increased since the 1990s and now seems stuck above 15%. In other words, single adults who are unable to find work in Quebec do not benefit from

Figure 5.10. Poverty rate of unattached individuals not working, Canada and select countries

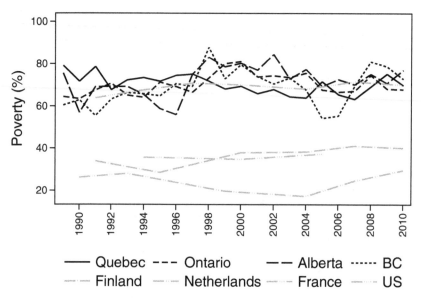

significantly better social protection than their counterparts elsewhere in North America. But even among those who do work more or less full time, the poverty rates are still higher than for working single-parent families. Quebec's combination of anti-poverty measures may have benefited families with children, however unequally, but it appears to have done very little, if anything at all, for single adults.

Conclusion

Now, has Quebec's *virage sociodémocratique* enabled it to combat poverty and social exclusion by 'making work pay' for those able to work and adequately protecting incomes for those who are not? Has Quebec managed to prevent the growth of a population of working poor, the ostensible consequence of the punitive workfare policies pursued by market-oriented Anglo-Saxon countries? Based on the evidence presented in this chapter, we think the answer to both has to be a qualified *yes*.

There is little doubt that a large part of Quebec's success in reducing the poverty rate is accounted for by the success of its activation policies. These policies have clearly contributed to the sharp rise in the labour force participation of women in Quebec, especially women with (young) children. With employment levels increasing sharply for families with children and poverty rates remaining stable for each level of labour force attachment, the overall poverty rate necessarily declines. *Both* trends contrast to varying degrees with what we see in the other Canadian provinces and the United States, so we can reasonably conclude that the reduced poverty rates are attributable to Quebec's distinctive policy mix. These findings are in line with a growing literature documenting the strong negative relationship between a variety of policies helping mothers reconcile employment with family care and maternal poverty (see Haddow 2015, 21 and the literature cited therein).

Chapter 3 shows that Quebec's strategy to combat poverty and social exclusion has primarily benefited families with children, in particular, families with two parents. The findings presented in this chapter lead us to think that much of the success in combating poverty among these families comes from the increased labour force participation of their members. This is true even for single-parent families. However, poverty rates for single-parent families with a near full-time income earner have remained stable while the proportion of their income accounted for by market earnings has declined, an effect offset by increased transfer payments.

Quebec's policies have been considerably less beneficial for households with little or no labour force attachment and for childless households, in spite of the relatively more generous social assistance benefits available to Quebeckers noted in Chapter 3 (see Tweddle, Battle, and Torjman 2014). That assistance, which should be of particular benefit to those with difficulty finding employment, has not prevented poverty rates among underemployed households, including single-parent households with children, to rise far above the levels common in Continental and Northern Europe. With respect to these households, Quebec's poverty rates are indistinguishable from those elsewhere in North America, and the *virage sociodémocratique* appears to have had little effect. While Quebec may have avoided the trend towards 'working poverty' characteristic of states and provinces pursuing a more punitive workfare strategy, for the un- and underemployed, and for childless adults, its strategy to combat poverty and social exclusion remains a job half done.

Chapter Six

How Exceptional *Is* Quebec?

Introduction

As Chapter 1 shows, since the early 2000s Quebec has far outspent the three other Canadian provinces on a range of social policies. We might expect this to have a major impact on provincial differences in poverty levels. When we look more closely, however, we find a paradox. On the one hand, Chapter 2 finds Quebec's overall poverty rates have diverged only moderately from those of British Columbia, Ontario, and especially Alberta. On the other hand, Chapters 3 and 4 clarify that for certain specific household types, especially those with children, Quebec's anti-poverty strategy has had impressive results. How can we account for these contradictory findings?

Poverty rates are routinely treated as summary measures of government performance in combating social exclusion. The fact that one province or country reports higher poverty rates than another is habitually interpreted as showing that the efforts to reduce poverty by the government of the former must have been less vigorous than those of the latter. But poverty reduction policies are only one factor among many likely to have an impact on actual poverty levels. And many of the other factors, such as family composition, are more or less beyond the purview of policymakers and service providers. Consequently, the typical comparative analysis that attributes the entire difference in output or performance – in poverty rates in our case – to differences in government policy overlooks the independent effects of factors more or less beyond the government's control.[1] Such analyses are quite likely to greatly overestimate the importance of government policies.

We may find an answer to the contradictory results in the differences in population compositions between provinces with respect to the kinds of demographic factors that render households prone to poverty. While we have looked at poverty rates for different family types in the preceding chapters, we have not actually controlled for their *relative prevalence* in the different provinces. If, for instance, Quebec had a much smaller proportion of single-parent households than, say, Alberta, its record of overall poverty reduction would look a lot less impressive than if the reverse were the case. In other words, to fully capture the effect of different policy regimes, we need to look not only at the policies themselves but also at the composition of the populations to whom those policies are applied. Or, to put it differently, to properly evaluate the impact of different policy approaches on overall poverty outcomes, we need a level playing field.

As we have seen throughout this book, some types of households are far more likely to experience poverty than others, however generous or restrictive the government's social policies. Well-known determinants of the risk of ending up in poverty include household size, family composition, and labour market participation (Blossfeld and Drobnic 2001; Budig, Misra, and Böckmann 2010; Misra, Budig, and Moller 2007; Misra and Moller 2005; Raïq, Bernard, and van den Berg 2011; Raïq, Plante, and van den Berg 2011; Raïq and van den Berg 2012; Sarfati and Bonoli 2002; Schmid and Gazier 2002). We are able to see these forces at work in the persistence of poverty gaps between lone- and two-parent families across developed nations. Whereas some states have been able to effect a considerable reduction in both overall poverty and the poverty gap between these two family types, lone-parent families are much more likely to be poor than two-parent families everywhere.

As it turns out, there are substantial differences between the provinces in household composition that may well affect overall poverty trends. This is true, for instance, for the proportions of two- and single-parent families. Whereas two-parent families made up roughly 40% of households in Alberta and Ontario in 2010, they represented 35% of households in British Columbia and Quebec. Similarly, since the early 1990s, the share of lone-parent families among all households has been about a fifth higher in Quebec than in the other large Canadian provinces. On the one hand, targeting poverty rates among lone-parent families in Quebec will have a greater impact on the province's overall poverty rate than if lone-parents made up a smaller share; on the other hand, if other provinces have greater shares of households that are much less likely to end up poor, such targeting will have much less effect on *their* overall poverty rates. Thus, jurisdictions with a greater share of household types more likely to be poor will post higher overall poverty rates than we would expect on the basis of their policies alone and those with a smaller share of such household types will post lower rates.

Similarly, as we have seen, historically there have been significant interprovincial differences in the rates of labour market participation, particularly of women with young children. And, as we have also seen, labour force participation is possibly the single most important determinant of poverty reduction. Undoubtedly, governments have some influence on the rate of labour force participation and Quebec has, as noted, employed a particularly successful strategy to raise the participation rate of women with children. At the same time, governments cannot fully control overall trends in labour force participation, as these depend on the state of the economy, changing cultural norms, and much more. Consequently, differences in labour force participation patterns are also likely to affect overall poverty rates, to some extent independently of government anti-poverty policies.

Thus, Quebec's performance in poverty reduction in comparison to the other large Canadian provinces is not just a function of how well the province is able to reduce poverty among working families, but also a function of how many working families there are in Quebec, and how many more or fewer working families there are in the other provinces. Working families are the most prevalent household type, but they still constitute only one of several types with varying poverty risks. Lone-parent working families might be doing better in Quebec than they are elsewhere, but they make up only a very small fraction of the province's population. And even though Quebec has reduced poverty among working families, other household types have not fared as well. The relatively high poverty levels of unattached non-working and working singles and couples will negatively affect the overall poverty rate, but the extent depends on the prevalence of such household types in the province. A province with a relatively high proportion of dual-earner households like Alberta will be able to keep poverty rates down with less public effort than a province where this proportion is lower.

In this chapter, we isolate the extent to which those poverty rates can be attributed to differences in government policies rather than to more or less fortuitous differences in demographic and employment patterns. Of course, a significant part of employment patterning is *not* 'more or less fortuitous,' but rather the result of deliberate government policy. In fact, in Chapter 5 we argue that much of Quebec's success in reducing poverty among families with children can be attributed to its ability to influence employment patterns. But since we do not know precisely what portion is due to government policies and what portion is independent of those policies, we cannot isolate them in our analyses.

To reiterate, in this chapter we are seeking to identify the effect of government policies net of demographic differences and *both* policy-induced and non-policy-induced employment patterns. To do this, we will control for demographic and employment pattern differences by standardizing the results with respect to these potentially confounding factors. We are trying to answer questions like the following: if Alberta had had the same population composition in terms of family types and labour force participation as Quebec, what, given its distinctive policy regime, would its poverty rates be?

As the chapter goes on to show, Quebec stands even farther apart from the other Canadian provinces than the unstandardized poverty rates that we have looked at so far would suggest. Once demographic composition and labour market participation are controlled for, the poverty rates of Ontario, Alberta, and British Columbia become similar – and they distance themselves even further from Quebec's rates. Quebec is striking out on its own, following a unique welfare path. Its lower poverty rates appear to be the result not just of greater (female) labour force participation in recent years, but also of greater benefit generosity. Quebec is clearly more generous towards its most needy families than are the other provinces. Interestingly, while compositional differences change our understanding of the differences in poverty between the Canadian provinces, they have relatively little impact on differences between the Canadian provinces and the other nations considered here and elsewhere in the book.

Note that when we interpret our standardized results as reflecting the *net* effects of differences in government policies, we are assuming that all effects left over after controlling for the effects of family composition and employment patterns are entirely due to differences in the generosity and effectiveness of governmental anti-poverty policies. Of course, this is likely to overstate the effect of those policies. But ours is a residual approach; that is, we isolate the residual effect of *all* differences in policies and conditions that may affect poverty outcomes, including a host of taxation and transfer policies unrelated to anti-poverty policy, trends in earnings distributions, immigration patterns and much else.

This important qualification must be borne in mind throughout this chapter. At the same time, while no standardization method can control for all relevant causal factors, we are standardizing here for the two most important extraneous factors affecting poverty outcomes; therefore, the standardized results provide a rough indication of the effect of differences in the generosity and effectiveness of the different poverty-combating policy regimes.

Standardizing Poverty Rates

Researchers comparing poverty rates between countries have not routinely controlled for differences in population composition. An exception is a study by Fritzell and Ritakallio (2010). They look at poverty trends in eleven countries while controlling for population composition differences between Sweden and the other ten countries and find most nations would have much lower poverty rates if they had populations similar to Sweden's. Fritzell and Ritakallio standardize for household composition, the age of the household head, and whether the head and his or her spouse are working. Their findings suggest a considerable portion of Sweden's relatively good performance compared to other European nations may be attributed to the composition and labour force attachment of its population, not to policies aimed directly at reducing poverty. Interestingly, the Netherlands and Belgium look a lot more like Nordic nations after standardization. Overall, 15% of cross-national variation in poverty levels is due to compositional differences, not to differences in policies. The most important of these compositional differences is household labour market participation. Specifically, dual-earner households are considerably more prevalent in the Nordic countries than in the rest of the developed world; this goes a long way to explaining their relatively good track record in reducing poverty.

The chapter follows Fritzell and Ritakallio by standardizing population composition characteristics for the provinces and countries whose poverty rates we have been comparing, taking Quebec's population composition as the baseline. In other words, we will estimate what the poverty rates in those other provinces and countries *would have been* if they had had Quebec's population composition but kept their own anti-poverty policy regimes. In effect, we will be simulating[2] poverty rates for each other province and country by applying that province's or country's own group-specific poverty rates – as identified in the preceding chapters – to a population with Quebec's compositional characteristics. If the simulated poverty rate turns out to be higher than the actual rate, this means the latter reflects the province's or country's good fortune of having a population composition that is less prone to poverty than Quebec's, not its unique policies. Conversely, it means Quebec has benefited from a favourable population composition without which its relative poverty reduction performance would have been less successful.

Earlier chapters examined two broad categories of poverty determinants: first, demographic composition, or how different types of households and families face different risks of poverty; and second, economic activity, or the extent to which the labour market participation of the members of these households and families reduces these risks. Now, neither of these factors is entirely beyond the control, or at least the influence, of government policy. While we routinely attribute patterns and trends in family formation and dissolution, fertility, and so on, to broadly cultural and historical trends, there is no question that government policies can and do have a considerable influence on citizens' behaviour in this domain as well (Moffit 1998). At the same time, government policies do not entirely determine demographic trends. Moreover, even when and where anti-poverty policies include efforts to influence the composition of families so as to reduce the proportion of the most poverty-prone family types – such as efforts to control the rise of single-parent families in the United States (Maynard et al. 1998) – it remains important to be able to distinguish the effects of changing family compositions from those of *other* policies intended to reduce poverty.

Much the same can be said about the degree of labour market participation of family members which we analysed in Chapter 5. There is no question that many governments try, with a whole range of policies, to influence the labour market behaviour of their citizens with a view of raising the income tax base, reducing poverty, reducing gender inequality, and much more. As we have seen, Quebec in particular has pursued a conscious policy of facilitating the labour force participation of women with (young) children as part of its overall strategy to combat poverty and social exclusion. But like family formation decisions, labour market participation choices are no doubt also the product of history and culture. And, again, whether or not there is a conscious policy in place to reduce poverty by stimulating greater labour force participation, it is of considerable importance to be able to distinguish the poverty-reducing effects of growing labour force participation from those of the generosity of governmental transfer programs. After all, not everyone is able to work, and for those who are not those programs may be all that can prevent them from falling into poverty. Standardizing for labour market participation permits us to compare provinces and countries as though they had the same proportions of economically active versus those excluded from the labour market. Nevertheless, we need to keep in mind that both family composition and labour market participation are at least *in part* the result of government policies as well.

In slightly more technical terms, then, each province's and country's overall poverty rate in a given year is a function of the distribution of different kinds of households within that province's or country's population, and the different likelihoods of each household type ending up in poverty in that province or country. When we standardize poverty rates, we retain differences in the likelihood of each household type ending up in poverty across states and years, but we ensure that the relative share of each household type in each population is the same. To do this we need to select the province or country whose population distribution will serve as the standard. Normally, one would choose a case that is particularly salient from the perspective of the issues we are interested in, as Fritzell and Ritakallio (2010) do when they select Sweden as the standard. Following this sensible strategy we choose Quebec's population distribution in terms of family type and labour force participation as our basis for standardization.

A related method to the standardization technique we use here to identify the effects of family composition and labour force participation patterns would be regression decomposition, a statistical technique favoured by many econometricians (see Fortin, Lemieux, and Firpo 2011; Jann 2008; Biewen and Jenkins 2005).[3] While regression decomposition is a more powerful method, we opt here for the simpler standardization approach because, first, its results are intuitively easier to grasp, and second, decomposition adds little additional information in our case.[4]

In what follows, we present two sets of standardized poverty rates. The first standardizes for demographic composition, the second for demographic composition *and* household labour market participation combined. We use the same variables and categories that we used to differentiate between household types and their levels of labour market participation in Chapters 3 and 5.

First, we begin by asking what the poverty rates in the other provinces and countries would have been if they had had the same distribution

Figure 6.1. Poverty rate and standardized poverty rate according to family types, Canadian provinces

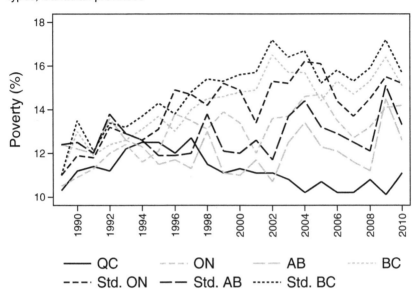

of family types (two-parent, single-parent, couples, singles, elderly, and 'other') as Quebec did in the year in question. Next, we ask what those poverty rates would have been if those other provinces and countries had had the same distribution of family types *as well as* the same distribution of labour market participation within each family type as described in Chapter 5 (i.e., not working, underemployed, single-earner equivalent, or dual-earner equivalent).

Family Composition

Figure 6.1 shows the poverty rates standardized according to the Quebec distribution of family types for each of the years considered for Alberta, British Columbia, and Ontario, as well as the actual poverty rates for each and for Quebec.[5]

Figure 6.1 shows differences in family type distributions are only a modest part of the explanation of the 4%–7% difference in overall poverty rates between Quebec and the other provinces. But family type distributions do play a role. For each of the three other provinces, the standardized poverty rates are between 1 and 2 percentage points higher than the actual rates. In other words, if these provinces had had Quebec's distribution of family types, their poverty rates would have been another 1 or 2 percentage points higher. Thus, when compared to the other Canadian provinces Quebec's actual poverty rates slightly *under*estimate the beneficial effects of its policies on reducing poverty,[6] as its distribution of family types is slightly less favourable with respect to typical poverty risks than those of the other provinces. By way of explanation, we point to the fact that Quebec has proportionately slightly more single-parent households and adults living alone than the other provinces, and a smaller proportion of two-parent families, particularly when compared to Alberta.

But Quebec is not at a compositional disadvantage in all respects. In fact, relative to Ontario and especially Alberta, Quebec benefits from a slightly larger elderly population that is, on average, considerably less likely to end up in poverty than the broader population. This 'advantage' speaks to the success of the federally implemented and managed Canada Pension Plan in the other three provinces and the Quebec Pension Plan, its provincial counterpart in Quebec (Schirle 2013). Nevertheless, when it comes to population-wide poverty statistics, this modest advantage is washed out by other differences in population composition between the provinces that are less favourable to Quebec.

Finally, the actual and the standardized curves for the three Anglophone provinces start very close to each other in the early 1990s but diverge until sometime during the second half of the 1990s, after which they continue to rise more or less parallel to each other. This is true for both sets of curves *as well as* for the discrepancy between the actual and the standardized curves for each of these three provinces. What this means, roughly, is that while they enjoyed little or no advantage in demographic composition at the beginning of the period, their advantage grew early on and then remained steady from the mid- to late 1990s onward.

Figure 6.2 gives the results for the four comparison countries: the United States, France, Finland, and the Netherlands. As the figure shows, the difference between poverty rates in France and Quebec has little or nothing to do with differences in the distribution of family types, as France's rates hardly change at all when we assume it has the same distribution as Quebec. The same can be said for the Netherlands, where the discrepancy between the actual and the standardized poverty rates never rises much above 1%. The patterns for the other

Figure 6.2. Poverty rate and standardized poverty rate according to family types, Quebec and select countries

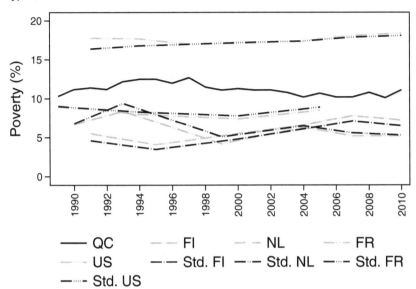

two countries are a little more interesting. The US standardized rates are about 2 percentage points *lower* than the actual rates at the beginning but they converge towards the end. Compared to Quebec, then, the United States suffers a slight disadvantage with respect to the distribution of family types early on but the two distributions gradually become more similar.

In Figure 6.2, the standardized rates for Finland remain slightly lower than its actual rates after the early 1990s.[7] This means Finland was and remains at a slight disadvantage in terms of family composition when compared to Quebec. Like the other Nordic countries, Finland has had a larger proportion of unattached single adults than Quebec. The proportion of elderly in the population is also larger in Finland than in Quebec. In spite of Finland's net compositional disadvantage, however, the standardized Finnish rates are still well below Quebec's rates, reflecting Finland's overall better performance among these relatively more poverty-prone household types.

On the whole, the changes in poverty rates when we compare standardized to actual rates are modest at best in Figures 6.1 and 6.2. That is, the difference in poverty reduction performance between Quebec and the other provinces and countries has relatively little to do with differences in the family composition of their populations. Our finding supports Brady's (2009) broader conclusion that, although some family types are more likely to suffer from poverty than others, comparative differences in the relative share of family types across nations are not great enough to explain the cross-sectional variations in poverty levels. Although we have seen substantial changes in the prevalence of different families over the past several decades (see Chapter 3), these shifts have been similar throughout the developed world. International differences in poverty trends have had little or nothing to do with any differences in the 'decline of the traditional family,' as some have claimed. As Brady points out, this is noteworthy because single motherhood has gotten far more attention than any other cause of poverty in many research and policy circles (2009, 162). Even if the United States were to completely eradicate lone-parent poverty, he says, it would still have some of the highest poverty levels in the world (ibid., 163).

Labour Market Participation

What happens when we enter the different degrees of labour force participation (see Chapter 5) for each household type into the standardization equation? What would the poverty rates have looked like in the other provinces and countries if they had not only had the same distribution of household types but if these households also had the same patterns of labour force participation as in Quebec? Figure 6.3 shows the standardized and actual rates for the four Canadian provinces controlling for both household type distribution *and* labour force participation.

When we add the standardization for labour force participation, the picture changes in interesting ways. Recall that both the actual and the standardized curves for the three Anglophone provinces (Figure 6.1) started very close together, diverged somewhat, and then rose in tandem. The pattern of the standardized curves in Figure 6.3 is quite different, as are, of necessity, the discrepancies between the actual and standardized curves.

Consider, first, what Figure 6.3 tells us about the differences in provincial patterns of labour market attachment and the respective poverty levels. The gap between the actual and standardized poverty rates for each province is particularly telling. Keep in mind that the curves in

Figure 6.3. Poverty rate and standardized poverty rate according to family and labour force participation types, Canadian provinces

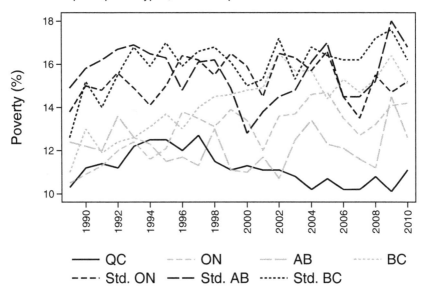

Figure 6.3 represent the *combined* effects of controls for family type *and* labour market attachment patterns. Remember also that controlling for family composition alone (Figure 6.1) rarely produces a change in the poverty rate of more than a percentage point; in the early years, in fact, there is no noticeable effect at all.

Now look at Figure 6.3. While the gaps between actual and standardized poverty rates for the English-speaking provinces in Figure 6.1 are virtually nil in the early years, they are quite large in Figure 6.3. Alberta's poverty rate would have been around 4 percentage points higher than the actual reported rate if its population had had the same labour market attachment pattern as the population of Quebec. This discrepancy remains relatively stable over the entire period, in spite of some minor fluctuations. In other words, Alberta relied and continues to rely on its very high labour force participation to keep poverty down.

By contrast, while Ontario's poverty rates would have risen by 3 to 4 percentage points throughout the 1990s if its population had had Quebec's labour market attachment pattern, the discrepancy falls to around 1 percentage point in recent years. The difference between British Columbia's standardized and actual rates follows a similar path over time, albeit at about a percentage point less than Ontario, with a virtually negligible gap in more recent years. In sum, then, while Alberta's poverty rate is held down by its very high labour force participation rates as compared to Quebec, differences in labour force participation are not a major determinant of the difference – or the similarity, actually – between Quebec and the other two provinces. If anything, the actual and standardized rates display a slight convergence towards the end of the period in both Ontario and British Columbia. In other words, the difference between Quebec and these two provinces in terms of labour market attachment patterns becomes less important over time. This makes sense, as during this period Quebec caught up with the other provinces in terms of the labour force participation of women with (young) children, boosting its initially relatively low proportions of single- and dual-earner equivalent families. As Quebec catches up, differences in labour market participation patterns become less important in accounting for differences in the poverty rates.

Now consider the standardized rates by themselves. As mentioned in the introduction to this chapter, if we have standardized for the two most important extraneous factors likely to affect the poverty rate, we can interpret the differences between the provincial standardized rates as a reasonable approximation of the differences in the level of generosity of the provinces' anti-poverty policies, always keeping in mind, of course, that our residual approach captures the effect of a host of other policies and conditions as well. Thus, the difference between Alberta's and the other two Anglophone provinces' standardized rates in the early 1990s suggests Alberta's anti-poverty regime was considerably less generous than Ontario's and British Columbia's at that time. With the same combination of family types and labour force behaviour, Alberta's poverty rate would have been about 3 percentage points higher than the other two provinces' rates and no less than 6% – rather than the actual 2% – higher than Quebec's poverty rate at the time.

In short, Alberta's regime was *considerably* harsher than Quebec's even then and somewhat more so than Ontario's and British Columbia's, even though they all *seem* about equally generous when we look only at the actual, non-standardized rates. By the end of the period, the difference between Alberta and British Columbia is shrinking while Ontario's standardized rate declines, possibly as a result of new anti-poverty initiatives.

Figure 6.4. Poverty rate and standardized poverty rate according to family and labour force participation types, Quebec and select countries

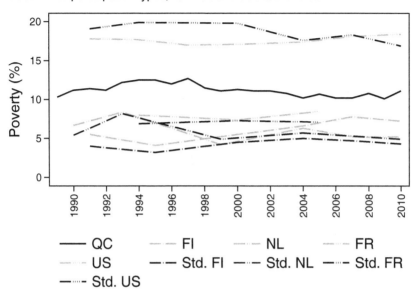

But what about Quebec? Quebec's poverty rates have declined since the mid-1990s while the standardized rates for the other three provinces have fluctuated around a relatively stable trend line. This means that Quebec's anti-poverty regime has become even more generous relative to those of British Columbia and Ontario than the already significant and rising differences in actual poverty levels suggest. We can get an idea of the magnitude of the difference in generosity by measuring the distance between the provinces' standardized rates. If Quebec had had Alberta's relatively ungenerous anti-poverty regime, its poverty rate would have been over 16.8% in 2010, not 11.1%. In other words, Quebec's regime is over 50% more generous than Alberta's![8]

In short, standardizing for family composition and labour market attachment emphasizes the growing distance between Quebec and the other Canadian provinces. But what about other countries? Figure 6.4 answers this question.

What is striking about the results in Figure 6.4 is how little difference adding controls for labour market participation makes when we are comparing Quebec to the four other countries. The basic pattern is remarkably similar to the pattern in Figure 6.2. For the Netherlands and France, controlling for both family type composition and labour market participation makes little difference. The actual and standardized curves remain very close to each other. This means differences in overall poverty rates between these countries and Quebec are due almost entirely to differences in the generosity of their respective anti-poverty regimes and other unmeasured factors, and not to population demographics or labour force participation patterns.

Interestingly, the pattern for the United States is now reversed. Whereas its standardized poverty rate in Figure 6.2 is, at least during the first half of the period, slightly lower than the actual rate, suggesting the United States is suffering a slight population composition disadvantage relative to Quebec, in Figure 6.4, the US standardized rate is one or two percentage points higher than the actual rate until the two begin to converge in the early 2000s. For most of the period, then, the United States has a relative labour force participation 'advantage' much like Alberta's: its poverty rates would have been several percentage points higher if its population had exhibited the same employment patterns as Quebec's. Proportionately, Quebec has fewer working single adults and single-parent families than the United States, and this may explain the findings.

For Finland, the pattern in Figure 6.2 suggests it has a family composition disadvantage, with proportionately more single parents and single adults living alone. In Figure 6.4, the pattern is amplified from about 2004 onwards. That is, Finland's labour force participation pattern has become less favourable than Quebec's in recent years.

The general conclusion to be drawn from Figure 6.4 is that any differences we have documented between Quebec's poverty rates and those of the European comparison countries are primarily the result of the relative generosity of their respective anti-poverty programs (and other unmeasured factors), not the result of differences in labour force participation of different family types.

In sum, standardizing for family composition and labour market participation leads us to qualify the findings of the preceding chapters. First, while Quebec has been slightly disadvantaged in terms of the distribution of family types more or less prone to the risk of poverty when compared to the other Canadian provinces, the difference is not so large as to necessitate a reassessment of our earlier findings on the gradual divergence of poverty policy regimes. With respect to the United States and the European countries, population composition seems to be even less of a factor in accounting for differences.

Second, differences in labour market participation by the different family types in the population appear to make a difference. If Quebec's population had displayed the same pattern of labour market participation as the populations of the other provinces, particularly Alberta, its poverty rates would have been lower still. In other words, the differences between Quebec and the other provinces in their actual, reported poverty rates considerably *under*state their respective differences in poverty regime generosity. As Quebec's pattern of labour market participation catches up with the pattern of the other provinces, the effect of this difference may diminish, but the magnitude of the difference in regime generosity remains as large as before.

Finally, and surprisingly, Quebec's family composition and labour market participation pattern has little or no modifying effect on the differences between its poverty rates and those of the European countries. That is, the admittedly modest difference is almost entirely a matter of differences in generosity. The United States is the exception, in that it would have had a significantly higher poverty rate during most of the period if it were not for its higher rates of labour market attachment.

Conclusion

With respect to social policy and its outcomes, Canada's provinces are moving in different directions. Whereas Quebec seems likely to join the industrialized nations with the lowest poverty levels, the other provinces seem likely to join those with the highest levels of poverty, notably the United States. In addition, standardizing the poverty rates of the other largest Canadian provinces for differences in levels of labour market participation reduces their observed differences. Rather than being the result of differences in approaches to poverty reduction, then, much of the observed differences in poverty outcomes among the Anglophone provinces can be traced to provincial economic fortunes. Taken together, these results support the bifurcation thesis: there are two emergent approaches to social policy and poverty outcomes among Canada's largest provinces.

By standardizing poverty rates with respect to demographic composition and labour market participation, we show that, thanks to a combination of activation and greater generosity, Quebec has moved even further away in its policy approach and outcomes from the other Canadian provinces than the actual reported poverty rates would have us believe, and closer to the European approach. We emphasize that our results suggest Quebec's success in bringing down poverty rates for families with dependent children is the result of a *combination* of relatively successful activation policies *and* greater generosity of welfare benefits for families in need. As mentioned in Chapter 3, total real welfare income available to families in Quebec has increased moderately over the past three decades, while it has declined or remained unchanged in the other three Canadian provinces (Tweddle, Battle, and Torjman 2014).

But poverty rates are always the complex result of a combination of factors, of which the policy we wish to evaluate is only one. In this chapter we have made a first attempt to assess the effect of the policy net of confounding factors. But any attempt to isolate the effects of the policies from those of all other potentially important factors is, almost by definition, imperfect and provisional. The aim of the standardization exercise is to control for as many confounding factors as we can think of between two populations and then attribute the residual effect to the policy differences between them. The two sets of factors we have controlled for here, though certainly important, do not and cannot exhaust the major structural differences in populations, institutions, and economic conditions likely to affect poverty rates.

As we have noted repeatedly, our standardization technique treats policy effects as a residual category. We attribute whatever proportion of the difference in outcomes that cannot be explained by compositional differences to the 'regime' effect. But the latter is simply the 'unexplained' residual. It does not estimate the effect of policy differences directly. Rather, it establishes the upper limit of what part of the variation could possibly be attributed to policy differences. The actual importance of policy differences may be far more modest, as many unmeasured systematic inter-jurisdictional differences other than policy differences may account for the remaining unexplained residual variation. Future research will have to refine the technique by controlling for additional factors of potential importance for poverty levels so as to isolate the 'pure' effect of government policies more precisely.

A second qualification points in the opposite direction. While family composition and labour force participation patterns may not be entirely under the control of governments, they are nonetheless affected by them to some extent. And, as we have seen, governments have good reasons to try and influence both with their policies. Consequently, at least *some* part of the evolution of family type composition and patterns of labour market participation is the result of government policy, not extraneous to it, as we have assumed here. Controlling for them as we have done to 'isolate' the effects of government policy may fail to capture some of those effects. But it would take an exceedingly sophisticated analysis and far more detailed comparative data than are currently available to sort out the exact mix of policy and non-policy factors in the evolution of family composition and employment behaviour.

Our findings, then, must remain tentative and suggestive. At the same time, as we move from chapter to chapter, our evidence is steadily building an ever stronger case for the claim that the Canadian welfare state is becoming more and more divided into two quite different regimes: the Quebec regime is approaching its goal of joining the European welfare states, while the rest of Canada is veering towards an American alternative.

Conclusion: Towards the Provincialization of the Social Union?

'In most matters of social policy, Canadian citizens are increasingly provincial citizens,' write Rice and Prince in their authoritative treatise on the politics of Canadian social policy (2013, 298). Our findings in this book support this view. More importantly, they raise a number of major questions, not just about the long-term prospects of continuing divergence between the provinces in their formulation of social and employment policy, but about the very character of the Canadian federation. We raised these broad questions in the Introduction and will return to them here. But first, it may be useful to summarize our findings.

The principal aim of this book has been to document and assess recent trends in social and employment policies in Canada's four largest provinces (Quebec, Ontario, British Columbia, and Alberta), as well as their outcomes, particularly in terms of poverty rates for different sections of the population. We analysed these trends and outcomes in the context of a number of issues that have recently been raised about the evolution of advanced welfare states, including Canada's. Among other things, we asked how far Canada's largest provinces have drifted apart as a result of Quebec's *virage sociodémocratique* and the neoliberal retrenchment of the other provinces and the federal government. We also asked how close that *virage* has brought Quebec to the Nordic social democratic model it seeks to emulate. We have been particularly interested in assessing how Quebec and the other major provinces have dealt with recent trends in family composition and labour market behaviour and the extent to which they have adopted the social investment rather than the workfare variant of activation policies.

We began, in Chapter 1, by comparing a broad range of social and employment policies in Ontario, Quebec, British Columbia, and Alberta since 2002, the year Quebec adopted its distinctive strategy to combat poverty and social exclusion. We found that in terms of their scope and range, Quebec's policies and programs clearly exceed those of the other provinces, particularly Alberta. Especially after the mid-2000s, the Quebec government's expenditures on these policies as a proportion of provincial GDP far surpass those of the other three provinces, with Alberta once again bringing up the rear. Finally, we noted that Quebec's policies are characterized by a strong emphasis on supporting families with children and encouraging activation, particularly on facilitating the labour force participation of women with (young) children. These emphases appear to reflect the aspiration of policymakers in Quebec to follow the social investment approach characteristic of the much-admired Nordic social democratic welfare state model.

Having established Quebec's distinctive approach in terms of the character and extent of its policies, in Chapter 2 we asked to what extent the various policies have produced the desired outcomes, most notably the reduction of poverty. Before doing so we addressed a number of technical issues having to do with the measurement of poverty. The most appropriate measure for cross-provincial and cross-national comparisons, we argued, is the provincially based low income measure, or LIM, with disposable household income equivalized for household size as the unit of analysis. Using this measure, we compared the poverty rates, based on the conventional 50% of median income threshold, and acute poverty rates, at 30% of the median, in the four provinces and a selection of comparison countries. In the aggregate – that is, without differentiating between different household types – Quebec's poverty and acute poverty rates exhibit a trend towards modest improvement over time that corresponds with the evolution of its distinctive policy approach; those same rates either remain stable or rise in the comparison provinces and countries.

But such aggregate poverty rates may hide significant differences between subpopulations. This is particularly relevant because Quebec's policies are heavily targeted at families with children. Accordingly, in Chapter 3 we analyse and compare poverty rates and trends for different household types. Much larger differences in poverty trends between Quebec and the other jurisdictions quickly become apparent, and the evidence suggests that Quebec's targeting of families with children has had considerable success. While poverty rates for two-parent families have drifted upward in the three other provinces and remained stable in the comparison countries, Quebec's rates have dropped, reaching the relatively low levels characteristic of some of Europe's most generous welfare states. Single-parent family poverty rates are much higher everywhere than the rates for two-parent families. But they have come down in all four Canadian provinces, albeit much more so in Quebec. By contrast, Quebec's policy mix has done little for childless households, particularly single adults for whom poverty rates remain among the worst of the comparative provinces and countries.

In Chapter 4 we extend our analysis of differences in possible policy outcomes by looking at poverty *duration*. Generous anti-poverty policies may help to pull some families out of poverty, but they may also create a culture of dependency on government support and inadvertently produce a new underclass of chronically poor. Moreover, chronic poverty presents policymakers with a far more serious problem, and one of a different order, than 'mere' transitory poverty. In Chapter 4 we examine 'poverty trajectories' of two-parent and single-parent families in the four Canadian provinces over a six-year period. Our findings do not support the existence of a trade-off between poverty levels and mobility. Again, Quebec does significantly better than the other provinces, with rates of chronic poverty much lower for both family types and higher proportions of those who are poor at some point but whose poverty turns out to be transitory. Only some of Alberta's figures come close to Quebec's in terms of the average duration of poverty spells. Since Alberta is also the province with the least comprehensive and least generous set of policies to combat poverty, the province's buoyant economy may have enabled those at risk of poverty to keep their poverty spells relatively short. In the absence of either a strong economy *or* Quebec's generous and elaborate anti-poverty strategy, as is the case in British Columbia, families are not only much more likely to fall into poverty but also, and more alarmingly, to remain poor for long periods of time.

In short, according to our findings, Quebec clearly stands out within Canada, or at least among its largest provinces, with respect to the character and extent of its social policies, and these policies appear to have had some of the intended effects. But correlation is not causation. In Chapters 5 and 6 we examine the relationship between Quebec's distinctive policies and the poverty outcomes documented in Chapters 2, 3, and 4. Part of Quebec's strategy, following the Nordic social investment model, is to reduce poverty levels by encouraging more people, particularly mothers with children, to work. In Chapter 5 we assess to what extent this strategy has actually succeeded in reducing poverty rates, rather than adding to the ranks of working poor. A large part of Quebec's success in bringing down the poverty rates of families with children is indeed related to increased labour force participation, particularly of women with (young) children. There is also some evidence that single-parent families and single-earner two-parent families have benefited from the more generous social transfer payments. However, such transfers have not prevented the poverty rates of underemployed households in Quebec, including single-parent families, from remaining at North American levels, far higher than those of the comparison countries in Europe that the province has sought to emulate.

But aggregate poverty rates are not simply the result of government policies. They are also affected by the composition of the population, particularly the proportions of different household types, and the state of the economy, both of which are beyond the direct control of the provincial government. In Chapter 6 we take such differences into account by 'standardizing' poverty rates with respect to Quebec's population composition and employment patterns. In effect, we are asking: what would the poverty rate have been in the other provinces and countries if they had had Quebec's composition of households and employment pattern? Our results reinforce the findings of the other chapters. When we standardize in this way, it turns out that the poverty rates in most other provinces and countries would have been even higher than they actually were. While we caution against over-interpretation of these results, they *are* compatible with the possibility that Quebec's measured poverty rates *under*state the extent to which the province has managed to steer a distinctive policy course that has brought poverty levels down to near-European levels, at least for families with children.

In summary, then, almost all of the evidence points in the same direction: over the past couple of decades Quebec has clearly and decisively veered away from the Anglo-Saxon liberal welfare state regime prevalent in the rest of North America and moved towards a regime that in its policy commitments and most of its outcomes is much closer to the European social democratic type. To be sure, as we noted in Chapter 1, a number of the other Canadian provinces have, partly in response to Quebec's initiative, declared and implemented their own broad strategies to combat poverty. But so far, these remain modest in terms of overall funding commitments or are simply declarations of intent yet to be followed by concrete policies. Moreover, given the current climate of fiscal prudence, none is likely to come close to matching Quebec in the near future. In fact, if anything, our evidence and that of others

(Banting and Myles 2013a; Béland and Daigneault 2015) suggest the other Canadian provinces are moving in the *opposite*, liberal market-oriented direction.[1]

But is Quebec not subject to the same pressures for fiscal prudence as the other provinces and the federal government? This is certainly what the theorists of globalization whom we discussed briefly in the Introduction would claim. Given the increasing importance of international trade, finance, and investment, so it is argued, governments can no longer afford to run deficits, and debts that are out of line with their countries' trading partners are seen as risky by the international financial industry. Consequently, they will be forced to cut taxes and expenditures in a competitive 'race to the bottom.' Sooner or later, according to this argument, Quebec will be forced by the pressures of globalization to abandon its eccentric *virage sociodémocratique* and join the other provinces in cutting back on expenditures and commitments.

There is no doubt that Quebec has accumulated the largest public debt of any province in the country, whether measured as dollars per capita or as a percentage of its provincial GDP. According to some calculations, the province's own public debt plus its share of the federal debt amount to 87% of its GDP (see, e.g., Doucet et al. 2015, 1; Institut de la statistique du Québec 2015; Mallet 2013). This is perilously close to the famous, though not exactly uncontested (see Cassidy 2013), 'tipping point' identified by Reinhart and Rogoff (2009), beyond which the debt allegedly becomes economically unsustainable. And there is no shortage of critics who have argued that it is unsustainable (Malvern, Mrozek, and Benesch 2011; Speer 2014; Vaillancourt and Laberge 2010; Van Praet 2011), a message Premier Couillard's Liberal government appears to have taken to heart.

Such critics from the political right have usually targeted social policies for cutbacks, as in their view, governments cannot afford the lavish and excessively generous policies of the type seen in Quebec. This kind of criticism usually rests on two widespread assumptions about the nature and effects of such policies. First, some say social policies, particularly those intended to provide material support for the poor, unavoidably pervert economic incentives in such a way as to produce the opposite of the intended outcome in the long run. According to this neo-Malthusian line of argument, financial transfers to the poor undermine the incentive to find proper employment and produce a culture of dependency on 'government handouts' that, in the long run, demoralizes the beneficiaries and keeps them in poverty (for one of the most discussed statements of this position, see Murray 1994; see also Dean and Taylor-Gooby 2014).

Second, conservative critics of welfare spending say practically all such spending is a net deadweight loss to the economy as a whole. Hence, the often-heard claim that social programs are 'a luxury that we cannot afford.' Ironically some critics from the *left* who have predicted an inevitable race to the bottom between advanced welfare states as a result of the ineluctable competitive pressures of globalization make the same basic assumption that social protection programs constitute a net burden on the economy that governments can ill afford in the age of intensified international competition (see, e.g., Bowles and Wagman 1997; Brady, Beckfield, and Seeleib-Kaiser 2005; Genschel 2004; Huber and Stephens 2001; Mishra 1999; Tanzi 2002).

The debate over the net costs and benefits of social and employment policies tends to be either highly ideologically driven or exceedingly technical, involving detailed program evaluations. Although we are not in a position to settle such issues in these final pages, a few points are worth keeping in mind when considering any strong claims about the need to cut back on the kinds of policies that we have documented and analysed.

First, the assumptions underlying conservative criticisms of 'excessive' welfare spending are the opposite of those made by recent advocates of the social investment approach and related perspectives mentioned in the Introduction (see, e.g., de Gier and van den Berg 2005; Gazier 2003; Jenson 2013; Morel, Palier, and Palme 2012; Schmid 2006; Schmid and Gazier 2002; van den Berg 2009). According to them, social protection policies, *if properly designed*, not only do not detract from economic growth and competitiveness but may very well *contribute* to them.[2] As we have noted throughout, Quebec's *virage sociodémocratique* was inspired by this social investment approach. Its main principles are an emphasis on employment as the first and most desirable path out of poverty and on targeting families with children to prevent the inter-generational persistence of social disadvantage. In effect, Quebec's strategy to combat poverty and social exclusion is more or less consciously *designed* to address the classical conservative objections to support for the poor, with activation rather than passive financial support a central component.

In other words, Quebec's strategy has sought to do the very opposite of creating a culture of dependency among the poor, encouraging them in various ways to pull themselves out of poverty through employment. And, as Chapter 5 tells us, this 'making work pay' strategy constitutes a considerable part of the explanation of Quebec's favourable performance with respect to poverty rates, at least for families with children. Nor, as Chapter 4 makes clear, is there any evidence of a large or growing population of permanently poor dependent on government handouts in Quebec as compared to the other large provinces. To the contrary, by whatever measure we care to use, on average, Quebec's poor escape poverty sooner, and therefore suffer shorter poverty spells, than the other provinces' poor, with the partial exception of Alberta.

The question of the net economic and budgetary burden or benefit of the policies examined in the preceding pages is a little more complicated. As noted, it is widely accepted by policymakers and observers that Quebec's cumulative public debt is a serious concern requiring measures to reduce its size lest the provincial government's budget be overwhelmed by the costs of servicing it (Fortin 2011; Godbout et al. 2012; Godbout et al. 2014; Speer 2014).[3] It is also true that aggregate social expenditures, certainly when we include expenditures on health care and education, constitute the lion's share of Quebec's provincial budget. Finally, there is no question that this kind of 'discretionary' spending represents the fastest growing expense category in recent years (Deslauriers and Gagné 2013).

But to conclude from this that Quebec should cut back on its social and employment programs and policies simply to balance its books could well be counterproductive for two reasons. First, these programs[4] account for only about 11% of total program expenditures,[5] whereas health care and education add up to over 70% of the province's total expenditures (see, e.g., Kneebone and Wilkins 2014, 21). Consequently, cutbacks would either have to be too little to have much of an impact on Quebec's fiscal position *or* be so draconian as to destroy most of the recent gains in poverty reduction.

Second, a significant proportion of the expenditures analysed in these pages, roughly 25%, is targeted at activating policies, that is, policies encouraging beneficiaries to join and/or stay in the labour force. First among these is Quebec's system of subsidized $7-a-day day-care centres. While the program is hardly uncontroversial (Allaire 2011; Richards 2011), it appears to have made a significant difference in helping to reduce the poverty rates of families with young children. What is more, according to careful estimates by Pierre Fortin and his colleagues, the system has been a net *contributor* to the government's coffers, not a net burden. The availability of relatively affordable day-care centres has enabled so many more women with young children to join the labour force that the additional taxes they have paid more than make up for the cost of the program (see Fortin, Godbout, and St-Cerny 2012, 2013). If this is indeed the case, cutting back on the government's expenditures on the program could actually end up *increasing* its deficit rather than reducing it!

Of course, there is plenty of room to debate these claims. Moreover, we have little or no information about the net fiscal effects of the province's other activating policies. Surely we can assume its passive support programs for the poor *are* a net burden to its finances. But again, to conclude that cutting back on these programs makes fiscal sense is not necessarily self-evident. Some of the other activating programs may also produce more government revenue than they cost, while others may not. Only careful evaluation of each program can determine this. Similarly, in view of the massive literature documenting the many undesirable – and costly – effects of poverty (see, e.g., Fleury and Fortin 2006, 4; Raphael 2007, Part 3), it is hardly obvious that all passive poverty-reducing programs are necessarily a net burden on the public purse. Again, only careful assessments of each measure, taking into account the broader effects and their costs to the community as a whole, will enable us to make an informed judgment as to the balance between their real costs and benefits.

So let us assume for a moment that Quebec will be able to pursue its distinctive approach to social and employment policy, despite globalization and fiscal pressures, while the rest of Canada continues on its path of neoliberal retrenchment and austerity. Such a scenario raises some interesting and, for some, alarming questions about the character and future of Canada's confederation as a whole. In the Introduction, we mention several researchers who have recently drawn attention to the close relationship between social policy and a sense of national identity and solidarity (Barbier 2013; Béland and Lecours 2008). The idea is that social policy involves the redistribution and sharing of resources which, in turn, presupposes a willingness to share, that is, the existence of some sense of social solidarity which, finally, is only likely to be felt towards the members of a community with whom one shares some kind of collective identity. But social policy doesn't just rest on a sense of shared identity; it also helps create that sense among the members of the redistributive community. Social policy, by marking off those with whom one shares resources from those with whom one does not, creates and sustains a sense of a distinct community separate from others.

According to Béland and Lecours (2005, 2006, 2008), nationalist movements, especially nationalist politicians in Quebec, are keenly aware of the intimate relationship between social policy and national identity. In fact, as they show in some detail (Béland and Lecours 2008, Ch. 2), Quebec's policymakers have deliberately used social policy as an instrument for the building of a Québécois identity in contradistinction to the proverbial 'rest of Canada.' This is particularly the case for the set of policies examined in this book (Béland and Lecours 2008, 68–71; Noël 2002, 106; Ulysse and Lesemann 2004, 294–8; Vaillancourt 2012, 129). In other words, these policies have not only been advocated as a manifestation of Quebec's distinctive and stronger egalitarian and solidary values; they have also been implemented with the aim of *creating* and *maintaining* a distinctively Québécois identity. Is this an instance of Boychuk's 'competitive state-building' (Boychuk 2013)?

In other words, is Quebec's divergent approach to social policy part of a deliberate attempt to create an ever more *distinct society* by stealth? And, if so, would it be able to drive the wedge between Quebec and the rest of Canada that the incessant constitutional wrangling and disputes over language rights have not? A number of observers fear it might. They warn that 'the provincialization of social policy' will result in the 'diminished saliency of pan-Canadian political sentiment,' which in turn will undermine any 'meaningful "social union" ' at the national level (Osberg 2000, 214; see also Jenson 2013, 50; Kershaw 2006; Wood and Klassen 2009, 267). Others are more sanguine about the potential effects on Canada's confederation of a growing divergence between provincial social policy regimes. 'As a country, Canada seems comfortable with greater regional variation in terms of social citizenship than do most federations,' Banting and Myles argue (Banting and Myles 2013c, 422; see also Boychuk 2013; Noël 2012).

Moreover, as Béland and Lecours themselves readily admit, 'it is difficult to assess whether or not there are actually significant differences between Quebeckers and other Canadians with respect to the importance allocated to values such as solidarity and equality of opportunity, and to general policy objectives like poverty reduction' (Béland and Lecours 2008, 70). It would necessarily be even harder to determine whether or to what extent those distinctive Québécois values, if they are that distinct to begin with, are the *cause* or the *result* of the province's distinctive social policies. While many Quebeckers feel somewhat distant from their fellow Canadians when it comes to issues like poverty, inequality, the gun registry, the long-form census or, for that matter, 'family values,' we simply do not know to what extent any or all of these add up to a sense of alienation sufficient to refuel separatist sentiment to any significant degree. At the time of writing, Quebec's *souverainiste* movement is in retreat, in part due to tactical errors in recent electoral campaigns, in part because of generational shifts in orientation that do not favour the cause. At the same time, the direction taken by Quebec since the mid-1990s in the realm of social and employment policy has set it apart from the rest of the Canadian confederation, and this is bound to have *some* effect on Quebec's sense of uniqueness within the confederation. At this point, we see no clear grounds for making an informed guess as to the long-term effect of this on the Canadian confederation and Quebec's place in it.

For all the centrifugal forces always lurking under the surface in the Canadian political landscape, we should never ignore the centripetal force exerted by Canada's federal government. As Banting (2005, 2008) shows, there has always been an element of 'competitive nation-building' (2008, 90) in the continuous federal-provincial tug of war over the making of social policy (see also van den Berg and Jensen 2015). And at least until the mid-1970s, the federal government's nation-building efforts, exemplified by the introduction of national health care, the Canada Pension Plan, and the Canada Assistance Plan, were clearly dominant. True, with the gradual retreat of the federal government's role in social policy since the late 1980s, this nation-building effort has inevitably weakened (see Banting and Myles 2013a). But the process is by no means necessarily irreversible.

In fact, at this point it is worth reflecting on how quickly the political landscape can change. Since we wrote the first draft of this chapter, Albertans have elected their first ever NDP government and the Liberal Party has regained power at the federal level with a program calling explicitly for massive federal deficit spending! And, if anything, the recent commodity bust in the oil-rich provinces of Alberta, Saskatchewan, and Newfoundland and Labrador highlights the importance of the federal government's role in providing support for the provinces who need it. Meanwhile, the Couillard government in Quebec continues to follow a policy of austerity to bring down the province's public debt. In other words, for all the concerns about Canada's fragmented welfare state, we may be witnessing the beginning of a trend towards convergence rather than divergence between the provinces and the federal government.

Thus, while Quebec may or may not persist in its distinctive approach to social and employment policy, it is not carved in stone that the other provinces and the federal government will forever continue down the road of neoliberal austerity. In fact, Rice and Prince end their comprehensive account of the politics of Canadian social policy on an optimistic note, *applauding* the provincialization of social policy as the beginning of a growing movement to compensate at the provincial level for the retreat from social policy at the federal level (Rice and Prince 2013, Ch. 11). They note that several provinces have recently announced their own poverty reduction strategies, some of which have apparently taken some of their cues from the Quebec example. Despite the neoliberal winds blowing across the Canadian political landscape, then, it is possible that the other provinces and perhaps even the federal government may come around to adopt at least some of Quebec's pioneering policies if and when they are seen to be successful and cost-effective. Much would depend, of course, on how convincing the evidence turns out to be for the positive effects of these policies. A great deal of social-scientific research remains to be done to carefully assess the positive and negative effects of each policy and program before such evidence would be capable of moving policymakers in one direction or another. But we firmly believe, as well we must, that such evidence can be a major positive factor in the debates surrounding them.

In this book, we present some of that evidence. Obviously, we cannot settle any of the larger questions. But we hope our findings and those of the researchers who continue to scrutinize the effects of Quebec's distinctive policies in the near future will inform this discourse. What we have been able to do in this book is document that, thanks in large part to its strategy to combat poverty and social exclusion, Quebec *is* fairer than its North American counterparts (Fortin 2010). In some respects at least, it has joined the 'industrialized nations having the least number of persons living in poverty.' But with the partial exception of Quebec's subsidized day-care system, we do not know which policies have had what effects exactly, and at what cost. Thus, we do not rule out the possibility that some of the current programs do not have the desired effect, are counterproductive or are excessively costly according to some reasonable weighing of the costs and benefits. Nonetheless, the overall strategy has produced some remarkably positive results. To be sure, much remains to be done, particularly for groups of the population who appear to have benefited very little if at all from Quebec's incomplete *virage sociodémocratique*. And the hard work of figuring out what works, to whose benefit, and at what cost has barely started.

Notes

Introduction

1 Simply put, 'decommodification' refers to the degree to which individuals' incomes are rendered independent of their market earnings.
2 For instance, Goodin (1999) proposes a four-type classification locating the Netherlands in the social democratic grouping with the Nordic countries, rather than with its Continental neighbours. For a good survey of the literature on the political economy of the welfare state up to about 2003, see Hicks and Esping-Andersen (2005).
3 An important exception is Ferrara's influential argument about the 'regionalization' of welfare regimes in the context of the expanding role of EU social policy (Ferrara 2005).
4 For a more sanguine view, stressing the continued presence of the federal government in the politics of redistribution in all of Canada as a result of the 'competitive state-building' characterizing Canada's territorial politics, see Boychuk (2013).
5 For a recent assessment see Haddow (2015, 17, and the literature cited in 293n57).

Chapter One

1 For a famous, harrowing account, see Polanyi (1944: Part 2).
2 In 1943, the federal government commissioned a *Report on Social Security in Canada*, better known as the 'Marsh Report' after its principal author, Leonard Marsh (Marsh 1975). The Report established 'the pillars of the social architecture of the welfare state in Canada' (Maioni 2004, 22) and was explicitly based on the famous British report published a year earlier by William Beveridge, who had been Marsh's mentor.

3 For the early history of Quebec social policy, see Vaillancourt (1988).
4 Federal funding began to decline as early as 1990, when the federal government put a cap on CAP (see Boychuk 2015, 73).
5 For a more detailed account of the politics of social assistance and child benefits in Ontario since the early 1980s see Haddow (2015, 113–25).
6 For a more detailed account of the evolution of Quebec's redistributive policies (primarily social assistance and child and family benefits) see Haddow (2015, 101–13).
7 That level of detail requires painstaking analysis of consecutive provincial budgets and other governmental documents as described in the methodological appendix to this chapter. For an analysis of the difficulties faced when trying to identify individual program expenditures over time from government sources, see Kneebone and White (2015, 96, 137–9).
8 As Haddow (2015, 41, 53–5, 126) shows, the pattern goes back to the early 1970s in the wake of the Quiet Revolution.
9 Respite services are services meant to give a break to the informal caregiver. This might consist of a daycare or homecare service that makes it possible for the caregiver to leave the home and his/her caregiving responsibilities for a few hours, even a few days.
10 These programs are: Support to Community Housing Providers (2002–4); Homeless Initiatives (2002–3, 2006–7); Canada/Alberta Affordable Housing Agreement (2002–7); Other Housing Grants (2002–9); Special Needs Housing (2002–10); Rent Supplement Program (2002–10); Assistance to the Alberta Social Housing Corporation (2002–11); Homeless Support (2003–6); Affordable Housing Partnership Initiative (2005–6); Off-reserve Aboriginal Housing Program (2006–9); Affordable Housing Program (2006–10); Emergency/Transitional Shelter Support (2006–12); Municipal Sustainability Housing Program (2007–8); Homeless and Eviction Prevention Fund (2007–10); Homeless Outreach Support Services (2007–12); and Housing Capital Programs (2010–12).
11 Devenir and Interagir were merged into the program Action in 2011.
12 This program was gradually phased out and replaced by the Ontario Child Benefit, a program we classify as a 'family income support' policy.
13 We do not include the Alberta Family Employment Tax Credit because we only found data for 2010.
14 For the remainder of this Chapter 'GDP' refers to *provincial* GDP unless explicitly indicated otherwise.
15 We include only programs providing positive incentives and resources for joining the labour force (i.e. workfare activation by tightening eligibility conditions for income support programs is excluded).

16 The province of Newfoundland and Labrador implemented a poverty reduction strategy in 2006, followed by Ontario in 2008, New Brunswick, Nova Scotia, and Manitoba in 2009, and Prince Edward Island in 2012 (Department of Advanced Education and Skills 2014; Government of Ontario 2008, 2013; Province of New Brunswick 2014; Government of Nova Scotia 2009; Government of Manitoba 2014). In New Brunswick, a second plan was released for 2014–19 (Province of New Brunswick 2014).

17 Expenditures from provincial budgets refer to fiscal years, while data from other sources were released for calendar years. We matched calendar years with fiscal years in such a way that nine months of the fiscal year are grouped with 12 months of the same calendar year; i.e., fiscal year 2008–9 is matched with calendar year data for 2008.

18 The program represents a small part of Alberta's overall expenditures on the programs we are interested in. For 2010 this tax credit was valued at approximately $117 million, which amounts to approximately 2% of Alberta's total expenditures on the social and labour market programs that we have included in the analysis.

Chapter Two

1 Poverty Solved. 2011. 'Chris Alexander announces that Poverty has been eliminated in Canada.' Retrieved from https://www.youtube.com/watch?v=ncUtF2E7D8Y.

2 We should note however that the World Bank uses its $2-a-day cut-off as a measure of absolute dire poverty only and does in effect take into consideration purchasing power at the national level in its comparative studies.

3 According to Kenworthy (2004), there is a strong correlation between welfare regimes and poverty levels when we use the relative conception of poverty. Those preferring an 'absolute' conception of poverty generally also have a negative view of extensive welfare states. A notable exception is Scruggs and Allan (2005), who maintain a favourable view of welfare states yet prefer the absolute notion of poverty. These authors report a relationship between poverty and absolute measures similar to that found by Kenworthy between poverty and relative measures.

4 As we point out in Chapter 4, the term 'social exclusion' is sometimes used in Canada to refer to chronic or long-duration *income* poverty.

5 Statistics Canada has been reluctant to use the term 'poverty,' preferring 'low-income' instead: 'As former chief statistician Ivan Fellegi puts it, "poverty is intrinsically a question of social consensus" and the determination of a poverty criterion ultimately "involves value judgments" and, as such, it is not the role of Statistics Canada to define and measure poverty' (Murphy, Zhang, and Dionne 2012, 11, 87). Statistics Canada has been criticized for this (Hunter and Miazdyck 2006).

6 A related poverty measure, the fixed low income measure, or 'fixed LIM,' suffers the same limitation. Like the MBM, the fixed LIM establishes a consumption standard based on the LIM threshold in a single time period and then corrects for inflation for subsequent time periods. The choice of the baseline time period and periodic rebasing of the measure are necessarily highly debatable. As there is broad agreement on the need for periodic rebasing, we might well ask what the advantage of this measure is over one that is rebased slightly and simply each period, as with the ordinary LIM. But see Zhang (2014) for a recent application of a fixed LIM.

7 For a similar comparison for Canada as a whole see Banting and Myles (2013b, 30–1).

8 For more discussion and results on this theme see Murphy, Zhang, and Dionne (2012).

9 The choice of equivalence scale may slightly affect poverty rates for select groups (Raïq 2012) and between countries (Buhmann et al. 1988). Whatever scale we use, however, poverty trends over time tend to remain robust, and differences in poverty rates between different family types and sizes remain broadly the same (Raïq 2012).

10 For the latest available poverty estimates (at a poverty line of 50% of the median) see http://stats.oecd.org/Index.aspx?QueryId=47991.

11 Recall that the LIS data are only available for a few of the years along the horizontal axis which accounts for the smoother curves for the comparison countries than for the provinces for which we have annual data from the SLID.

12 The LIS dataset does not contain data for Sweden beyond 2005. The figure for the Swedish poverty rate cited here is taken from the OECD dataset referred to in footnote 10.

Chapter Three

1 Although it has recently been argued that these countries have moved, however cautiously, towards a 'dual' system of protection incorporating some of those formerly excluded from social protection through a second, more modest set of social programs (Hemerijck 2013, 180–95; Palier 2010).

2 Statistics Canada defines a census family as 'composed of a married or common-law couple, with or without children, or of a lone parent living with at least one child in the same dwelling. Couples can be of the opposite sex or of the same sex' (Statistics Canada 2012b, 17). In 2001, same-sex common-law couples were first counted and in 2006 same-sex married couples were first counted. To see how the census family definition was broadened in 2001, see Statistics Canada (2012a).
3 Based on our own calculations with SCF and SLID.
4 Individuals aged 65 years and over.
5 Again, as noted in Chapter 2, this means our findings are not directly comparable to those using the 'economic family' as the unit of analysis, the most common approach in Canadian poverty studies.
6 We have taken averages for 2006 to 2010 for the Canadian provinces and the most recent year(s) available for the comparison countries from the LIS data set from 2005 onward.
7 Note that the proportion of individuals in the population living in households of a particular type is not the same as the proportion of all households of this type (e.g., lone-parent households). While single-parent households may represent around 16% of all households in Canada, as reported earlier in the chapter, only about 6% of Canada's population lives in such households. The difference is due, of course, to the fact that single-parent households have, by definition, relatively few members compared to others, in particular, the two-parent households who are still a plurality among household types.
8 While the gap for lone-parent families was numerically greater in the earliest years, it increased proportionately by 2010 as all poverty rates have been declining.
9 Our calculations. Figures available upon request.
10 The high degree of volatility for the Alberta and BC rates may be the result of small numbers in the sample. Alberta's average acute poverty rate for two-parent families between 2006 and 2010 was 3%.

Chapter Four

1 As we noted in chapter 2, the term 'social exclusion' has been used in the European context to refer to a broader syndrome of social deprivations than merely low income. By contrast, Canadian researchers tend to use the term to refer to chronic income poverty.
2 We insist on keeping our causal interpretations tentative. In the following chapters, we assess the extent to which Quebec's results are due to its distinctive policies rather than other possibly confounding factors.

3 As we are working with annual income data, the shortest amount of time a household can be classified as having been poor is one year.
4 Compare the numbers in Table 4.1 with the results displayed in Figure 3.2 of Chapter 3.
5 Since our information is necessarily limited to the six-year period under consideration, we cannot know what proportion of these families really are permanently poor. We use the term 'permanently' to distinguish this group of families from those we call 'chronically' poor.
6 Adding up the numbers for British Columbia in the columns for three years, four years, and five years yields a total of 26.8%.
7 In Quebec 4.6% of lone-parent families suffer one year of acute poverty, compared to 25.2% in Alberta.
8 Recall our qualification of this term in note 5.
9 They are infinitesimal in Table 4.2, as well. Therefore, we will not discuss acute poverty here but return to Table 4.1 instead.
10 We follow Valletta's (2006: 265) definition of 'chronic' poverty. See also Murphy, Zhang and Dionne (2012: 78–82).
11 Thus, for instance, for Quebec two-parent families this proportion is 13.2/(2.3+13.2)=85.2%.
12 While the six-year poverty rates for Alberta and Quebec are the same (0.9% in Table 4.1), the chronic rates in Table 4.3 are 2.3% for Quebec as opposed to 8.2% in Alberta. Another way of putting this is that while 1.4% (2.3–0.9) of Quebec's two-parent families were poor on average without being poor all the time, no less than 7.3% (8.2–0.9) of Alberta's two-parent families fall into this category.

Chapter Five

1 This is the explicit aim of the 'capabilities' approach proposed by Amartya Sen and others (Nussbaum 2011; Sen 1988) to which we briefly refer in Chapter 2.
2 The labour force participation rate is the proportion of a defined population which is either employed or looking for a job. Those who are neither are considered to be 'outside the labour force.'
3 Our 26-week cut-off roughly coincides with Statistics Canada's criterion of a minimum of 910 hours worked per year to qualify as 'working poor' (Lefèvre, Boismenu and Dufour 2011: 126–7; Roy, Fréchet and Savard 2008: 59; for a careful development of a similar measure, see Fleury and Fortin 2006: Ch.2).
4 The LIS database does not contain the requisite information about labour force participation patterns before the year 1994; therefore, the curves for

France start in that year in the figures in this chapter and in Chapter 6. In addition, please recall that the LIS data are only available for a few of the years along the horizontal axis, which accounts for the smoother curves for the comparison countries than for the provinces for which we have annual data from the SLID.

5 These households may include a small number in which the employment of members other than the lone parent accounts for the household accumulating enough working weeks during the year to be classified as a 'single-earner equivalent' household by our scheme.

6 As noted in Chapter 3, the volatility in the rates for Alberta and British Columbia from 2004 onward should be viewed with caution as they are probably the result of relatively small sample numbers.

7 While we lumped together single-earner and dual-earner equivalent lone-parent families in the preceding section to capture the total activation effect, we now restrict ourselves to single-earner equivalent households. We are interested in assessing to what extent single-parent households are able to escape poverty by one member, presumably the lone parent, working more or less full time. This yields a comparatively conservative estimate of Quebec's success in bringing down the poverty rate among lone-parent families because the proportion of *dual*-earner equivalent single-parent families grew the most during this period while their poverty rates have been close to 0%.

8 'Market earnings' include capital income, but the overwhelming majority consists of employment earnings. The residual non-market earnings are primarily social transfer payments and, particularly for single-parent families, a small proportion (less than 5%) consists of child support (alimony).

9 For a more sophisticated demonstration of the share and effectiveness of Quebec transfers in reducing poverty, see Bibi and Duclos (2011).

Chapter Six

1 A common approach is to compare incomes before and after taxes and transfers to infer the effect of government policies (see, e.g., Kenworthy 1999; Moller et al. 2003; Smeeding 2005b) and/or looking at the effects of specific social policies (e.g., Scruggs and Allan 2006; Smeeding 2006). For a thorough critique of such studies on the grounds that they cannot claim to directly measure the impact of government policy, see Brady (2009, 37–40). It should be noted, however, that some studies have in fact attempted to control for demographic and macroeconomic differences across countries (e.g., Caminada, Goudswaard, and Koster 2012).

2 Fritzell and Ritakallio call their standardized poverty rates, 'simulated poverty rates.' We prefer 'standardized results' because the process is identical to techniques referred to as 'standardization' in other disciplines.

3 See, for instance, Bhaumik et al. (2006) and Biewen and Jenkins (2005), who use regression decomposition to compare poverty rates.

4 In fact, in previous work (Plante and van den Berg 2011) we have followed an approach to standardizing poverty rates that draws on the Oaxaca-Blinder decomposition (Blinder 1973; Oaxaca 1973). The two approaches produce identical results. For theoretical treatments of the Oaxaca-Blinder decomposition, see Fairlie (2006), Jann (2008), Bauer and Sinning (2008) and Yun (2004, 2005).

5 For Quebec we show only one curve because its actual rate is identical to its 'standardized' rate.

6 Strictly speaking, our residual approach only allows us to infer something about the *combined* effects of Quebec's policies to reduce poverty *and* a host of unmeasured effects of differences in other policies and socio-economic conditions.

7 Recall that the LIS data are only available for a few of the years along the horizontal axis, which accounts for the smoother curves for the comparison countries than for the provinces for which we have annual data from the SLID.

8 'Poverty regime' captures a host of factors besides the policies that are part of the province's strategy to combat poverty and social exclusion.

Conclusion

1 For a more sanguine assessment, see Rice and Prince (2013, 297–301).

2 For two influential, empirically based studies supporting this position, see Kenworthy (2008) and Lindert (2004).

3 For a more sceptical position, see Haddow (2015, 282–5).

4 A number of the programs included in Chapter 1 are off-budget in the sense that they are self-financed or otherwise not a direct government expense. These include tax credits, the parental leave program, SAAQ, and CSST benefits. See Chapter 1 for more details.

5 Program expenditures exclude debt charges.

Works Cited

Aboriginal Relations. 2009. *First Nations economic partnerships initiative*. Retrieved from: http://open.alberta.ca/publications/4225671.

Abrahamson, P. 1999. 'The welfare modelling business.' *Social Policy & Administration* 33 (4): 394–415.

Achterberg, P., and M. Yerkes. 2009. 'One welfare state emerging? Convergence versus divergence in 16 western countries.' *Journal of Comparative Social Welfare* 25 (3): 189–201.

Allaire, L. 2011. 'Are Quebec's $7-a-day public daycare centres in danger?' *Inroads: The Canadian Journal of Opinion* (28): 100–6.

Allen, J., R. Amano, D.P. Byrne, and A.W. Gregory. 2009. 'Canadian city housing prices and urban market segmentation.' *Canadian Journal of Economics. Revue Canadienne d'Economique* 42 (3): 1132–49. http://dx.doi.org/10.1111/j.1540-5982.2009.01541.x.

Arts, W., and J. Gelissen. 2002. 'Three worlds of welfare capitalism or more? A state-of-the-art report.' *Journal of European Social Policy* 12 (2): 137–58. http://dx.doi.org/10.1177/0952872002012002114.

Atkinson, R., and S. Da Voudi. 2000. 'The concept of social exclusion in the European Union: Context, development and possibilities.' *JCMS: Journal of Common Market Studies* 38 (3): 427–48.

Bambra, C. 2005. 'Cash versus services: 'Worlds of welfare' and the decommodification of cash benefits and health care services.' *Journal of Social Policy* 34 (02): 195–213. http://dx.doi.org/10.1017/S0047279404008542.

Bambra, C. 2006. 'Decommodification and the worlds of welfare revisited.' *Journal of European Social Policy* 16 (1): 73–80. http://dx.doi.org/10.1177/0958928706059835.

Bane, M.J., and D.T. Ellwood. 1986. *Slipping into and out of poverty: The dynamics of spells*. Cambridge, MA: National Bureau of Economic Research.

Banting, K. 1982. *The welfare state and Canadian federalism*. Kingston, ON: McGill-Queen's University Press.

Banting, K. 2005. 'Canada: Nation-building in a federal welfare state.' In *Federalism and the welfare state: New world and European experiences*, edited by H. Obinger, S. Leibfried, and F.G. Castles, 89–137. Cambridge: Cambridge University Press. http://dx.doi.org/10.1017/CBO9780511491856.005.

Banting, K. 2006. 'Disembedding liberalism: The social policy trajectory in Canada.' In *Dimensions of Inequality in Canada*, edited by David A. Green and Jonathan R. Kesselman, 417–52. Vancouver: UBC Press.

Banting, K. 2008. 'The three federalisms: Social policy and intergovernmental decision-making.' In *Canadian federalism: Performance, effectiveness, and legitimacy*, 2nd ed., edited by H. Bakvis and G. Skogstad, 137–60. Don Mills, ON: Oxford University Press.

Banting, K. 2012. 'Introduction: Debating Employment Insurance.' In *Making EI work: Research from the Mowat Centre Employment Insurance Task Force*, edited by K. Banting and J. Medows, 1–34. Kingston, ON: School of Policy Studies, McGill-Queen's University Press.

Banting, K., and J. Myles. 2013a. *Inequality and the fading of redistributive politics*. Vancouver: UBC Press.

Banting, K., and J. Myles. 2013b. 'Introduction.' In *Inequality and the fading of redistributive politics*, edited by K. Banting and J. Myles, 1–42. Vancouver: UBC Press.

Banting, K., and J. Myles. 2013c. 'Conclusion.' In *Inequality and the Fading of Redistributive Politics*, edited by K. Banting and J. Myles, 413–28. Vancouver: UBC Press.

Banting, K., and J. Myles. 2015. 'Framing the new inequality: The politics of income redistribution in Canada.' In *Income inequality: The Canadian story*, vol. 5, edited by D.A. Green, W.C. Riddell, and F. St-Hilaire, 509–36. Montreal: Institute for Research on Public Policy.

Banting, K.G., and J. Medow. 2012. *Making EI work: Research from the Mowat Centre Employment Insurance Task Force*. Kingston, ON: School of Policy Studies McGill-Queen's University Press.

Barbier, J.-C. 2009. 'Le workfare et l'activation de la protection sociale, vingt ans après: Beaucoup de bruit pour rien? Contribution à un bilan qui reste à faire.' *Lien social et Politiques* (61): 23–36.

Barbier, J.-C. 2013. *The road to social Europe: A contemporary approach to political cultures and diversity in Europe*. Abingdon, UK: Routledge.

Bauer, T.K., and M. Sinning. 2008. 'An extension of the Blinder-Oaxaca decomposition to nonlinear models.' *AStA. Advances in Statistical Analysis* 92 (2): 197–206. http://dx.doi.org/10.1007/s10182-008-0056-3.

Beaujot, R., C.J. Du, and Z. Ravanera. 2013. 'Family policies in Quebec and the rest of Canada: Implications for fertility, child-care, women's paid work, and child development indicators.' *Canadian Public Policy* 39 (2): 221–40. http://dx.doi.org/10.3138/CPP.39.2.221.

Béland, D., and P.-M. Daigneault. 2015. 'Conclusion.' In *Welfare reform in Canada: Provincial social assistance in comparative perspective*, edited by D. Béland and P.-M. Daigneault, 555–76. Toronto: University of Toronto Press.

Béland, D., and A. Lecours. 2004. 'Nationalisme et protection sociale: Une approche comparative.' *Analyse de Politiques* 30 (3): 319–31.

Béland, D., and A. Lecours. 2005. 'The politics of territorial solidarity: Nationalism and social policy reform in Canada, the United Kingdom, and Belgium.' *Comparative Political Studies* 38 (6): 676–703. http://dx.doi.org/10.1177/0010414005275600.

Béland, D., and A. Lecours. 2006. 'Sub-state nationalism and the welfare state: Québec and Canadian federalism.' *Nations and Nationalism* 12 (1): 77–96. http://dx.doi.org/10.1111/j.1469-8129.2006.00231.x.

Béland, D., and A. Lecours. 2008. *Nationalism and social policy: The politics of territorial solidarity*. Oxford: Oxford University Press.

Bengtsson, M. 2014. 'Towards stand-ability: Swedish and Danish activation policies in flux.' *International Journal of Social Welfare* 23: S54–70. http://dx.doi.org/10.1111/ijsw.12075.

Bernard, P. 2007. 'The interconnected dynamics of population change and life-course processes.' *Horizons* 9 (4): 13–16.

Bernard, P., and S. McDaniel. 2009. 'Life course as policy lens: Challenges and opportunities for human development.' Paper presented at the HRSDC Policy Dialogue, Ottawa, ON.

Bernard, P., and H. Raïq. 2011. 'Le Québec est-il une société égalitaire?' In *L'État du Québec 2011*. Montreal: Institut du nouveau monde/Boréal

Bernard, P., and S. Saint-Arnaud. 2004. 'Du pareil au même? La position des quatre principales provinces canadiennes dans l'univers des régimes providentiels.' *Canadian Journal of Sociology/Cahiers canadiens de sociologie* 29 (2): 209–39. http://dx.doi.org/10.2307/3654694.

Berthet, T., and C. Bourgeois. 2014. 'Towards "activation-friendly" integration? Assessing the progress of activation policies in six European countries.' *International Journal of Social Welfare* 23:S23–39. http://dx.doi.org/10.1111/ijsw.12088.

Bhaumik, S.K., I.N. Gang, and M.-S. Yun. 2006. *A note on decomposing differences in poverty incidence using regression estimates: Algorithm and example*. Bonn, DE: IZA Discussion Papers.

Bibi, S., and J.-Y. Duclos. 2011. 'L'effet des prélèvements fiscaux et des transferts aux particuliers sur la pauvreté au Québec et au Canada.' *Canadian Public Policy* 37 (1): 1–24.

Biewen, M., and S.P. Jenkins. 2005. 'A framework for the decomposition of poverty differences with an application to poverty differences between countries.' *Empirical Economics* 30 (2): 331–58. http://dx.doi.org/10.1007/s00181-004-0229-1.

Bird, K. 2007. *The intergenerational transmission of poverty: An overview*. London, UK: Chronic Poverty Research Centre.

Björklund, A., and M. Jäntti. 1997. 'Intergenerational income mobility in Sweden compared to the United States.' *American Economic Review* 87 (5):1009–18.

Blanden, J. 2013. 'Cross-country rankings in intergenerational mobility: A comparison of approaches from economics and sociology.' *Journal of Economic Surveys* 27 (1): 38–73. http://dx.doi.org/10.1111/j.1467-6419.2011.00690.x.

Blanden, J. 2014. 'Inequality restricts opportunities.' *Journal for a Progressive Economy* (2): 49–54.

Blinder, A.S. 1973. 'Wage discrimination: reduced form and structural estimates.' *Journal of Human Resources* 8 (4): 436–55. http://dx.doi.org/10.2307/144855.

Blossfeld, H.-P., and S. Drobnic. 2001. *Careers of couples in contemporary society: From male breadwinner to dual-earner families*. New York: Oxford University Press.

Bonoli, G. 1997. 'Classifying welfare states: A two-dimension approach.' *Journal of Social Policy* 26 (3): 351–72. http://dx.doi.org/10.1017/S0047279497005059.

Bonoli, G. 2012. 'Active labour market policy and social investment: A changing relationship.' In *Towards a social investment welfare state*, edited by N. Morel, B. Palier, and J. Palme, 181–204. Bristol, UK: Policy Press.

Bonoli, G., and D. Natali. 2012. 'The politics of the "new" welfare states: Analysing reforms in Western Europe.' In *The politics of the new welfare states*, edited by G. Bonoli and D. Natali, 3–17. Oxford: Oxford University Press.

Bowles, P., and B. Wagman. 1997. 'Globalization and the welfare state: Four hypotheses and some empirical evidence.' *Eastern Economic Journal* 23 (3): 317–36.

Boychuk, G.W. 1998. *Patchworks of purpose: The development of provincial social assistance regimes in Canada*. Montreal: McGill-Queen's University Press.

Boychuk, G.W. 2013. 'Territorial politics and the new politics of redistribution.' In *Inequality and the fading of redistributive politics*, edited by K. Banting and J. Myles, 234–55. Vancouver: UBC Press.

Boychuk, G.W. 2015, forthcoming. 'Federal policies, national trends, and provincial systems: A comparative analysis of recent developments in social assistance in Canada, 1990–2013.' In *Welfare reform in Canada: Provincial social assistance in comparative perspective*, edited by D. Béland and P.-M. Daigneault. Toronto: University of Toronto Press.

Brady, D. 2003. 'Rethinking the sociological measurement of poverty.' *Social Forces* 81 (3): 715–51. http://dx.doi.org/10.1353/sof.2003.0025.

Brady, D. 2009. *Rich democracies, poor people: How politics explain poverty.* Oxford: Oxford University Press. http://dx.doi.org/10.1093/acprof:o so/9780195385878.001.0001.

Brady, D., J. Beckfield, and M. Seeleib-Kaiser. 2005. 'Economic globalization and the welfare state in affluent democracies, 1975–2001.' *American Sociological Review* 70 (6): 921–48. http://dx.doi.org/10.1177/000312240507000603.

Bretschger, L., and F. Hettich. 2002. 'Globalisation, capital mobility and tax competition: Theory and evidence for OECD countries.' *European Journal of Political Economy* 18 (4): 695–716. http://dx.doi.org/10.1016/S0176-2680(02)00115-5.

Brochu, P., P. Makdissi, and L.L. Tahoan. 2011. 'Québec, champion canadien de la lutte contre la pauvreté?' In *L'État du Québec 2011.* Montreal: Institut du nouveau monde/Boréal.

Brooks, C., and J. Manza. 2007. *Why welfare states persist: The importance of public opinion.* Chicago: University of Chicago Press. http://dx.doi. org/10.7208/chicago/9780226075952.001.0001.

Budig, M., J. Misra, and I. Böckmann. 2010. 'The motherhood penalty in cross-national perspective: The importance of work-family policies and cultural attitudes.' Luxembourg Income Study Working Paper No. 542.

Buhmann, B., L. Rainwater, G. Schmaus, and T.M. Smeeding. 1988. 'Equivalence scales, well-being, inequality, and poverty: Sensitivity estimates across ten countries using the Luxembourg Income Study (LIS) Database.' *Review of Income and Wealth* 34 (2): 115–42. http://dx.doi. org/10.1111/j.1475-4991.1988.tb00564.x.

Caminada, K., K. Goudswaard, and F. Koster. 2012. 'Social income transfers and poverty: A cross-country analysis for OECD countries.' *International Journal of Social Welfare* 21 (2): 115–26. http://dx.doi.org/10.1111/j.1468-2397.2011.00815.x.

Cantillon, B. 2011. 'The paradox of the social investment state: Growth, employment and poverty in the Lisbon era.' *Journal of European Social Policy* 21 (5): 432–49. http://dx.doi.org/10.1177/0958928711418856.

Cassidy, J. 2013. 'The Reinhart and Rogoff controversy: A summing up.' *The New Yorker*, 26 April 2013. Retrieved from: http://www.newyorker.com/ news/john-cassidy/the-reinhart-and-rogoff-controversy-a-summing-up

Castles, F. 1985. *The working class and welfare: Reflections on the political development of the welfare state in Australia and New Zealand, 1890–1980.* London: Allen & Unwin.

Castles, F., and D. Mitchell. 1993. 'Worlds of welfare and families of nations.' In *Families of nations*, edited by F. Castles, 93–128. Aldershot, UK: Dartmouth Publishing Company.

CEPE. 2009. *Taking the measure of poverty: Proposed indicators of poverty, inequality and social exclusion to measure progress in Quebec.* Quebec: Centre d'étude sur la pauvreté et l'exclusion sociale.

Christopher, K. 2001. 'Welfare state regimes and mothers' poverty.' Luxembourg Income Study Working Paper No. 286.

Corak, M. 2006. 'Do poor children become poor adults? Lessons from a cross-country comparison of generational earnings mobility.' In *Dynamics of Inequality and Poverty (Research on Economic Inequality)*, vol. 13, edited by J. Creedy and G. Kalb, 143–88. Bingley, UK: Emerald Group Publishing. http://dx.doi.org/10.1016/S1049-2585(06)13006-9.

Corak, M. 2013. 'Income inequality, equality of opportunity, and intergenerational mobility.' *Journal of Economic Perspectives* 27 (3): 79–102. http://dx.doi.org/10.1257/jep.27.3.79.

Daigneault, P.-M. 2014. 'Three paradigms of social assistance.' *SAGE Open* 4 (4): 1–8. http://dx.doi.org/10.1177/2158244014559020.

Daly, M. 2010. 'Families versus states and markets.' In *The Oxford handbook of the welfare state*, edited by F.G. Castles, S. Leibfried, J. Lewis, H. Obinger, and C. Pierson, 139–51. Oxford: Oxford University Press.

Dandurand, R., and F.R. Ouellette. 1992. *Parenté et soutien aux familles avec jeunes enfants: Entre l'autonomie et la solidarité, Comprendre la famille au Québec.* Montreal: Presse de l'Université du Québec.

Dandurand, R.B., and M. Kempeneers. 2002. 'Pour une analyse comparative et contextuelle de la politique familiale au Québec.' *Recherches Sociographiques* 43 (1): 49–78. http://dx.doi.org/10.7202/009446ar.

de Gier, E., and A. van den Berg. 2005. *Managing social risks through transitional labour markets: Towards an enriched European Employment Strategy.* Amsterdam: Het Spinhuis.

de la Porte, C., and K. Jacobsson. 2012. 'Social investment or recommodification? Assessing the employment policies of the EU member states.' In *Towards a social investment welfare state?: Ideas, policies and challenges*, edited by N. Morel, B. Palier, and J. Palme, 117–51. Bristol, UK: Policy Press.

Dean, H., and P. Taylor-Gooby. 2014. *Dependency culture.* Oxford: Routledge.

Department of Advanced Education and Skills. 2014. *2010 poverty reduction strategy consultations.* Retrieved from: http://www.aes.gov.nl.ca/poverty/consultations/poverty_reduction_strategy_consultations.pdf.

Deslauriers, J., and R. Gagné. 2013. *Dépenses publiques au Québec: Comparaisons et tendances.* Montreal: Centre sur la Productivité et la Prospérité.

Dingeldey, I. 2007. 'Between workfare and enablement – The different paths to transformation of the welfare state: A comparative analysis of activating labour market policies.' *European Journal of Political Research* 46 (6): 823–51. http://dx.doi.org/10.1111/j.1475-6765.2007.00712.x.

Dostal, J.M. 2008. 'The workfare illusion: Re-examining the concept and the British case.' *Social Policy and Administration* 42 (1): 19–42.

Doucet, M., E. Marion, D. Rothwell, C. Roy, N. Trocmé, and J. Wegner-Lohin. 2015. *Reorganizing health and social services in Québec in the name of austerity: Too much, too fast and too centralized?* Montreal: Centre for Research on Children and Families, McGill University.

Dufour, P., A. Noël, and G. Boismenu. 2003. *L'aide au conditionnel: La contrepartie dans les mesures envers les personnes sans emploi en Europe et en Amérique du Nord.* Montréal: Les Presses de l'Université de Montréal.

Duncan, G.J., W.J. Yeung, J. Brooks-Gunn, and J.R. Smith. 1998. 'How much does childhood poverty affect the life chances of children?' *American Sociological Review* 63 (3): 406–23. http://dx.doi.org/10.2307/2657556.

Esping-Andersen, G. 1985. *Politics against markets: The social democratic road to power.* Princeton: Princeton University Press.

Esping-Andersen, G. 1990. *The three worlds of welfare capitalism.* Cambridge, UK: Polity Press.

Esping-Andersen, G. 1996a. 'Welfare states without work: The impasse of labour shedding and familialism in continental European social policy.' In *Welfare states in transition: National adaptations in global economies,* edited by G. Esping-Andersen, 66–87. London: Sage Publications. http://dx.doi.org/10.4135/9781446216941.n3.

Esping-Andersen, G. 1996b. 'After the golden age? Welfare state dilemmas in a global economy.' In *Welfare states in transition: National adaptations in global economies,* edited by G. Esping-Andersen, 1–31. London: Sage Publications. http://dx.doi.org/10.4135/9781446216941.n1.

Esping-Andersen, G. 1999. *Social foundations of postindustrial economies.* Oxford: Oxford University Press. http://dx.doi.org/10.1093/0198742002.001.0001.

Esping-Andersen, G, ed. 2002. *Why we need a new welfare state.* Oxford: Oxford University Press. http://dx.doi.org/10.1093/0199256438.001.0001.

Esping-Andersen, G. 2009. *The incomplete revolution: Adapting to women's new roles*. Cambridge, UK: Polity.

Esping-Andersen, G. 2014. 'How family change and income inequality affect children's life chances.' *Journal for a Progressive Economy* (2): 18–22.

Faid, P. 2009. *Poverty reduction policies and programs: Extending the Alberta advantage*. Kanata, ON: Canadian Council on Social Development.

Fairlie, R.W. 2006. 'An extension of the Blinder-Oaxaca decomposition technique to logit and probit models.' *Journal of Economic and Social Measurement* 30 (4): 305–16.

Ferrera, M. 1996. 'The "southern model" of welfare in social Europe.' *Journal of European Social Policy* 6 (1): 17–37.

Ferrara, M. 2005. *The boundaries of welfare: European integration and the new spatial politics of social protection*. Oxford: Oxford University Press. http://dx.doi.org/10.1093/0199284660.001.0001.

Finnie, R., and A. Sweetman. 2003. 'Poverty dynamics: Empirical evidence for Canada.' *Canadian Journal of Economics. Revue Canadienne d'Economique* 36 (2): 291–325. http://dx.doi.org/10.1111/1540-5982.t01-1-00002.

Fleckenstein, T., and S.C. Lee. 2014. 'The politics of postindustrial social policy: Family policy reforms in Britain, Germany, South Korea, and Sweden.' *Comparative Political Studies* 47 (4): 601–30. http://dx.doi.org/10.1177/0010414012451564.

Fleury, D., and M. Fortin. 2006. *When working is not enough to escape poverty: An analysis of Canada's working poor*. Ottawa: Human Resources and Social Development Canada.

Förster, M., and M. D'Ercole. 2012. *The OECD approach to measuring income distribution and poverty*. Oxford: Oxford University Press.

Fortin, M., and J. Gauthier. 2011. 'Measuring social exclusion in Canada: An exploratory study of cumulative disadvantage.' In *Social statistics, poverty and social exclusion: Perspectives from Quebec, Canada and abroad*, edited by G. Fréchet, D. Gauvreau, and J. Poirier, 125–38. Montreal: Les Presses de l'Université de Montréal.

Fortin, N., and T. Lemieux. 2015. 'Changes in wage inequality in Canada: An interprovincial perspective.' *Canadian Journal of Economics. Revue Canadienne d'Economique* 48 (2): 682–713. http://dx.doi.org/10.1111/caje.12140.

Fortin, N., T. Lemieux, and S. Firpo. 2011. 'Decomposition methods in economics.' *Handbook of labor economics*, vol. 4, 1–12. Amsterdam: Elsevier Science. http://dx.doi.org/10.1016/S0169-7218(11)00407-2.

Fortin, P. 2010. 'Quebec is fairer: There is less poverty and less inequality in Quebec.' *Inroads: The Canadian Journal of Opinion* (26): 58–65.

Fortin, P. 2011. 'Staying the course: Quebec's fiscal balance challenge.' *CD Howe Institute* (325). http://dx.doi.org/10.2139/ssrn.1808146.

Fortin, P., L. Godbout, and S. St-Cerny. 2012. *Impact of Quebec's universal low fee childcare program on female labour force participation, domestic income, and government budgets.* Sherbrooke, QC: Université de Sherbrooke.

Fortin, P., L. Godbout, and S. St-Cerny. 2013. 'L'impact des services de garde à contribution réduite du Québec sur le taux d'activité féminin, le revenu intérieur et les budgets gouvernementaux.' *Revue Interventions économiques. Papers in Political Economy* (47).

Fouarge, D., and R. Layte. 2005. 'Welfare regimes and poverty dynamics: The duration and recurrence of poverty spells in Europe.' *Journal of Social Policy* 34 (03): 407–26. http://dx.doi.org/10.1017/S0047279405008846.

Fourastié, J. 1979. *Les trente glorieuses: Ou la Révolution invisible de 1946 à 1975.* Paris: Hachette.

Fraser, N. 1994. 'After the family wage: Gender equity and the welfare state.' *Political Theory* 22 (4): 591–618. http://dx.doi.org/10.1177/0090591794022004003.

Fritzell, J., O. Bäckman, and V.-M. Ritakallio. 2012. *Income inequality and poverty: Do the Nordic countries still constitute a family of their own?* Bristol, UK: Policy Press.

Fritzell, J., and V.-M. Ritakallio. 2010. 'Societal shifts and changed patterns of poverty.' *International Journal of Social Welfare* (19): S25–41. http://dx.doi.org/10.1111/j.1468-2397.2010.00728.x.

Gallie, W.B. 1955. 'Essentially contested concepts.' *Proceedings of the Aristotelian Society* 56: 167–98.

Gauvreau, M. 2005. *Catholic origins of Quebec's Quiet Revolution, 1931–1970,* vol. 2. Montreal: McGill-Queen's Press-MQUP.

Gazier, B. 2003. *Tous sublimes: Vers un nouveau plein emploi.* Paris: Flammarion.

Genschel, P. 2004. 'Globalization and the welfare state: A retrospective.' *Journal of European Public Policy* 11 (4): 613–36. http://dx.doi.org/10.1080/1350176042000248052.

Gibson, D. 2007. *The spoils of the boom: Incomes, profits and poverty in Alberta.* Edmonton: Parkland Institute, University of Alberta.

Godbout, L., and S. St-Cerny. 2008. *Le Québec, un paradis pour les familles?: Regards sur la famille et la fiscalité.* Québec: Presses de l'Université Laval.

Godbout, L., S. St-Cerny, M. Arsenau, N.H. Dao, and P. Fortin. 2014. *La soutenabilité budgétaire des finances publiques du gouvernement du Québec.* Sherbrooke, QC: Chaire de recherche en fiscalité et en finances publiques, Université de Sherbrooke.

Godbout, L., S. St-Cerny, P.-A. Bouchard St-Amant, P. Fortin. 2012. 'Quebec's public finances between demographic changes and fiscal responsibility.' In *The family, the market or the state: Intergenerational support under pressure in ageing societies*, edited by Gustavo De Santis, 59–79. New York: Springer. http://dx.doi.org/10.1007/978-94-007-4339-7_3

Goldberg, G.S. 2009. *Poor women in rich countries: The feminization of poverty over the life course*. Oxford: Oxford University Press. http://dx.doi.org/10.1093/acprof:oso/9780195314304.001.0001.

Goldin, C. 2006. 'The quiet revolution that transformed women's employment, education, and family.' *American Economic Review* 96 (2): 1–21. http://dx.doi.org/10.1257/000282806777212350.

Goodin, R.E. 1999. *The real worlds of welfare capitalism*. Cambridge: Cambridge University Press. http://dx.doi.org/10.1017/CBO9780511490927.

Government of Alberta. 2009. *Widows' Pension Act: revised statutes of Alberta 2000, chapter W-7*. Edmonton: Alberta Queen's Printer.

Government of Alberta. 2013. *Together we raise tomorrow: Alberta's poverty reduction strategy discussion paper*. Retrieved from: http://povertyreduction.alberta.ca/Document/Poverty_Reduction_Strategy_Discussion_Guide.

Government of Manitoba. 2014. *All aboard: Manitoba's poverty reduction and social inclusion strategy*. Retrieved from: http://www.gov.mb.ca/allaboard/.

Government of Nova Scotia. 2009. *Preventing poverty. Promoting prosperity. Nova Scotia's poverty reduction strategy*. Retrieved from: http://www.phans.ca/cmsAdmin/uploads/NS-Poverty-Reduction-Strategy-2009.pdf.

Government of Ontario. 2008. *Breaking the cycle: Ontario's poverty reduction strategy*. Retrieved from: http://www.children.gov.on.ca/htdocs/English/documents/breakingthecycle/Poverty_Report_EN.pdf.

Government of Ontario. 2013. *Breaking the cycle: The fifth progress report*. Retrieved from: http://www.children.gov.on.ca/htdocs/English/documents/breakingthecycle/2013AnnualReport.pdf

Graefe, P. 2015, forthcoming. 'Social assistance in Ontario.' In *Welfare reform in Canada: Provincial social assistance in comparative perspective*, edited by D. Béland and P.-M. Daigneault. Toronto: University of Toronto Press.

Graham, S., J. Atkey, C. Reeves, and M. Goldberg. 2009. *The best place on Earth?: Contemporary and historical perspectives on poverty reduction policies and programs in British Columbia*. Kanata, ON: Canadian Council on Social Development.

Guest, D. 1980. *The emergence of social security in Canada*. Vancouver: University of British Columbia Press.

Haddow, R. 2015. *Comparing Quebec and Ontario: Political economy and public policy at the turn of the millennium*. Toronto: University of Toronto Press.

Hakovirta, M. 2001. 'The income sources of single parents: A comparative analysis.' Luxembourg Income Study Working Paper No. 282.

Harper, C., R. Marcus, and K. Moore. 2003. 'Enduring poverty and the conditions of childhood: Lifecourse and intergenerational poverty

transmissions.' *World Development* 31 (3): 535–54. http://dx.doi.
org/10.1016/S0305-750X(03)00010-X.

Hemerijck, A. 2013. *Changing welfare states*, 1st ed. Oxford: Oxford University Press.

Hick, S. 2004. *Social welfare in Canada: Understanding income security*, 3rd ed. Toronto: Thompson Educational Publishing.

Hicks, A., and G. Esping-Andersen. 2005. 'Comparative and historical studies of public policy and the welfare state.' In *The handbook of political sociology: States, civil societies, and globalization*, edited by T. Janoski, R. Alford, A. Hicks, and M.A. Schwartz, 509–25. Cambridge: Cambridge University Press.

Huber, E., and J.D. Stephens. 2001. *Development and crisis of the welfare state: Parties and policies in global markets*. Chicago: University of Chicago press. http://dx.doi.org/10.7208/chicago/9780226356495.001.0001.

Hunter, G., and D. Miazdyck. 2006. 'Current issues surrounding poverty and welfare programming in Canada.' In *Social fabric or patchwork quilt: The development of social policy in Canada*, edited by R. Blake and J. Keshen, 383–418. Peterborough, ON: Broadview Press.

Huo, J., M. Nelson, and J.D. Stephens. 2008. 'Decommodification and activation in social democratic policy: Resolving the paradox.' *Journal of European Social Policy* 18 (1): 5–20.

Hyman, I., R. Mercado, G. Grace-Edward, and D. Patychuk. 2011. 'A critical review of social exclusion and social inclusion indicators: Implications for the development of a Canadian framework.' In *Social statistics, poverty and social exclusion: Perspectives from Quebec, Canada and abroad*, edited by G. Fréchet, D. Gauvreau, and J. Poirier, 139–51. Montréal: Les Presses de l'Université de Montréal.

Imbeau, L., R. Landry, H. Milner, F. Petry, J. Crete, P.-G. Forest, and V. Lemieux. 2000. 'Comparative provincial policy analysis: A research agenda.' *Canadian Journal of Political Science/Revue canadienne de science politique* 33(04): 779–804.

Institut de la statistique du Québec. 2015. *Comparaisons interprovinciales*, section 13, *Les finances publiques*, http://www.stat.gouv.qc.ca/statistiques/economie/comparaisons-economiques/interprovinciales/

Jann, B. 2008. 'The Blinder-Oaxaca decomposition for linear regression models.' *Stata Journal* 8 (4): 453–79.

Jenkins, S.P., and T. Siedler. 2007. 'The intergenerational transmission of poverty in industrialized countries.' London, UK: Chronic Poverty Research Centre.

Jenson, J. 2002. 'Against the current: Child care and family policy in Quebec.' In *Child care policy at the crossroads: Gender and entitlements at the crossroads*, edited by R. Mahon and S. Michel, 309–32. New York: Routledge.

Jenson, J. 2013. 'Historical transformations of Canada's social architecture: Institutions, instruments, and ideas.' In *Inequality and the fading of redistributive politics*, edited by K. Banting and J. Myles, 43–64. Vancouver: UBC Press.

Jenson, J., and D. Saint-Martin. 2006. 'Building blocks for a new social architecture: The LEGO™ paradigm of an active society.' *Policy and Politics* 34 (3): 429–51. http://dx.doi.org/10.1332/030557306777695325.

Kenworthy, L. 1995. 'Equality and efficiency: The illusory tradeoff.' *European Journal of Political Research* 27 (2): 225–54. http://dx.doi.org/10.1111/j.1475-6765.1995.tb00637.x.

Kenworthy, L. 1999. 'Do social-welfare policies reduce poverty? A cross-national assessment.' *Social Forces* 77 (3): 1119–39. http://dx.doi.org/10.1093/sf/77.3.1119.

Kenworthy, L. 2004. *Egalitarian capitalism: Jobs, incomes and growth in affluent countries*. New York: Russel Sage Foundation.

Kenworthy, L. 2008. *Jobs with equality*. New York: Oxford University Press. http://dx.doi.org/10.1093/acprof:oso/9780199550593.001.0001.

Kershaw, P. 2006. 'Weather-vane federalism: Reconsidering federal social policy leadership.' *Canadian Public Administration* 49 (2): 196–219. http://dx.doi.org/10.1111/j.1754-7121.2006.tb01979.x.

Kim, J.W., and Y.J. Choi. 2013. 'Feminisation of poverty in 12 welfare states: Consolidating cross-regime variations?' *International Journal of Social Welfare* 22 (4): 347–59. http://dx.doi.org/10.1111/j.1468-2397.2012.00874.x.

Kneebone, R., and K. White. 2015, forthcoming. 'An overview of social assistance trends in Canada.' In *welfare reform in Canada: Provincial social assistance in comparative perspective*, edited by D. Béland and P.-M. Daigneault. Toronto: University of Toronto Press.

Kneebone, R., and M. Wilkins. 2014. *Who, or what, is to blame for the accumulation of debt in Ontario and Quebec (and what will it take to stop the bleeding?)*. University of Calgary, School of Public Policy, SPP Research Paper No. 7-17. http://dx.doi.org/10.2139/ssrn.2487525.

Kolkman, J. 2011. *Issue update: The market basket measure rebased or debased. fACTivist*. Edmonton: Edmonton Social Planning Council.

Korpi, W. 1983. *The democratic class struggle*. London: Routledge & Kegan Paul.

Korpi, W., and J. Palme. 2003. 'New politics and class politics in the context of austerity and globalization: Welfare state regress in 18 countries, 1975–95.' *American Political Science Review* 97 (03): 425–46. http://dx.doi.org/10.1017/S0003055403000789.

Laïdi, Z. 1999. 'Qu'est ce que la troisième voie?' *Esprit* (Paris) 251 : 31–9.

Larsen, C.A. 2007. 'The institutional logic of welfare attitudes: How welfare regimes influence public support.' *Comparative Political Studies* 41 (2): 145–68. http://dx.doi.org/10.1177/0010414006295234.

Le Bourdais, C., and É. Lapierre-Adamcyk. 2004. 'Changes in conjugal life in Canada: Is cohabitation progressively replacing marriage?' *Journal of Marriage and the Family* 66 (4): 929–42. http://dx.doi.org/10.1111/j.0022-2445.2004.00063.x.

Lefaucheur, N. 1993. 'Les familles dites monoparentales.' *Autrement* 134: 27–37.

Lefebvre, P., and P. Merrigan. 2008. 'Child-care policy and the labor supply of mothers with young children: A natural experiment from Canada.' *Journal of Labor Economics* 26 (3): 519–48. http://dx.doi.org/10.1086/587760.

Lefèvre, S., G. Boismenu, and P. Dufour. 2011. *La pauvreté: Quatre modèles sociaux en perspective*. Montréal: Les Presses de l'Université de Montréal.

Leisering, L., and R. Walker. 1998. 'New realities: The dynamics of modernity.' In *The dynamics of modern society: Poverty, policy and welfare*, edited by L. Leisering and R. Walker, 3–16. Bristol, UK: Policy Press.

Letablier, M.-T. 2003. 'Les politiques familiales des pays nordiques et les ajustements aux changements socio-économiques des années quatre-vingt dix.' *Revue Francaise des Affaires Sociales* (4): 485–514.

Lindert, P.H. 2004. *Growing public: Volume 1, the story: Social spending and economic growth since the eighteenth century*. Cambridge: Cambridge University Press.

Lindvall, J. 2010. *Mass unemployment and the state*. Oxford: Oxford University Press. http://dx.doi.org/10.1093/acprof:oso/9780199590643.001.0001.

Lødemel, I., and H. Trickey, eds. 2001. *An offer you can't refuse: Workfare in international perspective*. Bristol, UK: Policy Press. http://dx.doi.org/10.1332/policypress/9781861341952.001.0001.

Lu, Y., R. Morissette, and T. Schirle. 2011. 'The growth of family earnings inequality in Canada, 1980–2005.' *Review of Income and Wealth* 57 (1): 23–39. http://dx.doi.org/10.1111/j.1475-4991.2010.00377.x.

Lund, R., C. Nilsson, and K. Avlund. 2010. 'Can the higher risk of disability onset among older people who live alone be alleviated by strong social relations? A longitudinal study of non-disabled men and women.' *Age and Ageing* 39 (3): 319–26. Medline:20208073 http://dx.doi.org/10.1093/ageing/afq020.

Mahon, R. 2013. 'Childcare, new social risks, and the new politics of redistribution.' In *Inequality and the fading of redistributive politics*, edited by K. Banting and J. Myles, 359–80. Vancouver: UBC Press.

Maioni, A. 1998. *Parting at the crossroads: The emergence of health insurance in the United States and Canada*. Princeton: Princeton University Press.

Maioni, A. 2004. 'New century, new risks: The Marsh Report and the post-war welfare state in Canada.' *Policy Options* 25 (7): 20.

Mallet, T. 2013. 'Canadian debt levels aren't as they appear.' *Financial Post* (Toronto), 10 June 2013, http://business.financialpost.com/entrepreneur/cfib/canadian-debt-levels-arent-as-they-appear?__lsa=cba8-8590

Malvern, P., A. Mrozek, and C. Benesch. 2011. *A Québec family portrait*. Ottawa: Institute of Marriage and Family Canada.

Maquet, I., and D. Stanton. 2012. 'Income indicators for the EU's social inclusion strategy.' In *Counting the poor: New thinking about European poverty measures and lessons for the United States*, edited by D. Besharov and K. Couch, 59–78. New York: Oxford University Press.

Marchand, J. 2015. 'The distributional impacts of an energy boom in western Canada.' *Canadian Journal of Economics. Revue Canadienne d'Economique* 48 (2): 714–35. http://dx.doi.org/10.1111/caje.12141.

Marsh, L.C. 1975. *Report on social security for Canada*. Toronto: University of Toronto Press.

Mau, S., and B. Veghte. 2007. *Social justice, legitimacy and the welfare state*. Aldershot, UK: Ashgate Publishing, Ltd.

Maynard, R., E. Boehnen, T. Corbett, G. Sandefur, and J. Mosley. 1998. 'Changing family formation behavior through welfare reform.' In *Welfare, the family, and reproductive behavior: Research perspectives*, edited by A.M. Robert, 50–97. Washington, DC: National Academy Press.

McBride, S., and K. McNutt. 2007. 'Devolution and neoliberalism in the Canadian welfare state ideology, national and international conditioning frameworks, and policy change in British Columbia.' *Global Social Policy* 7 (2): 177–201. http://dx.doi.org/10.1177/1468018107078161.

Michaud, S., C. Cotton, and K. Bishop. 2004. *Exploration of methodological issues in the development of the market basket measure of low income for Human Resources Development Canada*. Statistics Canada, Income Research Paper Series. Retrieved from: http://www.statcan.gc.ca/pub/75f0002m/75f0002m2004001-eng.pdf.

Milan, A. 2000. 'One hundred years of families.' *Canadian Social Trends* 56: 2–12.

Millar, J. 1996. 'Mothers, workers, wives: Comparing policy approaches to supporting lone mothers.' In *Good enough mothering? Feminist perspectives on lone mothering*, edited by S.E. Bortolaia, 97–113. London: Routledge.

Ministère de l'emploi et de la solidarité sociale du Québec. 2012. *Plan d'action gouvernemental en matière de lutte contre la pauvreté et l'exclusion sociale 2004–2010*. http://www.mess.gouv.qc.ca/grands-dossiers/lutte-contre-la-pauvrete/plan.asp.

Mishra, R. 1999. *Globalization and the welfare state*. Northampton, MA: Edward Elgar Publishing.

Misra, J., M.J. Budig, and S. Moller. 2007. 'Reconciliation policies and the effects of motherhood on employment, earnings and poverty.' *Journal of Comparative Policy Analysis* 9 (2): 135–55. http://dx.doi.org/10.1080/13876980701311588.

Misra, J., and S. Moller. 2005. 'Familialism and welfare regimes: Poverty, employment and family policies.' Luxembourg Income Study Working Paper No. 399.

Moffit, R.A. 1998. 'The effect of welfare on marriage and fertility.' In *Welfare, the family, and reproductive behavior: Research perspectives*, edited by R.A. Moffit, 50–97. Washington, DC: National Academy Press.

Moller, S., E. Huber, J.D. Stephens, D. Bradley, and F. Nielsen. 2003. 'Determinants of relative poverty in advanced capitalist democracies.' *American Sociological Review* 68 (1): 22–51. http://dx.doi.org/10.2307/3088901.

Mondou, M. 2009. 'Comment éviter la politique du blâme et les instruments punitifs? Une analyse comparée des politiques québécoise et terre-neuvienne de lutte contre la pauvreté et l'exclusion sociale.' *Lien social et Politiques* (61): 61–77.

Morel, N., B. Palier, and J. Palme. 2012. *Towards a social investment welfare state?: Ideas, policies and challenges.* Bristol, UK: Policy Press.

Morel, S. 2002. *The insertion model or the workfare model?: The transformation of social assistance within Quebec and Canada.* Ottawa: Status of Women Canada.

Muffels, R.J., P. Tsakloglou, and D.G. Mayes. 2002. *Social exclusion in European welfare states.* Cheltenham, UK: Edward Elgar Publishing.

Murphy, B.B., X. Zhang, and C. Dionne. 2012. *Low income in Canada: A multiline and multi-index perspective.* Ottawa: Statistics Canada.

Murray, C. 1994. *Losing ground: American social policy, 1950–1980.* New York: Basic Books.

Myles, J., F. Hou, G. Picot, and K. Myers. 2009. 'The demographic foundations of rising employment and earnings among single mothers in Canada and the United States, 1980–2000.' *Population Research and Policy Review* 28 (5): 693–720. http://dx.doi.org/10.1007/s11113-008-9125-2.

Noël, A. 2002. 'Une loi contre la pauvreté: La nouvelle approche québécoise de lutte contre la pauvreté et l'exclusion sociale.' *Lien social et Politiques* 48 (48): 103–14. http://dx.doi.org/10.7202/007895ar.

Noël, A. 2011. 'Une lutte inégale contre la pauvreté et l'exclusion sociale.' In *L'État du Québec 2011*, edited by M. Fahmy, 103–10. Montréal: Boréal.

Noël, A. 2012. 'Assymetry at work: Quebec's distinct implementation of programs for the unemployed.' In *Making EI work: Research from the Mowat Centre Employment Insurance Task Force*, edited by K. Banting and J. Medow, 421–48. Montreal: McGill-Queen's University.

Noël, A. 2013. 'Quebec's new politics of redistribution.' In *Inequality and the fading of redistributive politics*, edited by K. Banting and J. Myles, 256–82. Vancouver: UBC Press.

Noël, A. 2015, forthcoming. 'Québec: The Ambivalent politics of social solidarity.' In *Welfare reform in Canada: Provincial social assistance in comparative perspective*, edited by D. Béland and P.-M. Daigneault. Toronto: University of Toronto Press.

Nolan, B. 2013. 'What use is "social investment"?' *Journal of European Social Policy* 23 (5): 459–68. http://dx.doi.org/10.1177/0958928713499177.

Nolan, B., and C.T. Whelan. 2010. 'Using non-monetary deprivation indicators to analyze poverty and social exclusion: Lessons from Europe?' *Journal of Policy Analysis and Management* 29 (2): 305–25. http://dx.doi.org/10.1002/pam.20493.

Nussbaum, M.C. 2011. *Creating capabilities*. Cambridge: Harvard University Press. http://dx.doi.org/10.4159/harvard.9780674061200.

O'Rand, A. 2009. 'Cumulative processes in the life course.' In *The craft of life course research*, edited by G.H. Elder and J.Z. Giele, 121–40. New York: The Guilford Press.

Oaxaca, R. 1973. 'Male-female wage differentials in urban labor markets.' *International Economic Review* 14 (3): 693–709. http://dx.doi.org/10.2307/2525981.

Olsen, G.M. 2002. *The politics of the welfare state: Canada, Sweden and the United States*. Don Mills, ON: Oxford University Press.

Orloff, A.S. 1993. 'Gender and the social rights of citizenship: The comparative analysis of gender relations and welfare states.' *American Sociological Review* 58 (3): 303–28. http://dx.doi.org/10.2307/2095903.

Osberg, L. 2000. 'Poverty trends and the Canadian "social union." ' In *Toward a new mission statement for Canadian fiscal federalism*, edited by H. Lazar, 213–31. Montreal: McGill-Queen's University Press.

Osberg, L., and A. Sharpe. 2011. *Beyond GDP: Measuring economic well-being in Canada and the provinces, 1981–2010. CSLS Research Reports*. Ottawa: Centre for the Study of Living Standards.

Oxley, H., D. Thai-Thanh, and P. Antolín. 2000. 'Poverty dynamics in six OECD countries.' *OECD Economic Studies* 30: 7–52.

Palier, B., ed. 2010. *A long goodbye to Bismarck? The politics of welfare reforms in continental Europe*. Amsterdam: Amsterdam University Press. http://dx.doi.org/10.5117/9789089642349.

Paquin, S., and P.-L. Lévesque, eds. 2014. *Social-démocratie 2.0: Le Québec comparé aux pays scandinaves*. Montreal: Les Presses de l'Université de Montréal.

Pascual, A.S., and L. Magnusson. 2007. *Reshaping welfare states and activation regimes in Europe*, vol. 54. Frankfurt, DE: Peter Lang.

Peck, J. 2001. *Workfare States*. New York: Guilford Press.

Picot, W., and J. Myles. 2005. *Income inequality and low income in Canada: An international perspective*. Ottawa: Statistics Canada.

Pierson, P. 2001. *The new politics of the welfare state*. Oxford: Oxford University Press. http://dx.doi.org/10.1093/0198297564.001.0001.

Plante, C., and A. van den Berg. 2011. 'How much poverty can't the government be blamed for? A counterfactual decomposition of poverty rates among Canada's largest provinces.' In *Statistiques Sociales, pauvreté et exclusion sociale, perspectives québécoises, canadiennes et internationales*, edited by G. Fréchet, D. Gavreau, and J. Poirier, 164–75. Montréal: Presses de l'Université de Montréal.

Polanyi, K. 1944. *The great transformation: The political and economic origins of our time*. Boston: Beacon Press.

Province of New Brunswick. 2014. *Overcoming poverty together: The New Brunswick Economic and Social Inclusion Plan 2014–2019*. Retrieved from: http://www2.gnb.ca/content/dam/gnb/Departments/esic/pdf/NBEconomicSocialInclusionPlan2014–2019.pdf.

Pulkingham, J. 2015, forthcoming. 'Social assistance in British Columbia.' In *Welfare reform in Canada: Provincial social assistance in comparative perspective*, edited by D. Béland and P.-M. Daigneault. Toronto: University of Toronto Press.

Quebec National Assembly. 2002. *Bill 112: An act to combat poverty and social exclusion*. Quebec: Quebec Official Publisher. Retrieved from: http://www2.publicationsduquebec.gouv.qc.ca/dynamicSearch/telecharge.php?type=5&file=2002C61A.PDF.

Raïq, H. 2012. 'Pauvreté monoparentale: Le Canada et le Québec dans l'univers des régimes providentiels.' PhD diss., Département de Sociologie, Université de Montréal.

Raïq, H., P. Bernard, and A. van den Berg. 2011. 'Family type and poverty under different welfare regimes: A comparison of Canadian provinces and select European countries.' In *Statistiques Sociales, pauvreté et exclusion sociale, perspectives québécoises, canadiennes et internationals*, edited by G. Fréchet, D. Gavreau, and J. Poirier, 190–202. Montréal: Presses de l'Université de Montréal.

Raïq, H., and C. Plante. 2013. 'Trajectoires de pauvreté et monoparentalité: Le Québec dans une perspective comparative.' *Sociologie et Sociétés* 45 (1): 67–90. http://dx.doi.org/10.7202/1016396ar.

Raïq, H., C. Plante, and A. van den Berg. 2011. 'Les interactions entre la famille et l'emploi: Les enjeux et les risques de pauvreté au Québec dans une perspective comparative.' In *Statistiques Sociales, pauvreté et exclusion sociale, perspectives québécoises, canadiennes et internationals*, edited by G. Fréchet, D. Gavreau and J. Poirier, 190–204. Montréal: Presses de l'Université de Montréal.

Raïq, H., and A. van den Berg. 2012. 'Quebec's distinct welfare state.' *Inroads: The Canadian Journal of Opinion* (31): 59–67.

Raïq, H., and A. van den Berg. 2014. 'La lutte contre la pauvreté au Québec: Vers une social-démocratie nordique?' In *Social-démocratie 2.0: Le Québec comparé aux pays scandinaves*, edited by Stéphane Paquin and Pier-Luc Lévesque, 337–54. Montreal: Presses de l'Université de Montréal.

Raphael, D. 2007. *Poverty and policy in Canada: Implications for health and quality of life*. Toronto: Canadian Scholars' Press.

Reichwein, B.P. 2003. *Benchmarks in Alberta's public welfare services: History rooted in benevolence, harshness, punitiveness and stinginess*. Edmonton: Alberta College of Social Workers.

Reinhart, C.M., and K. Rogoff. 2009. *This time is different: Eight centuries of financial folly*. Princeton: Princeton University Press.

Rice, J.J., and M.J. Prince. 2013. *Changing politics of Canadian social policy*. Toronto: University of Toronto Press.

Richards, J. 2010. *Reducing lone-parent poverty: A Canadian success story*. Toronto: C.D. Howe Institute. Retrieved from: http://www.cdhowe.org/reducing-lone-parent-poverty-a-canadian-success-story/4425

Richards, J. 2011. 'Quebec's $7-a-day universal childcare: Introducing a few doubts.' *Inroads: The Canadian Journal of Opinion* (28): 107–9.

Ringen, S. 1988. 'Direct and indirect measures of poverty.' *Journal of Social Policy* 17 (03): 351–65. http://dx.doi.org/10.1017/S0047279400016858.

Rothwell, D.W., and R. Haveman. 2013. 'Definition and measurement of asset poverty in Canada.' Retrieved from: http://ssrn.com/abstract=2367057 or http://dx.doi.org/10.2139/ssrn.2367057

Rovny, A. 2014. *The capacity of social policies to combat poverty among new social risk groups*. LIS Working Paper Series. http://dx.doi.org/10.1177/0958928714542732.

Roy, L., and J. Bernier. 2006. *La politique familiale, les tendances sociales et la fécondité au Québec: Une expérimentation du modèle nordique?* Québec: Direction des relations publiques et des communications, Ministère de la famille, des aînés et de la condition féminine.

Roy, M.-R., G. Fréchet, and F. Savard. 2008. 'Le Québec, à l'avant-garde de la lutte contre la pauvreté au Canada.' *Policy Options* 29, (9): 57–61.

Saint-Martin, D. 2000. 'De l'État-providence à l'État d'investissement social?' In *How Ottawa spends 2000–2001: Past imperfect, future tense*, edited by L.A. Pal, 33–58. Toronto: Oxford University Press.

Sarfati, H., and G. Bonoli, eds. 2002. *Labour market and social protection reforms in international perspective: Parallel or converging tracks?* Aldershot, UK: Ashgate Publishing.

Sarlo, C.A. 2001. *Measuring poverty in Canada.* Vancouver: Fraser Institute.

Schirle, T. 2013. 'Senior poverty in Canada: A decomposition analysis.' *Canadian Public Policy* 39 (4): 517–40. http://dx.doi.org/10.3138/CPP.39.4.517.

Schmid, G. 2006. 'Social risk management through transitional labour markets.' *Socio-economic Review* 4 (1): 1–33. http://dx.doi.org/10.1093/SER/mwj029.

Schmid, G., and B. Gazier. 2002. *The dynamics of full employment: Social Integration through transitional labour markets and the European social model: Towards a new employment compact.* Northampton, MA: Edward Elgar.

Scruggs, L., and J. Allan. 2005. 'The Material consequences of welfare states benefit generosity and absolute poverty in 16 OECD countries.' Luxembourg Income Study Working Paper No. 409.

Scruggs, L., and J. Allan. 2006. 'Welfare-state decommodification in 18 OECD countries: A replication and revision.' *Journal of European Social Policy* 16 (1): 55–72. http://dx.doi.org/10.1177/0958928706059833.

Sen, A. 1983. 'Poor, relatively speaking.' *Oxford Economic Papers* 35 (2): 153–69.

Sen, A. 1988. *The standard of living.* Cambridge: Cambridge University Press.

Sen, A. 1999. *Commodities and capabilities.* Oxford: Oxford University Press.

Smeeding, T. 2006. 'Poor people in rich nations: The United States in comparative perspective.' *Journal of Economic Perspectives* 20 (1): 69–90. http://dx.doi.org/10.1257/089533006776526094.

Smeeding, T.M. 2005a. 'Public policy, economic inequality, and poverty: The United States in comparative perspective.' *Social Science Quarterly* 86 (S1): 955–83. http://dx.doi.org/10.1111/j.0038-4941.2005.00331.x.

Smeeding, T.M. 2005b. 'Government programs and social outcomes: Comparison of the United States with other rich nations.' In *Public policy and the income distribution,* edited by A.J. Auerbach, D. Card, and J.M. Quigly, 149–218. New York: Russell Sage Foundation.

Smith, A. 1776. *An inquiry into the nature and causes of the wealth of nations.* London: Home University Library. http://dx.doi.org/10.1093/oseo/instance.00043218.

Solon, G. 2002. 'Cross-country differences in intergenerational earnings mobility.' *Journal of Economic Perspectives* 16 (3): 59–66. http://dx.doi.org/10.1257/089533002760278712.

Somers, M.R., and F. Block. 2005. 'From poverty to perversity: Ideas, markets, and institutions over 200 years of welfare debate.' *American Sociological Review* 70 (2): 260–87. http://dx.doi.org/10.1177/000312240507000204.

Speer, S., ed. 2014. *Quebec's government indebtedness: Unnoticed, uncontrolled.* Vancouver: Fraser Institute.

Stalker, G., and M. Ornstein. 2013. 'Quebec, daycare, and the household strategies of couples with young children.' *Canadian Public Policy* 39 (2): 241–62. http://dx.doi.org/10.3138/CPP.39.2.241.

Starke, P. 2006. 'The politics of welfare state retrenchment: A literature review.' *Social Policy and Administration* 40 (1): 104–20. http://dx.doi.org/10.1111/ j.1467-9515.2006.00479.x.

Statistics Canada. 2010a. *Low income lines, 2008–2009* (Catalogue No. 75F0002M 2–No. 005). Income Research Paper Series. Ottawa: Statistics Canada.

Statistics Canada. 2010b. *Population projections for Canada, provinces and territories 2009 to 2036* (Catalogue No. 91–520-X). Ottawa: Statistics Canada.

Statistics Canada. 2011. *Census dictionary*. Ottawa: Statistics Canada.

Statistics Canada. 2012a. *Fifty years of families in Canada: 1961 to 2011* (Catalogue no. 98–312–X2011003). Ottawa: Statistics Canada.

Statistics Canada. 2012b. *Portrait of families and living arrangements in Canada* (Catalogue no. 98–312–X2011001). Ottawa: Statistics Canada.

Statistics Canada. 2013. *Low income lines, 2011–2012* (Catalogue no. 75F0002M — No. 002.). Ottawa: Statistics Canada.

Statistics Canada. 2014. *Table 202–0802: Persons in low income families, annual.* CANSIM.

Stevens, A. 1994. 'The dynamics of poverty spells: Updating Bane and Ellwood.' *The American Economic Review* 84 (2): 34–7.

Sundberg, T., and P. Taylor-Gooby. 2013. 'A systematic review of comparative studies of attitudes to social policy.' *Social Policy and Administration* 47 (4): 416–33. http://dx.doi.org/10.1111/spol.12027.

Svallfors, S. 1997. 'Worlds of welfare and attitudes to redistribution: A comparison of eight western nations.' *European Sociological Review* 13 (3): 283–304. http://dx.doi.org/10.1093/oxfordjournals.esr.a018219.

Svallfors, S. 2003. 'Welfare regimes and welfare opinions: A comparison of eight western countries.' *Social Indicators Research* 64 (3): 495–520.

Svallfors, S., ed. 2012. *Contested welfare states: Welfare attitudes in Europe and beyond.* Stanford: Stanford University Press. http://dx.doi.org/10.11126/ stanford/9780804782524.001.0001.

Swank, D. 2005. 'Globalisation, domestic politics, and welfare state retrenchment in capitalist democracies.' *Social Policy and Society* 4 (02): 183–95. http://dx.doi.org/10.1017/S1474746404002337.

Tanzi, V. 2002. 'Globalization and the future of social protection.' *Scottish Journal of Political Economy* 49 (1): 116–27. http://dx.doi.org/10.1111/1467- 9485.00224.

Taylor-Gooby, P. 1985. *Public opinion, ideology, and state welfare*. Oxford: Routledge.

Taylor-Gooby, P. 2011. 'Security, equality and opportunity: Attitudes and the sustainability of social protection.' *Journal of European Social Policy* 21 (2): 150–63. http://dx.doi.org/10.1177/0958928710385735.

Tellier, G. 2005. *Les dépenses des gouvernements provinciaux canadiens: L'influence des partis politiques, des élections et de l'opinion publique sur la variation des budgets publics*. Saint-Nicolas, QC: Presses de l'Universite Laval; Distribution de livres Univers.

Théret, B. 2002a. *Protection sociale et fédéralisme l'Europe dans le miroir de l'Amérique du Nord*. Montréal: Presses de l'Université de Montréal.

Théret, B. 2002b. 'L'union sociale canadienne dans le miroir des politiques sociales de l'Union européenne.' *Policy Matters* 3 (9): 3–47.

Théret, B. 2003. 'Canada's social union in perspective: Looking into the European Mirror.' In *Forging the Canadian social union: SUFA and beyond*, edited by S. Fortin, A. Noël, and F. St-Hilaire, 197–234. Montreal: IRPP.

Torjman, S. 2008. *Poverty policy*. Ottawa: Caledon Institute of Social Policy.

Torjman, S. 2010. *Poverty reduction in Québec: The first five years*. Ottawa: Caledon Institute of Social Policy.

Townsend, P. 1979. *Poverty in the United Kingdom: A survey of household resources and standards of living*. Berkeley: University of California Press.

Tweddle, A., K. Battle, and S. Torjman. 2014. *Welfare in Canada 2013*. Ottawa: Caledon Institute of Social Policy.

Ulysse, P.-J., and F. Lesemann. 2004. *Citoyenneté et pauvreté: Politiques, pratiques et stratégies d'insertion en emploi et de lutte contre la pauvreté*. Sainte-Foy, QC: Les Presses de l'Université du Québec.

Vaillancourt, F., and M. Laberge. 2010. 'Quebec: Equitable yes, sustainable no.' *Inroads: The Canadian Journal of Opinion* (26): 74–83.

Vaillancourt, Y. 1988. *L'évolution des politiques sociales au Québec, 1940–1960*. Montréal: Presses de l'Université de Montréal.

Vaillancourt, Y. 2012. 'The Quebec model of social policy, past and present.' In *Canadian social policy*, edited by A. Westheus and B. Wharf, 115–44. Waterloo, ON: Wilfrid Laurier University Press.

Valletta, R.G. 2006. 'The ins and outs of poverty in advanced economies: Government policy and poverty dynamics in Canada, Germany, Great Britain, and the United States.' *Review of Income and Wealth* 52 (2): 261–84. http://dx.doi.org/10.1111/j.1475-4991.2006.00187.x.

van den Berg, A. 2009. 'Flexicurity: What can we learn from the Scandinavian experience.' *European Journal of Social Security* 11 (3): 245–70.

van den Berg, A., B. Furåker, and L. Johansson. 1997. *Labour market regimes and patterns of flexibility: A Sweden-Canada comparison*. Lund, SE: Arkiv.

van den Berg, A., and J. Jensen. 2015. 'A tale of two federalisms: Social policy in Canada and the European Union.' In *Social Europe: A dead end. what the Eurozone crisis is doing to Europe's social dimension*, edited by A. Lechevalier and J. Wielgohs, 103–32. Copenhagen, DK: DJØF Forlag.

van den Berg, A., and H. Raïq. 2014. 'Les familles, inégalement protégées par la redistribution.' In *Miser sur l'égalité*, edited by M. Fahmy and A. Noël, 79–90. Montreal: Fides.

van den Berg, A., C.-H.v. Restorff, D. Parent, and A.C. Masi. 2008. 'From unemployment to Employment Insurance: Towards transitional labour markets in Canada?' In *Flexibility and work security in Europe: Labour markets in transition*, edited by R. Muffels, 307–41. Cheltenham, UK: Edward Elgar Publishing. http://dx.doi.org/10.4337/9781781007693.00020.

Van Kersbergen, K. 2003. *Social capitalism: A study of Christian democracy and the welfare state*. Oxford: Routledge.

van Oorschot, W., M. Opielka, and B. Pfau-Effinger. 2008. *Culture and welfare state: Values and social policy in comparative perspective*. Cheltenham, UK: Edward Elgar Publishing. http://dx.doi.org/10.4337/9781848440234.

Van Praet, N. 2011. 'Crushing debt jeopardizes Quebec's welfare state.' *National Post* (Toronto), 4 November 2011. Retrieved from: http://business.financialpost.com/2011/11/04/crushing-debt-jeopardizes-quebecs-welfare-state/

Walker, R. 1995. 'The dynamics of poverty and social exclusion.' In *Beyond the threshold: The measurement and analysis of social exclusion*, edited by G. Room, 102–28. Bristol, UK: Policy Press.

Warburton, J., and E.J. Grassman. 2011. 'Variations in older people's social and productive ageing activites across different social welfare regimes.' *International Journal of Social Welfare* 20 (2): 180–91.

Wood, D., and T.R. Klassen. 2009. 'Bilateral federalism and workforce development policy in Canada.' *Canadian Public Administration* 52 (2): 249–70. http://dx.doi.org/10.1111/j.1754-7121.2009.00074.x.

Wood, D.E. 2013. 'Comparing employment policy governance regimes in Canada and the European Union.' *Canadian Public Administration* 56 (2): 286–303. http://dx.doi.org/10.1111/capa.12019.

Wood, D.E. 2015, forthcoming. 'The state of social assistance in Alberta.' In *Welfare reform in Canada: Provincial social assistance in comparative perspective*, edited by D. Béland and P.-M. Daigneault. Toronto: University of Toronto Press.

Worts, D., A. Sacker, and P. McDonough. 2010. 'Falling short of the promise: Poverty vulnerability in the United States and Britain, 1993–2003.' *AJS* 116 (1): 232–71. Medline:21560510 http://dx.doi.org/10.1086/653542.

Yun, M.-S. 2004. 'Decomposing differences in the first moment.' *Economics Letters* 82 (2): 275–80. http://dx.doi.org/10.1016/j.econlet.2003.09.008.

Yun, M.-S. 2005. 'Hypothesis tests when decomposing differences in the first moment.' *Journal of Economic and Social Measurement* 30 (4): 295–304.

Zhang, X. 2010. *Low income measurement in Canada: What do different lines and indexes tell us?* Ottawa: Statistics Canada, Income Statistics Division.

Zhang, X. 2014. *What can we learn about low-income dynamics in Canada from the Longitudinal Administrative Databank?* Ottawa: Statistics Canada, Income Statistics Division.

Index

Studies in Comparative Political Economy and Public Policy

Lightning Source UK Ltd.
Milton Keynes UK
UKHW04n0722150718
325717UK00007B/264/P